IBSEN:

PILLARS OF SOCIETY
A DOLL'S HOUSE
GHOSTS

IBSEN : PLAYS

PILLARS OF SOCIETY

A DOLL'S HOUSE

GHOSTS

Translated with an Introduction by
JAMES WALTER McFARLANE

OXFORD UNIVERSITY PRESS
LONDON   OXFORD   NEW YORK
1970

Oxford University Press

LONDON OXFORD NEW YORK

GLASGOW TORONTO MELBOURNE WELLINGTON

CAPE TOWN SALISBURY IBADAN NAIROBI LUSAKA DAR ES SALAAM ADDIS ABABA

BOMBAY CALCUTTA MADRAS KARACHI LAHORE DACCA

KUALA LUMPUR SINGAPORE HONG KONG TOKYO

First published by Oxford University Press, London, 1961

First issued as an Oxford University Press paperback 1970

The text of this edition of *Pillars of Society*, *A Doll's House*, and *Ghosts* is taken from Volume V (1961) of The Oxford Ibsen, an edition of the plays newly translated and edited by J. W. McFarlane. That volume also contains earlier drafts of *Pillars of Society* and *A Doll's House*, an alternative ending to the latter, a commentary on each of the three plays giving dates of composition and contemporary reception, and a list of productions of Ibsen in English on stage, radio, and television, together with a full bibliography.

Printed in Great Britain

CONTENTS

PREFACE

The translations of the plays in this volume are based on the Norwegian text as printed in the Centenary Edition (*Hundreårsutgave*, 21 vols., 1928–57, edited by Francis Bull, Halvdan Koht, and Didrik Arup Seip). The plays themselves have not been in any way cut or condensed. For purposes of study, the need for a complete text is of course obvious; and when it comes to the theatre, I find myself recalling what Shaw once wrote about the cutting of Shakespeare: 'The simple thing to do with a Shakespeare play is to perform it. The alternative is to let it alone. If Shakespeare made a mess of it, it is not likely that Smith or Robinson will succeed where he failed.' Even in circles where this is felt to be too stern or perfectionist a doctrine, there is still likely to be wide support for the view that cutting is in any case not the *translator's* job.

All three plays represented here have been translated a number of times before, and I have not left these earlier versions unregarded—in addition to the Archer versions, I might mention in particular those of R. Farquharson Sharp, Una Ellis-Fermor and Eva Le Gallienne—but neither have I paid them importunate attention, preferring to approach them rather as a possible contributor to their fascinating conversation than as a potential borrower; and it is as such that I feel I owe them a general debt of gratitude for their company rather than specific debts in respect of particular items. Nevertheless, there are of course frequent coincidences, not a few of which are there as a result of a decision I early made not to alter a phrase merely because (as naturally quite often happened) it turned out to have been used in one or another of the earlier versions.

The best translation, says the man with no knowledge of the original, is one that does not read like a translation; for anybody familiar with the original, on the other hand, it is imperative that he should be reminded of it at every stage, and in every possible particular. If I have had any definable policy in shaping the present versions, it was to reconcile as far as I was able these two factors—making something that to the knowledgeable was recognizably a 'translation' and not a 'free-rendering' or 'adaptation' or something equally undisciplined, and yet at the same time making the lines 'sayable'. One other point may be referred to here: in deciding whether characters should address each other by first name or surname, I have chosen what seemed appropriate to the equivalent English context of situation, rather than follow the Norwegian conventions mechanically; titles such as 'Adjunkt', 'Frøken', and so on, have been similarly treated; and I have also tried to exploit this device to the point where it would, I hoped, deal relatively unobtrusively with the perennial problem of 'De' and 'du', the formal and familiar modes of address.

In connection with the staging of Ibsen's plays, there is one point of some interest: 'left' and 'right' in the stage directions mean 'as seen from the point of view of the audience'. In a letter of 22 November 1884 to the Swedish actor-manager, August Lindberg, Ibsen wrote: 'In answer to your question, I hasten to inform you that *The Wild Duck* is disposed from the auditorium and not from the stage, as indeed all my plays are. I position everything as I see it in my mind's eye as I am writing it down.'

J. W. McF.

SCHOOL OF EUROPEAN STUDIES
UNIVERSITY OF EAST ANGLIA
NORWICH.
June 1969

INTRODUCTION

Pillars of Society appeared in 1877, *A Doll's House* in 1879, and *Ghosts* in 1881. But it is more than chronology alone that orders them thus, as Ibsen himself insisted. 'You say that the translation of *Ghosts* will soon be complete,' he wrote on 14 September 1882 in connection with a plan to bring out English translations of his works in America, 'but I would not consider it appropriate for this play to come out *first*. Of the three works you mention, this one is the most extreme [lit. 'furthest going'], and ought therefore to be the last of the series. This should, I suggest, open with *Pillars of Society*, after which should come *A Doll's House*, since this forms as it were an introduction to, or preparation for, *Ghosts*.' Ordered in this fashion, the plays constitute a series, the terms of which are a succession of curses, increasing by a kind of anathematical progression. The things Ibsen thought merited his abuse, how he abused them, and the manner in which his denunciations became successively more extreme while at the same time sharing a common alignment—to inquire into these matters is to ask the crucial questions.

Generally the condemnation in them is directed against those aspects of contemporary living, and particularly of life as currently lived in the remoter north of Europe, that put obstacles in the way of free and unfettered self-realization: the hypocrisies of commerce, the dead hand of convention, the compulsion to do the done thing, the fear of what people will think, the bigotries of institutionalized religion, and all those related factors which, under the guise of duty or loyalty or moral obligation, stunt the personality, inhibit a natural development in the individual, and shut him off from genuine living. In these three dramas—as also, of course, in so many other of Ibsen's works, particularly from *Brand* (1865) onwards—the deeper preoccupations are with a proper definition of freedom. Freedom, he repeatedly insisted in these years, was essentially a matter of individual decision and individual responsibility, something personal which was striven for without ever being fully realizable, something which steadily expanded and proliferated as one tried to make it one's own, so that (as he put it in a letter to Georg Brandes, 17 February 1871) 'if . . . in the course of the struggle [for freedom] a man stops and says: "Now

I have it"—all he does in fact is show that he has lost it.' Much of the fabric of contemporary society he saw made up of out-dated attitudes and opinions, something that was now quite inappropriate for the new individual. It caught him up in a mesh of prescriptive duties; it saddled him with an intolerable burden of incumbencies largely obsolescent; it coerced him and bemused him into a belief that suffering and joylessness were necessarily predominant in the good life. Above all, Ibsen was anxious to revise current thinking about what one owed to oneself; he noted the tendency to suppose that *any* concern for oneself was unworthy, and he was eager to point out instead that a proper concern for one's own self was rather one of the supreme duties.

All three plays document a process of emancipation by ordeal; and all three principals, Bernick and Nora and Mrs. Alving, are driven on from some earlier and more rudimentary stage of personal integrity and freedom (intellectual or spiritual or moral or social) to a more advanced and enlightened one. But they move in echelon, perhaps even in relay; for they have widely separate points of departure, they finish up at different termini, and they cover different ground; only the direction in which they move is common to them. Bernick starts furthest back, in the sense that his career is a sham even by the most commonplace standards of public morality let alone by the standards of 'advanced' thought; and the progress he is able to make is limited by the very nature of his political role in society, and the constitution of that society: 'You can't imagine . . . how I've been forced year after year to whittle down any hopes I might have had of living a full and satisfying life', he says to Lona Hessel. 'What in fact *have* I achieved, however much it may seem? Bits and pieces . . . trivialities. But here they won't tolerate anything else . . . or anything more. If I wanted to take one step in advance of the current views and opinions of the day, that would put paid to any power I have.' Nora, by contrast, comes to the point where she does take a very drastic step ahead of her time; the route of her emancipation begins at a point less remote than Bernick's, in the sense that her life is less obviously inauthentic at the opening of the play than his; her position as the wife of a bank manager, cosseted and seemingly insulated against the more hurtful impact of life, needed a crisis of a different kind to persuade her that she must get away from it all; and she leaves far behind the more conventional ideas of what it was thought proper to do. It is not straining things too far to see Mrs. Alving's emancipation as beginning just here; hers is the career of one who also slammed the door on her husband and ran off into the night, but who was persuaded to return to the path of duty, with all its alarming consequences. The course of her career—of revulsion, of rebellion, and of re-appraisal—takes her so far ahead of her day that even her author dared go no further for the time being. It had been his deliberate intention with this play to extend a few frontiers (as he said), but this was for the moment the ultimate: 'I agree absolutely with you', he wrote to Sophie Adlersparre on 24 June 1882, 'when you say that further than *Ghosts* I dare not go. I felt myself that the general state of mind in our country would not permit it; nor do I feel any stimulus to go further. A writer must not leave his people so far behind that there is no longer any understanding between them and him. But *Ghosts had* to be written; I couldn't remain standing at *A Doll's House*; after Nora, Mrs. Alving of necessity had to come.'

Bernick, it was suggested above, does not go impressively far in his advance towards the Ibsenist ideal. He may even have advanced less than critics in the past have generally assumed. In the course of the play he is discovered to have transgressed in the past even by the most ordinary standards of mass morality: to have trampled on others in his scramble for power and influence, to have slandered and exploited his fellows for the sake of material advancement. But at the same time there is recognition of the fact that Bernick's deeper crime is not so much the harm he has done to others, but the injury he has thereby done to himself. Johan, with his more liberal outlook, suffers no real hurt from Bernick's lies; and what injury there is, is soon healed by Dina's courage in deciding to run away with him in defiance of public opinion. It is Bernick's own integrity that suffers most from these lies, and he has to be taught the necessity—or at least taught to admit the advantages—of obeying some rather more human compulsion than the pressure of public opinion or the craving for prestige. Under close scrutiny, however, Bernick's moral rehabilitation is a good deal less impressive than he would like it to appear, and even—and this is perhaps the real point—a good deal less effective than either he himself or Lona Hessel believes. In other words, one wonders just how much irony Ibsen meant to be read into the curtain scene. Although Bernick publicly renounces any intention of trying to run the railway for private profit, he nevertheless (one imagines) succeeds in retaining administrative power over it, and at the same time manages very nicely to get rid of his three earlier collaborators. After it has been made reasonably clear that Martha was done out of her inheritance, he says nothing about making any restitution. And although after fifteen years he finally, under considerable direct pressure, confesses to a youthful indiscretion, to having sheltered behind the magnanimity of his brother-in-law, and to having done nothing to discourage the slanderous rumours that got about concerning Johan, he is nevertheless careful to keep very quiet about the most monstrous thing of all: that he was ready to send a whole ship's company to their deaths merely to save his own respectability. He still seems to be working to the principle that the worst crime of all is to be found out. There is simply no guarantee that the salvage work done on him has brought about any real redemption. At the very moment of confession, indeed, there is in his words an involuntary betrayal of the fact that his thoughts still run on much the same lines as before, that he is still prepared to calculate in terms of what *profit* this might bring him: 'I ask each one of you to go to his home . . . to compose himself . . . to look into his heart,' he says, 'and when we have all calmed down, it will be seen whether I have lost or gained by speaking out.' Indeed, as the play moves into the final moments, and after the carefully phrased admissions, the equally careful suppressions, the sentimental family reconciliation, the gush of moralizing, one waits expectantly for some characteristic dash of Ibsenist cynicism, for the sting of some Relling-like remark such as cuts across Hjalmar's attitudinizing at the end of *The Wild Duck*, for something that would underline the fact that by the sterner principles of *A Doll's House* and *Ghosts* Bernick still has a long way to go.

Where Bernick is reprehensibly culpable, Nora's crime is in essence only a legal offence; it is not a shameful thing to be hushed up like Bernick's, but a source of pride and joy to her, an insurance even against the day when she is no longer young and beautiful, a lien on Torvald's affection. She is, to adapt an idea of Schiller's, a 'sublime criminal', a person whose transgression is against the unfeeling and unsympathetic laws created by male-dominated society, but whose deeper motives are honourable and admirable. It is true that here again the discovery brings things to a crisis, but it is a crisis of a very different kind from Bernick's, and lights up not (as before) the murky parts of a guilty soul but rather the wrongness of her situation as a chattel-wife. Nora's emancipation is much nearer the vanguard of social progress, and her final solution one that took her far in advance of public opinion, and not merely into line with it as Bernick's did.

The implications of *Ghosts* are even more extreme. Nora, in spite of the firmness of her resolution, is left confused; she cannot be sure, she says, how she will turn out, and all she knows is that the attempt must be made. Mrs. Alving's ordeal, or at least the first instalment of what proves to be a double ordeal, is endured in the name of duty. She in the past has done all that convention demanded of her, and more. After running away from her husband, she returned to him; she remained loyal to him, guarding his reputation with selfless devotion at enormous cost to herself and her own happiness; she sent her son away from home to escape the evil influence of his father, thereby denying her own maternal instincts, and drawing the accusation of being an unnatural and heartless mother. She puts all her late husband's money into an orphanage to his memory, in order to scotch any possible suspicion about his way of life. And this is the measure of how far *Ghosts* has progressed beyond *Pillars of Society*. Bernick's violence to his own Self is the direct consequence of selfishness, his violation of the standards of common decency; by contrast, Mrs. Alving's offence is her very selflessness. Her crime is a self-inflicted wound, an outrage which she commits upon her own individuality in the interest of a misdirected altruism and for the preservation of appearances. She, the most dutiful of persons, is guilty of dereliction of the most important duty of all: to herself. In living out her marriage, she shows a power of will that is almost inhuman, comparable with Brand's austerely purposeful career; but she comes to realize, as indeed he too is finally instructed, that the warmth of charity was lacking, that she had left no room for 'joie de vivre'. Mrs. Alving's emancipation is indeed a long and painful one, of which only the final rapid stages are presented in the drama. Her first act of rebellion was against the falsity of her marriage and its cruel domination; yet when the opportunity came, her solution was imperfect in that she merely substituted a different kind of domination in place of the earlier one: *she* took control of things as soon as she had a weapon she could use against her husband, she dictated what should be done, and she ran what she was later ready to admit was a sunless, joyless home. Her emancipation, although rooted in the disillusionment that accompanied her marriage, and fed by her reading of 'advanced' books, is left for Oswald to complete. Her attitude to marriage and to the relationship between men and women moves from a general condemnation of the loveless, dutiful relationship as characterized by her own married life, beyond a readiness to condone or approve free-love, to a point where she is prepared to contemplate even an incestuous relationship if she could be convinced it would bring happiness to her son. She is compelled to give drastic revision to her ideas of duty: not merely to reject the loyalty that wives were conventionally expected to show (no matter what the circumstances) to their husbands, not merely to repudiate the idea that children should unconditionally honour their parents, but even to acknowledge a new and terrifying interpretation of a mother's duty as something that must be prepared to countenance euthanasia even, if need be. The most devastating aspect of it all, however, is that her own son is destined to serve as proof that the past cannot be put away by a mere act of will, no matter how prodigious. She cannot run away from the past as Nora could run away from home. She is forced to recognize that the 'ghosts' of the past, whether they happen to be moribund ideas or outworn conventions or inherited characteristics or the latent hideousness of disease, continue to inhabit the living cells of the new, young life, in spite of the most tremendous efforts to deny them; that there are things against which no inoculation of the liberal spirit is proof. In spite of the tremendous advantages Oswald has enjoyed—held by his mother in scrupulous quarantine away from any contamination his poisoned home atmosphere might have for him, given freedom to travel and the choice of a satisfying career, and with everything that had to do with the less admirable side of his father cut as far as humanly possible out of his life—nevertheless his whole career is fated to be nothing more than a demonstration that, notwithstanding, the past *does* live on, and that it can in some cases quite overwhelm. In all this, the pattern is almost Nietzschean in its suggestion of 'eternal recurrence': Mrs. Alving encounters a situation terribly familiar from before, only that now a son substitutes for his father—both of them full of the joy of life, both of them fond of the bottle and with an eye for the women, both of them turning sour in the joylessness of the home she provides; and although she herself has radically changed, although her reactions are different, the pain is the same. Life, coming not quite full circle, completes a spiral turn.

To live in the present, to live for the future, one must escape from the past. Inevitably, however, the effort to break free brings the individual into immediate conflict with organized society and its institutions, with the established *mores* that derived from past ages and stubbornly lived on. Clearly implicit in *Pillars of Society* is the author's conviction that to lead a life attuned to the degenerate form of contemporary society was necessarily to involve oneself in falsehood; the play is disposed to show that the really magnanimous people, all the liberal minds and the generous hearts, all the more thoroughly integrated personalities, the essentially honest ones are those who got away; they have been able to reach a community with no crippling burden to bear from the past, they found America where the horizons are wider and the wind blows free. Only among those who remained behind does one find the twisted ones, the unfulfilled, the corrupt and the contaminated. Actually Bernick, the chief representative of this false way of living, had had his opportunity: as a young man, he too (like Oswald) had been to Paris, had seen what life was like beyond the narrow valleys of his own country; but the tainting effect of the society he settles down in is inescapable. (This insistence on the tainting effect of society on normally generous minds—and the more generous the mind, the greater the tainting effect—is also something strongly reminiscent of the young Schiller, incidentally.) Bernick, it was noted above, explains to Lona Hessel how isolated he feels in the 'shrivelled stunted little community' that provides the context of his life, how each year he has been forced to abandon more and more of the hopes he has had of living a full and satisfying life, because the community would not tolerate any kind of tampering with its set ways. Mrs. Alving says very nearly the self-same thing when enlightenment comes to her, when she realizes what made her late husband lead the kind of life he did: 'There was this lively, happy boy—and at the time he *was* still like a boy—having to eat his heart out here in this little provincial town; pleasures of a kind it had to offer, but no real joy; no chance of any proper vocation, only an official position to fill; no sign of any kind of work he could throw himself into heart and soul, only business.' No opportunity here beyond that of cashing in on things, of making private gain out of what passed for public good, a playing for status, as Bernick did; or of having to make do with substitutes instead of the genuine thing, with a forced gaiety instead of happiness, with the sterilities of routine instead of the satisfactions of honest work, as the late Captain Alving did. If you cannot escape, you must make do with escapism.

Nora, in the more intimate context of her married life, comes to realize the same thing; she too, as she says at the moment of revelation, has been gay only, not happy. And in tracing through the technical treatment of this idea, one becomes aware of the specialized range of meaning that Ibsen is able to attach to the concept of 'home', the symbolic use he makes of it, and the ambivalence that surrounds it: the home country, the home town, the childhood home, the marital home, the family home, the Children's Home, the Seamen's Home. These dramas make a penetrating analysis of the nature of such 'home' conditions, of the conventional organization of domestic and local affairs, and of the assumptions upon which the regulation of home life was currently based. One begins to notice how much of *Pillars of Society* and *Ghosts* is made to turn about the axis *'herhjemme'*—*'derute'* ('here at home'—'over there'). How to leave home is 'just the thing for a bright lad', and an essential part of the process of self-assertion, a necessary step on the way to self-reliance. To escape from home is to win release from the insidious authority of 'mother (or father) knows best'; it is to flee the place that stunts one's growth, stifles one's breath, distorts one's values, and kills one's opportunities. It gives rise to a particularly obnoxious kind of self-satisfaction, it inhibits the development of a true humility, and it will, if given half a chance, shut the door on the outside world, cut itself off from outside contact, and live on in its own smug self-sufficiency.

The fact that Ibsen himself was, in this special sense, a 'homeless' person has naturally a direct relevance to this aspect of his work, and needs no underlining. At the time of writing these plays, and indeed for the greater part of his creative life, he was a voluntary exile from the North, and he had all the expatriate's eagerness to pass on the lessons exile had taught him, to point out to the stay-at-homes what they had missed, as well as a strong but guarded nostalgia for his native land. He tended (or pretended) to look back pityingly on those who had stayed put; and behind many of his characters' remarks there is the quietly irritating superiority of one who had been over the hill, who had seen it all and knows what's what, and who insists that they order things better abroad—a quality in his work that in many cases roused the fury of his countrymen quicker than anything else. Ibsen is untiring in his insistence that contact with the outside world broadens the mind and liberates the spirit; and he laboured hard to undermine the assumption he found in so many of his compatriots that geographical remoteness is in itself an admirable thing, providing welcome insulation against the world's wickedness and the sophisticated corruption of the greater nations. And although Ibsen repeatedly and very rightly denied that any of his characters had acted as mouthpieces for him, it is surely true nevertheless that the role of wanderer returned, the role of a Johan or an Oswald, was one that gave him a good deal of vicarious pleasure.

The more specifically domestic aspects of 'home' are taken up and scrutinized in *A Doll's House*.[1] Here, as in its other senses, 'home' is seen as an institution that tends to inhibit the development of the authentic Self. For a child to be treated by its father as Nora was, for example, or Olaf—as a mere extension of the father's own life, a repository for his own ideas, and perhaps as the ultimate heir to his own life's work—is to suffer a complete eclipse of personality. As Nora puts it, and as the title of the play echoes, it is to endure becoming a doll for the gratification of others, not unlike the way Bernick in his 'home' surroundings becomes a puppet moving not by its own volition but in obedience to the pull of private gain or public esteem, a lay figure to be dressed up with the insignia of office or the trappings of power. For the married woman of Nora's day, the 'home' could be just as disabling as for the child; Nora finds herself reduced to the level of a home-comfort, something that merely contributes to the husband's domestic well-being and flatters *his* ego at the cost of destroying hers. She becomes a possession. Possessiveness is the keynote of such homes; and crisis, it seems, serves only to amplify it: 'For a man [Helmer says], there's something indescribably moving and very satisfying in knowing that he has forgiven his wife. . . . It's as though it made her his property in a double sense: he has, as it were, given her a new life, and she becomes in a way both his wife and at the same time his child.' So immediately marriage becomes a microcosm of the prevailing male-dominated society at large, in which—as the preliminary notes to *A Doll's House* put it—'a woman cannot be herself. . . . It is an exclusively male society with laws drafted by men, and with counsel and judges who judge feminine conduct from the male point of view.' Nora's inbred faith in authority and in male domination clashes with her natural instincts, and it is very largely this that makes the drama. Relentlessly, Ibsen builds up by such means his case against the 'home': as the source of bigotry and hypocrisy and blinkered vision; as the abode of tyrannical affection and possessiveness; snug, smug places that confine, enfold, demand; ostensibly well-regulated institutions, such as the Captain

---

[1] A more literal translation of the title, incidentally, would be 'A Doll's Home' which brings it even more obviously into line. On the other hand, in *Ghosts*, the Orphanage or Children's Home is only once specifically referred to in the Norwegian as a 'home'; the term most used is 'asyl' [lit. 'asylum', 'refuge'].

Alving Home was meant to be, which deservedly burn down; façades, like Engstrand's Seamen's Home, which conceal obscenities; ways of life such as any right-thinking person slams the door on.

Small wonder that strange things happen to truth in such surroundings; the suppressions, distortions, perversions that take place, the garbling and the dissembling that goes on, the sham and the pretence. Consider even *A Doll's House* alone, how much of the lives of the characters is spent in tampering in some way or other with the truth. Suppression first: Nora's big secret is of course the pivot about which the action turns, exploited by Krogstad, shared with Mrs. Linde, and withheld in terror from Torvald; and Rank's mortal secret is similarly a matter to share with some and withhold from others, entering into things by a kind of counterpoint. Then secondly, both Torvald and Nora need the opiate of day-dreams to help them to bear the reality of their lives: Torvald indulges himself with the pretence that he and Nora are secret lovers newly and clandestinely wed; and Nora dreams of a rich admirer who will leave her all his money. And while they knowingly day-dream, they also unknowingly deceive themselves: Torvald with an image of himself as the broad-shouldered courageous male, longing only for the opportunity to save his wife from distress; and Nora with a belief that her marriage is a source of genuine happiness when in reality it is nothing but a hollow sham. The fancy dress ball at their neighbour's is not the only masquerade here, nor the tarantella the only performance Nora puts on. All the time she is acting a part, playing up to the role of irresponsible, scatter-brained wife that her marriage seems to have cast her for, masquerading as the helpless little thing so utterly dependent on her strong husband. The entire ménage is based on misrepresentation, deception, falsity, in small things as well as big; it was a fraud that had to be exposed.

Not all three plays seem, however, equally confident that improvement, even using drastic Ibsenist methods, is possible. The degree of optimism built into them steadily diminishes over the range. In *Pillars of Society* the optimism is at its maximum and its most naïve. The suggestion seems to be that merely to have done with falsehood is to create a vacuum which truth and goodness will inevitably rush in to fill; that given light and air and space, the human soul will necessarily grow true and straight and tall, like a tree in a clearing. To clear up and clear out, it seems to say, is the best thing; and that to leave home for the wider world and its more spacious patterns of living is to find an ever-ready solution to the problems of living. Optimism is also there to a considerable degree in *A Doll's House*, but a little dimmed by comparison; the conviction that truth and goodness and self-realization *can* follow an act of breaking free is there, but is not held unconditionally. Nora cannot feel entirely sure that positive gain will follow for her; she hopes to be able to make something of herself, but realizes there can be no guarantee. Yet, as was made clear above, the implications of her career are bright compared with those that follow from Oswald's.

Accompanying these variations in theme are a number of more specifically technical changes of great fascination, particularly in the demands Ibsen made on language. The most conspicuous break with his own past in this respect had actually already taken place, at the time when he deliberately rejected verse as a mode of dramatic speech valid for his own day; but his desire to discover still more about the possibly unsuspected resources of prose dialogue led him unceasingly on. In the intertexture[1] of the three plays here under review, there is clear evidence of Ibsen's continuingly audacious experimentation in the dramatic use of language. Taking as the characteristic intertexture of drama some compounding of the elements of speech, gesture, and situation, one notes in moving from play to play through the series certain distinct changes in the relative importance attached to the separate constituent parts. To claim, *tout court*, that each is allowed dominance in turn—that speech predominates in the intertexture of *Pillars of Society*, gesture in *A Doll's House*, and situation in *Ghosts*—would be to over-simplify and in some measure to distort what is in any event a highly complex matter; but it opens up an approach to the technical nature of these separate dramas that is not without promise.

Clearly the climax of *Pillars of Society* is massively and expansively verbal. The tension that has been built up is discharged not by any sharp encounter of expostulation and rejoinder, not by any quick cut and thrust of impassioned argument, not by any stichomythiac exchange, but—of all things—by a vote of thanks and a speech in reply. Rörlund takes nearly 900 cliché-ridden words to provoke Bernick into speech, and Bernick takes nearly 800 words to reply, both speeches being very largely uninterrupted except by the noises

---

[1] To use a convenient term from Coleridge, happily revived and most penetratingly analysed by Ronald Peacock in his study *The Art of Drama* (London, 1957).

and asides of audience participation and reaction. Could Ibsen have found anything more unpromisingly ponderous, more monumentally rhetorical, more sheerly wordy to accompany the essentially verbal nature of the dramatic mode within which he is here operating? The final confrontation is between men wielding nothing more deadly than a knack for public speaking, a gift of the gab, and indulging themselves in their few well-chosen words. The speech rhythms are —for the dramatic crisis of a modern realistic play—quite astonishingly slow-moving. Prolix, verbose, it is nevertheless a form of climax wholly appropriate to a drama in which so much of the motive force is provided by what is, and was, *said*: where so many of the characters step forward and declare themselves, where the past is brought up to date by gossiping tongues, where rumour is one of the mainsprings of social change, and the liberating effect of public confession is made clear.

To pass from this to *A Doll's House* is to leave a predominantly verbal mode of drama for a much more pronouncedly gestural one. It is not merely that the high-point of the whole play, Nora's final exit and her slamming the door, is a 'gesture' of a particularly expressive kind, the first purposeful gesture of the new individualist; nor even that certain incidents and episodes—of which the business with Rank and the flesh-coloured stockings, the practice tarantella, and the change of costume in Act III are the most obvious—are so economically and laconically effective by virtue of their near wordlessness; but that throughout the entire drama there is an exploitation of the dramatic resources of gesture and posture and movement so unrelenting and so ingenious as to make the accompanying words in many cases almost superfluous. The point has been made before[1] that much of (for example) the first Act of *A Doll's House* would not merely have sufficient non-verbal quality to interest a deaf person, but would in fact be in unusually high degree intelligible to him, too: how Nora enters with the Christmas parcels, supervises the delivery of the Christmas tree, takes out her purse and tips the porter with obvious show of generosity, secretly helps herself to macaroons from a paper bag which she takes from her pocket, stealthily tiptoes across to one of the doors in the room, listens apprehensively, addresses some shouted remarks to the person within, guiltily stuffs the paper bag in her pocket and wipes her mouth as a man puts his head through the doorway; how she drags him across to show him the parcels,

[1] Particularly by Daniel Haakonsen, *Henrik Ibsens realisme* (Oslo, 1957).

meets his reproachful glances, pouts, tosses her head, wheedles; how she plays romping games with the children, how her attitude visibly changes when a stranger interrupts their games; and so on. Nora's role is composed quite differently from Bernick's, is much less an exercise in declaration, much less enunciative, less dependent on vocal utterance. To a very considerable extent she enacts what she had to communicate.

It is, however, not until the final moments of *Ghosts* that Ibsen showed how far it was possible to go in reducing the role of speech in the general interdependence of parts. Compared with the verbalistic climax of *Pillars of Society*, compared with the final show-down, the gesturally enriched wrangle, between Nora and Torvald in *A Doll's House*, *Ghosts* reaches its culmination in a situation from which conceptual language has been pared almost clean away, and where ultimately the only gesture is a negation of gesture. The language no longer informs, it marshals; it commands a situation fully realizable only in terms of dramatic production—which may very well explain why, of all Ibsen's plays, it is the one that reads least promisingly, or improves most on being acted. The entire weight of the drama bears down on this one select, refined moment of terror, where words fail and speech has become an idiot's babble and a mother's wounded cry of pain, where gesture has been paralysed by seizure and the torment of excruciating indecision. After the stolid monumentality of *Pillars of Society*, after the daring *bouleversement* of *A Doll's House*, Ibsen built up *Ghosts* to a fateful, final situation, then knocked away the props to leave it desperately balanced on a knife-edge of infinite irresolution and of unspeakable distress.

The other main point of technical interest concerns the dramatic function of a particular kind of Ibsenist character. It is a commonplace to remark that Ibsen's world is populated with characters, of whom many show among themselves a strong family resemblance; and it is always a revealing matter to trace the metamorphoses through which they pass as Ibsen moves on from play to play. *Pillars of Society*, as the first of his 'modern' plays—discounting for the moment the rather ambiguous position of *The League of Youth*—is particularly rich in characters which obviously continued to exert a steady fascination for Ibsen; yet the other plays too provide plenty of examples of how Ibsen continued to modify and adapt for subsequent pieces characters that had obviously meant much to him. One notes, for example, how a good deal of Rörlund reappears in Pastor Manders, and again in Kroll in *Rosmersholm*; how Bernick's easy assumption of male superiority comes out again in Helmer, and his sheer pomposity in Peter Stockmann, the Mayor in *An Enemy of the People*; how Hilmar Tönnesen's comic capacity for self-deception becomes pathetic in Hjalmar Ekdal in *The Wild Duck*, and vastly more subtle; how the character of the 'Old Badger' was, in the draft versions, originally part of *Pillars of Society*, but was eventually withdrawn and kept as Morten Kiil in *An Enemy of the People*; and how also the mortal sickness of Rank reappears in Oswald, as well as among the notes of jottings for *The Wild Duck*. But for present purposes, perhaps the most rewarding thing is to note what happened, in the three plays in this volume, to what might reasonably be called 'the agent'. This is the term by which I mean to indicate the person or force that promotes or initiates or precipitates the various crises of emancipation —acting upon the situation in a way not unlike the way (at a more rudimentary level perhaps) the declared 'villain' of melodrama is traditionally supposed to act. In *Pillars of Society* the office is quite unambiguously held by Lona Hessel, with intentions that are expressly altruistic. The play is so constructed to allow her to be fed by the dramatist into the prevailing state of affairs from without; she imposes her altruism upon an egoist who has forgotten what his obligations to his fellows should be (however much he may protest to the contrary), and who has so far neglected the more fundamental decencies of social behaviour that his career has become the enactment of a lie. Lona Hessel is the self-appointed agent of improvement, a kind of 'anti-villain': she is permitted on her first appearance to announce her intention of 'letting in some air', and is given further opportunity at the end to explain how she has acted with but one aim in view: to rescue her girlhood hero from the falsity of the position he had worked himself into. Her life has been built on devotion to others, first to Johan in America and now to Bernick; and nowhere is there any suggestion that this is incompatible with genuine self-realization. Martha's sacrifices, incidentally, are essentially different; for although admirable in one way, they have inevitably prevented her from realizing herself completely. (In passing, it might also be remarked that Gregers Werle in *The Wild Duck* is obviously a later and more complex variation on this idea of the altruistic agent; he is—dare one say?—in view of the consequences of his action a kind of anti-villain *manqué*.) The rest of the pattern of *Pillars of Society* is then built round Lona Hessel's design: the developments in the railway scheme, the complications of the shipyard repairs, and finally Olaf's running away all help to increase the pressure that is deliberately and consciously and purposely applied to effect Bernick's rehabilitation. In *A Doll's House*, on the other hand, the altruism is very largely involuntary, the chief agent in this instance being Krogstad. It is admittedly *through* him that the emancipating ordeal is engineered, but he is no declared altruist; indeed, by a stroke of authentic Ibsenist irony, he represents an egoism of the most conventional and bourgeois kind; he wants, he explains, to preserve at any cost what little respectability he has been able to win since the time of his own misdemeanours. The transformation in the Helmer household is thus obliquely, less obviously, less personally contrived. Yet there still is some slight trace of the Lona Hessel role in the person of Mrs. Linde (and with it, many would claim, a structural weakness in the architecture of the drama). In the last Act there is a moment when it seems the Helmers might be able to withdraw from the brink; if Krogstad were to do what was possibly the most natural thing, and ask for his letter back unopened, matters need never come to a head between husband and wife. But Mrs. Linde has seen 'quite incredible' things in their house, and insists that Helmer be forced to recognize how things are in reality; she dissuades Krogstad from asking for his letter back and thus deliberately precipitates the clash. In *Ghosts* the agency is vested in Pastor Manders; and much more important than his role as an embodiment of Ibsen's anti-sacerdotal bias is this function of his as an *agent provocateur*: 'A Pastor Manders will always provoke some Mrs. Alving or other into being', Ibsen once remarked. And a measure of the difference in *Ghosts* compared with *Pillars of Society* is that Bernick's moral improvement comes as a consequence of his capitulating to Lona Hessel's altruism, while Mrs. Alving's comes from a revulsion against Pastor Manders's. To show consideration for others is what Bernick is asked to accept as the surest way of being true to oneself; Mrs. Alving reverses the order, and brings her conduct rather into line with Polonius's advice to Laertes, or with Leslie Stephen's rather more contemporary concern for the 'health of the organism'. Manders's provocation belongs of course in the main to the past, particularly when he 'won a victory' over himself and helped Mrs. Alving to a similar 'victory' by returning her to the path of marital duty; he represents an attitude of mind that cannot accept the idea that circumstances alter cases, and sees only a code of behaviour. He becomes a kind of emancipator *malgré lui*. And the fact that Mrs. Alving undermines her own faith in altruism by obeying the call to duty so unremittingly contributes to the unexpected fluctuations in this play in the validity of first- and second-person responsibilities. Moreover, Manders's provocation is kept deliberately subdued in order not to clash too stridently with the idea of there also being some impersonal agency at work. The sins of the fathers are, in a very literal sense, visited here upon the children; nevertheless the fact that in the end Mrs. Alving is persuaded that these very sins themselves have their origin in the tainting influence of the narrow community her husband was forced to live in, plus the joylessness of the duty-ridden home environment she had created for him, all help to make the crisis seem self-engendered, or at least not imposed on the principals from without, as in *Pillars of Society* and to a lesser extent in *A Doll's House*.

It was because Ibsen was a dramatist and not a philosopher, and also because—as he was never tired of indicating—he was interested in using drama to ask questions rather than supply answers, that he left undefined except by implication those principles he felt might happily govern our actions, either as individuals or as social beings. It would perhaps not be difficult to separate out in his work a broad streak of Utilitarianism, an inclination to believe that what makes people happy is best. Although cynicism is an important ingredient in his dramas, he was never for very long cynical about man's capacity for good; there is below the surface of these plays a certain exhilaration at the thought of destroying all the apparitions, the delusions, the hallucinations of the past; there is a confidence, sometimes clearly expressed and sometimes only intimated, in the possibility of improvement; a belief that although things can go wrong, the potential integrity of man is something to be believed in. These dramas make the point that we often give our approval to things too easily, or else allow our unthinking consent. They insist that authority is not something established once and for all, but needs to establish itself ever anew; that filial affection is to be won and deserved, and never merely assumed; that marriage is an association by free choice, and held together by mutual trust; that patriotism needs more to justify it than a mere geographical accident of birth; that religion has to earn individual acceptance; and that social, political, cultural, and national institutions have ultimately to be shaped by individual conviction. The need to judge for oneself what is right and what is wrong is made paramount. Take as little as possible 'on trust' or 'on authority', these plays command; and in particular hold yourself independent of all instruments of human servitude: the codifications of the law, the precepts of dogma, the ingrained responses of habit, the prohibitions of convention, the tyranny of superstition, and the demands of any loyalty that takes itself for granted.

PILLARS OF SOCIETY

[Samfundets Støtter]

PLAY IN FOUR ACTS

(1877)

CHARACTERS

KARSTEN BERNICK, a consul

MRS. BETTY BERNICK, his wife

OLAF, their son, aged 13

MISS MARTHA BERNICK, the consul's sister

JOHAN TÖNNESEN, Mrs. Bernick's younger brother

MISS LONA HESSEL, Mrs. Bernick's elder step-sister

HILMAR TÖNNESEN, Mrs. Bernick's cousin

RÖRLUND, a schoolteacher

RUMMEL, a business man

VIGELAND, a tradesman

SANDSTAD, a tradesman

DINA DORF, a young girl living with the Bernicks

KRAP, chief clerk

AUNE, shipyard foreman

MRS. RUMMEL

MRS. HOLT, the postmaster's wife

MRS. LYNGE, the doctor's wife

MISS HILDA RUMMEL

MISS NETTA HOLT

Townspeople and other residents, foreign sailors, ship's passeng
etc.

The action takes place in the house of Consul Bernick, in a small Norwe:
coastal town

ACT ONE

A spacious conservatory in the house of CONSUL BERNICK. *A door, left front, leads to the Consul's room; further back on the same wall is a similar door. In the middle of the opposite wall is a fairly big entrance door. The rear wall is almost entirely glass; an open door gives on to a veranda with steps down, over which is stretched an awning. Part of the garden can be seen at the bottom of the steps, surrounded by railings with a little garden gate. Beyond the fence is a street, on the far side of which is a row of small, gaily painted timber houses. It is summer, and the sun is warm. Occasionally people pass along the street, some stop and talk, others call at a little corner shop, and so on.*

Within the conservatory, a group of ladies is seated round a table. At the middle of the table sits MRS. BERNICK. *On her left sit* MRS. HOLT *and her daughter, then* MRS. RUMMEL *and* MISS RUMMEL. *On* MRS. BERNICK'S *right sit* MRS. LYNGE, MISS MARTHA BERNICK *and* DINA DORF. *All the ladies are busy sewing. The table is piled high with bits of material, cut out and partly made-up, and with other articles of clothing. Further back, at a little table on which stand two pot plants and a glass of fruit juice, sits* RÖRLUND, *a schoolteacher; he is reading aloud from a book with gilt edges, but the audience is only able to catch an occasional word.* OLAF BERNICK *is running about outside in the garden, playing with a toy cross-bow.*

Presently AUNE, *a shipyard foreman, comes in quietly through the door on the right. The reading is momentarily interrupted;* MRS. BERNICK *nods to him and points to the door, left.* AUNE *walks quietly across and quietly knocks once or twice at the Consul's door, pausing in between.* KRAP, *the chief clerk, with his hat in his hand and papers under his arm, comes out of the room.*

KRAP. Oh, it's you knocking, is it?

AUNE. Mr. Bernick sent for me.

KRAP. He did. But he can't see you now. He authorized me . . .

AUNE. You? I'd much rather . . .

KRAP. . . . authorized me to tell you what it was. These week-end lectures of yours to the workmen have got to stop.

AUNE. Oh? I should have thought how I used my own free time was . . .

KRAP. You are not to go using your free time to make the men useless during working hours. Look what you told them last Saturday: that the new machinery and the new methods in the shipyard were a threat to the workers! Why do you do it?

AUNE. I do it in the interests of society.

KRAP. How interesting! Mr. Bernick says it's anti-social.

AUNE. My society isn't Mr. Bernick's society, Mr. Krap. Speaking as head of the Working Men's Society, I must . . .

KRAP. First and foremost you are foreman of Mr. Bernick's shipyard. First and foremost you've got your duty to the society known as Bernick and Co. On *that* all our livelihoods depend. . . . Well, now you know what Mr. Bernick had to say to you.

AUNE. Mr. Bernick wouldn't have put it quite like *that*, Mr. Krap! But I know what I have to thank for this. It's that damned American boat in for repair. These people want the work doing the way they are used to having it done over there, and that . . .

KRAP. Yes, yes, yes. I can't go into all these things now. You know now what Mr. Bernick's views are, and that's that! You'd better get back to the yard, you are probably needed. I'll be down there myself shortly. Excuse me, ladies.

[*He bows, and goes out through the garden down to the street.* AUNE *goes silently out, right.* RÖRLUND, *who has continued to read aloud during the whole of the previous subdued exchange, finishes the book and shuts it with a bang.*]

RÖRLUND. There, dear ladies, that's the end.

MRS. RUMMEL. Oh, what an edifying story!

MRS. HOLT. And so moral!

MRS. BERNICK. A book like that certainly makes you think.

RÖRLUND. Ah, yes. It makes a welcome contrast to those regrettable things that face us every day in the newspapers and the magazines. The gilded, painted façade which these big nations present to the world . . . what in fact does it conceal? Hollowness and decay, if I may say so. No moral foundation beneath their feet. In a word, they are nothing but whited sepulchres, these bigger nations of today!

MRS. HOLT. Yes, that is very true.

MRS. RUMMEL. You've only to look at the crew of this American boat that's in at the moment.

RÖRLUND. Scum of humanity, such as they are, I don't care to discuss. But even among the better classes—how are things *there*? Suspicion and ferment rife everywhere! Discontented minds and a complete lack of stability! The way family life is being undermined over there! Not even the most solemn truths are safe from impudent and subversive attack!

DINA [*without looking up*]. But plenty of great things do get done, don't they?

RÖRLUND. Great things . . . ? I don't understand. . . .

MRS. HOLT [*astonished*]. Good heavens, Dina. . . .

MRS. RUMMEL [*simultaneously*]. But Dina, how can you . . . ?

RÖRLUND. I don't think it would be to our advantage if any of these things were introduced here. No, we who live here ought to thank God that things are as they are. Not but what there aren't some tares among the wheat here too, I'm sorry to say; but these we honestly try to weed out as best we can. The thing that counts is to keep society pure, ladies . . . to keep at bay all these new-fangled things that an impatient age wants to force upon us.

MRS. HOLT. And unfortunately there are more than enough of those.

MRS. RUMMEL. Yes, last year the town was within a hairsbreadth of getting the railway.

MRS. BERNICK. Ah well, Karsten managed to put a stop to that.

RÖRLUND. Providence, Mrs. Bernick! You may be sure your husband was an instrument in the hand of a higher power when he refused to have anything to do with that scheme.

MRS. BERNICK. Yes, they said such nasty things about him in the papers. But we are quite forgetting to thank you, Mr. Rörlund. It really is more than kind of you to give up so much of your time to us.

RÖRLUND. Nonsense! While the school's on holiday. . . .

MRS. BERNICK. Ah yes, but it is a great sacrifice, nevertheless, Mr. Rörlund.

RÖRLUND [*moving his chair nearer*]. Please don't mention it, dear lady. Aren't you all making sacrifices in a good cause? And making them willingly and gladly? These moral delinquents whose rehabilitation we are working for, might be regarded as soldiers lying wounded on the field of battle. You, dear ladies, are the nurses, sisters of mercy, preparing the lint for these unfortunate casualties, placing the bandages gently round their wounds, tending and healing them. . . .

MRS. BERNICK. What a great blessing it must be to be able to see everything in such a beautiful light.

RÖRLUND. That sort of thing is largely inborn, but it can often be acquired. It's all a question of having some serious purpose in life, and seeing things in *that* light. What do you say to that, Miss Bernick? Don't you find that devoting yourself to school-work has given you, as it were, a firmer foundation to stand on?

MARTHA BERNICK. Oh, I don't know what to say. Often when I am down there in the schoolroom, I wish I were far out on the stormy sea.

RÖRLUND. There you see, such is temptation, dear Miss Bernick. But the thing is, one must bar the door to such unruly guests. The stormy sea . . . of course, you don't mean that literally. You mean the great surging tide of human society upon which so many are wrecked. That life you hear roaring, surging past outside, do you really value it so highly? Just look down into the street . . . people going about in the heat of the sun, sweating and straining over their petty affairs. No, we are certainly better off in here, sitting nice and cool and able to turn our backs on all these disturbing things.

MARTHA BERNICK. Heavens, yes, I'm sure you are absolutely right. . . .

RÖRLUND. And in a house like this . . . in a good and pure home, where family life is seen in its fairest form . . . where peace and harmony prevail. . . . [*To* MRS. BERNICK.] What are you listening for, Mrs. Bernick?

MRS. BERNICK [*turned to face the door downstage, left*]. How loud their voices are getting in there.

RÖRLUND. Is anything special going on?

MRS. BERNICK. I don't know. I can hear there's somebody in with my husband.

[HILMAR TÖNNESEN, *a cigar in his mouth, comes in through the door, right, but stops at the sight of all the ladies.*]

HILMAR TÖNNESEN. Oh, I beg your pardon. . . . [*He turns to withdraw.*]

MRS. BERNICK. Do come in, Hilmar, you aren't disturbing us. Was there something you wanted?

HILMAR TÖNNESEN. No, I just thought I'd look in. Good morning, ladies. [*To* MRS. BERNICK.] Well, what's going to be the upshot of all this?

MRS. BERNICK. What?

HILMAR TÖNNESEN. Bernick has drummed up a meeting, hasn't he?

MRS. BERNICK. Oh? But what's it all about?

HILMAR TÖNNESEN. It's all this stupid railway business again.

MRS. RUMMEL. No! Is that possible?

MRS. BERNICK. Poor Karsten, does he have to be bothered again . . . ?

RÖRLUND. But what sense does this make, Mr. Tönnesen? Mr. Bernick made it perfectly clear last year that he wouldn't have any railway.

HILMAR TÖNNESEN. Yes, that's what I thought, too. But I ran into Krap, and he said the question of the railway was on the cards again, and that Bernick was having a meeting with three of our local plutocrats.

MRS. RUMMEL. Ah, I *thought* I heard my husband's voice.

B

HILMAR TÖNNESEN. Yes, Mr. Rummel's in on it of course, and so is Mr. Sandstad from up the hill, and Michael Vigeland—'Holy Michael', as they call him.

RÖRLUND. H'm. . . .

HILMAR TÖNNESEN. I beg your pardon, Mr. Rörlund.

MRS. BERNICK. Just when everything was nice and peaceful.

HILMAR TÖNNESEN. Well, personally I wouldn't mind if they did start their squabbling again. It makes a bit of a diversion, at any rate.

RÖRLUND. Oh, that kind of diversion one could well do without, I should say.

HILMAR TÖNNESEN. Depends how you are made. Some types need a fight occasionally to shake them up. Unfortunately, small-town life hasn't a great deal to offer in that line, and it's not everybody who . . . [*Turns over the pages of* RÖRLUND'S *book.*] *Women in the Service of Society.* What sort of drivel is this?

MRS. BERNICK. Good heavens, Hilmar! You mustn't say that. I'm sure you haven't read the book.

HILMAR TÖNNESEN. No, and I don't intend reading it, either.

MRS. BERNICK. You don't seem quite on top of yourself today.

HILMAR TÖNNESEN. No, I'm not.

MRS. BERNICK. Didn't you sleep well last night?

HILMAR TÖNNESEN. No, I slept very badly. I went for a little walk last night for the sake of my health, and I finished up at the Club reading an account of an expedition to the North Pole. There's something invigorating about sharing in men's battles with the elements.

MRS. RUMMEL. I'm sure that wasn't very good for you, Mr. Tönnesen.

HILMAR TÖNNESEN. No, it was very bad for me. I lay all night tossing and turning, half-asleep and dreaming a horrible walrus was after me.

OLAF [*who has come up on the veranda*]. Were you being chased by a walrus, Uncle?

HILMAR TÖNNESEN. I dreamt it, stupid! Are you still going around playing with that ridiculous cross-bow? Why don't you get yourself a proper gun?

OLAF. Ah, I wish I could, but . . .

HILMAR TÖNNESEN. There's some point in having a real gun. There's always something terribly thrilling about firing it.

OLAF. Then I could shoot bears, Uncle. But Father won't let me.

MRS. BERNICK. Really, you mustn't go giving him ideas like that, Hilmar.

HILMAR TÖNNESEN. H'm. I don't know what's happening to the young people of today! Everybody talks about the wide open spaces, but —good Lord—it's all just a game. Never a spark of that old keenness for seeking out danger and facing up to it like a man—they don't want to be tough. Don't stand pointing that thing at me, you blockhead. It might go off.

OLAF. Oh, Uncle, there's no arrow in.

HILMAR TÖNNESEN. You can never be sure; there might be an arrow in all the time. Take it away, I tell you! . . . Why the devil is it you've never gone over to America in one of your father's boats? Then you might have seen a buffalo hunt, or a fight with the Redskins.

MRS. BERNICK. Now, Hilmar . . . !

OLAF. Yes, I'd love to, Uncle. And then perhaps I might meet Uncle Johan and Aunt Lona.

HILMAR TÖNNESEN. H'm . . . rubbish!

MRS. BERNICK. Off you go out into the garden again now, Olaf.

OLAF. Mother, can I also go out in the street?

MRS. BERNICK. Yes, but don't go too far. [OLAF *runs out through the garden gate.*]

RÖRLUND. You shouldn't put such wild ideas into the child's head, Mr. Tönnesen.

HILMAR TÖNNESEN. Oh no, of course not! He has to stay sitting here at home, like all the rest of them.

RÖRLUND. Why don't you go over yourself, then?

HILMAR TÖNNESEN. Me? In my state of health? Of course, nobody pays much attention to that in this town. All the same . . . one does have certain obligations towards the society one belongs to. *Somebody* here at any rate must keep the flag of the ideal flying. Ugh! There he goes bellowing again!

THE WOMEN. Who's bellowing?

HILMAR TÖNNESEN. Oh, I don't know. They've got their voices raised in there, and that makes me jumpy.

MRS. RUMMEL. It's probably my husband, Mr. Tönnesen. He's so used to addressing public meetings, you know. . . .

RÖRLUND. I wouldn't have said the others were particularly quiet-spoken, either.

HILMAR TÖNNESEN. My God, no! The moment anything touches their pockets, they . . . Everything here comes down to petty, material considerations. Ugh!

MRS. BERNICK. At least that's better than before, when everything went on pleasure-seeking.

MRS. LYNGE. Was it really as bad as all that here before?

MRS. RUMMEL. Believe me, it was, Mrs. Lynge. You can thank your lucky stars you weren't living here then.

MRS. HOLT. Ah, there have been some changes here all right! When I think back to when I was a girl. . . .

MRS. RUMMEL. Oh, you've only got to think back fourteen or fifteen years. Heavens above, the things that went on here! That was the time there was both a Dancing Club and a Music Society. . . .

MARTHA BERNICK. And a Dramatic Society. I remember that well.

MRS. RUMMEL. Yes, that was where your play was produced, Mr. Tönnesen.

HILMAR TÖNNESEN [*walks upstage*]. Oh, really now . . . !

RÖRLUND. Mr. Tönnesen! A play!

MRS. RUMMEL. Yes, that was long before *you* came here, Mr. Rörlund. And anyway, it was only done once.

MRS. LYNGE. Wasn't *that* the play where you told me you took the part of one of the young lovers, Mrs. Rummel?

MRS. RUMMEL [*glancing at* RÖRLUND]. Me? I really don't remember, Mrs. Lynge. But what I do remember is all the hectic social life that went on in some families.

MRS. HOLT. Yes, I even know of houses where they gave big dinner parties twice a week.

MRS. LYNGE. And haven't I heard about a theatrical company being on tour here?

MRS. RUMMEL. Yes, that was the worst thing of all. . . .

MRS. HOLT [*uneasily*]. H'm, h'm. . . .

MRS. RUMMEL. Actors? No, I don't remember that at all.

MRS. LYNGE. Yes, surely. They say they did all sorts of mad things, those people. What's the real truth behind these stories?

MRS. RUMMEL. Actually it's nothing, Mrs. Lynge.

MRS. HOLT. Dina, my sweet, hand me that piece of linen there, please.

MRS. BERNICK [*at the same time*]. Dina, my dear, please go and ask Katrine to bring in the coffee.

MARTHA BERNICK. I'll come with you, Dina.

[DINA *and* MARTHA BERNICK *go out by the door, upstage left.*]

MRS. BERNICK [*rising*]. And if you will excuse me a moment, ladies, I think we'll have our coffee outside.

[*She goes out on the veranda and lays a table;* RÖRLUND *stands in the doorway talking to her.* HILMAR TÖNNESEN *sits outside smoking.*]

MRS. RUMMEL [*in a low voice*]. Heavens, Mrs. Lynge, but you had me frightened!

MRS. LYNGE. I had?

MRS. HOLT. Yes, but really it was you yourself who started it, Mrs. Rummel.

MRS. RUMMEL. Who, me? Oh, how can you say such a thing, Mrs. Holt? Not so much as a single word crossed my lips.

MRS. LYNGE. But what *is* all this?

MRS. RUMMEL. How *could* you start talking about . . . ! Really! Didn't you see Dina was sitting there?

MRS. LYNGE. Dina? But, good heavens is anything wrong with . . . ?

MRS. HOLT. And in *this* house, too! Don't you know it was Mrs. Bernick's brother . . . ?

MRS. LYNGE. What about him? I know absolutely nothing. I haven't been here very long, you know. . . .

MRS. RUMMEL. You've never heard how . . . H'm. [*To her daughter.*] Hilda, you can go into the garden for a little while.

MRS. HOLT. You run along, too, Netta. And see you behave nicely to poor Dina when she comes back.

[MISS RUMMEL *and* MISS HOLT *go out into the garden.*]

MRS. LYNGE. Now, what was all this about Mrs. Bernick's brother?

MRS. RUMMEL. Don't you know he's the one all the scandal was about?

MRS. LYNGE. Scandal? About our Mr. Tönnesen?

MRS. RUMMEL. Good Lord, no! *He's* her cousin. I'm talking about her brother. . . .

MRS. HOLT. The ne'er-do-well one!

MRS. RUMMEL. His name was Johan Tönnesen. He ran away to America.

MRS. HOLT. *Had* to run away, you know.

MRS. LYNGE. So *he's* the one all the scandal was about?

MRS. RUMMEL. Yes, there was something . . . How shall I put it? It had something to do with Dina's mother. Oh, I remember it as if it were yesterday. Old Mrs. Bernick had the business then, and Johan Tönnesen was in the office. Karsten Bernick had just come back from Paris . . . he still wasn't engaged then . . .

MRS. LYNGE. But what about the scandal?

MRS. RUMMEL. Well, you see . . . that was the winter Möller's theatrical company was in town . . .

MRS. HOLT. . . . And among the actors in the company was a man called Dorf, together with his wife. All the young men fell for her completely.

MRS. RUMMEL. God only knows why they thought *she* was pretty. But then this man Dorf comes home late one evening . . .

MRS. HOLT. Quite unexpectedly. . . .

MRS. RUMMEL. . . . and what does he find but. . . . No, I really can't bring myself to tell you.

MRS. HOLT. In fact he didn't find anything, Mrs. Rummel, because the door was locked from the inside.

MRS. RUMMEL. That's just what I'm saying. He found the door locked. And what do you think? The man inside had to jump out of the window.

MRS. HOLT. Right down from an attic window.

MRS. LYNGE. And that was Mrs. Bernick's brother?

MRS. RUMMEL. Of course it was.

MRS. LYNGE. And then he ran away to America?

MRS. HOLT. Yes, then he *had* to run away, don't you see?

MRS. RUMMEL. Because they discovered something else afterwards that was nearly as bad. D'you know, he'd gone and helped himself out of the cash-box. . . .

MRS. HOLT. We don't really know if he did, Mrs. Rummel. Perhaps it was only a rumour.

MRS. RUMMEL. Well, I must say . . . ! Didn't the whole town know? Didn't it nearly bankrupt old Mrs. Bernick? My husband told me about it himself. But far be it from me to gossip about it!

MRS. HOLT. Well, none of the money came Mrs. Dorf's way, at any rate, because she . . .

MRS. LYNGE. Yes, how were things between Dina's parents after that?

MRS. RUMMEL. Well, Dorf went and left his wife and child. But madam had the nerve to stay on here for another year. Of course, she didn't dare show herself in the theatre any more, but she managed to keep herself by taking in washing and sewing. . . .

MRS. HOLT. Then she tried to get a school of dancing going.

MRS. RUMMEL. That was a flop, of course. What parents would trust their children to a person like that? Anyway, she didn't last much longer. She wasn't used to hard work, you see, fine lady that she was. She got a bad chest, and she died.

MRS. LYNGE. Really! What a dreadful story!

MRS. RUMMEL. Yes, it all weighed pretty heavily on the Bernicks, as you might imagine. It's the one dark spot in the sunshine of their lives, as my husband once put it. That's why you must never mention these things in this house, Mrs. Lynge.

MRS. HOLT. And don't, for heaven's sake, say anything about that step-sister, either!

MRS. LYNGE. Ah, yes, Mrs. Bernick has a step-sister too, hasn't she?

MRS. RUMMEL. *Used* to have—fortunately. They've broken off all connection now, those two. Ah, what a character she was! Would you believe it, she cut her hair short, and when it rained she used to walk about in men's boots!

MRS. HOLT. And when her step-brother . . . the ne'er-do-well one . . . had run away, and the whole town was naturally up in arms about him . . . d'you know what she does? She goes and joins him over there!

MRS. RUMMEL. Yes, but the scandal she caused before she left, Mrs. Holt!

MRS. HOLT. Hush! Don't talk about it!

MRS. LYNGE. Heavens, did she create a scandal, too?

MRS. RUMMEL. Wait till I tell you, Mrs. Lynge. Bernick had just got himself engaged to Betty Tönnesen; and he'd just come in, with her on his arm, to announce it to her aunt . . .

MRS. HOLT. The Tönnesens were orphans, you know. . . .

MRS. RUMMEL. . . . when Lona Hessel got up from the chair she was sitting in and gave the elegant Karsten Bernick such a slap in the face that his head rang.

MRS. LYNGE. Well, did you ever!

MRS. HOLT. That's absolutely true.

MRS. RUMMEL. Then she packed her bags and off she went to America.

MRS. LYNGE. She must have had an eye on him herself.

MRS. RUMMEL. Yes, that's pretty certain. She'd been going around with the idea that they'd make a match of it when he came home from Paris.

MRS. HOLT. Imagine thinking a thing like that! Bernick . . . a young man of the world . . . the perfect gentleman . . . the idol of all the girls. . . .

MRS. RUMMEL. . . . And yet so proper, too, Mrs. Holt! So moral!

MRS. LYNGE. But this Miss Hessel, what became of her in America?

MRS. RUMMEL. Ah! Over that there hangs a veil—as my husband once put it—which it would be better not to raise.

MRS. LYNGE. What do you mean by that?

MRS. RUMMEL. She is quite cut off from the family now, of course. But this much the whole town knows: that she used to sing for money in the saloons out there . . .

MRS. HOLT. . . . and she's given public lectures . . .

MRS. RUMMEL. . . . and published a quite outrageous book.

MRS. LYNGE. Fancy!

MRS. RUMMEL. Yes, indeed! Lona Hessel is another one of those dark spots in the sunlight of the Bernicks' lives. Well, now you know all about it, Mrs. Lynge. Of course I'm only saying this to put you on your guard, heaven knows!

MRS. LYNGE. Don't worry, I shall be. But poor Dina Dorf! I do feel sorry for her, really I do.

MRS. RUMMEL. But, after all, she's fallen on her feet. Think what would have happened if she'd remained in her parents' hands! Naturally, we all took an interest in her, and gave her all the good advice we could. Eventually Miss Bernick arranged for her to come and live in here.

MRS. HOLT. But she's always been a difficult child. It's not surprising—after such a bad example. It isn't as if she were like one of ours. You have to make allowances for her, Mrs. Lynge.

MRS. RUMMEL. Sh! She's coming. [*Aloud.*] Yes, she's a really clever girl, is Dina. Oh, is that you, Dina? Here we are just finishing off.

MRS. HOLT. Oh, how lovely that coffee of yours smells, Dina, my sweet. A cup of coffee like this in the middle of the morning. . . .

MRS. BERNICK [*on the veranda*]. Coffee is ready, ladies!

[MARTHA BERNICK *and* DINA *have in the meantime helped the maid with the coffee things. All the ladies go and sit outside; they talk with exaggerated kindliness to* DINA. *After a while she comes into the room to look for her sewing.*]

MRS. BERNICK [*out at the coffee table*]. Dina, don't you want . . . ?

DINA. No thanks. I don't want any.

[*She sits down at her sewing.* MRS. BERNICK *and* RÖRLUND *exchange a few words; a moment later he comes into the room.*]

RÖRLUND [*pretending to look for something on the table, speaks in a low voice*]. Dina!

DINA. Yes?

RÖRLUND. Why won't you come out?

DINA. When I came in with the coffee, I could see from that new visitor's face they'd been talking about me.

RÖRLUND. But then didn't you see how nice she was to you afterwards.

DINA. That's just what I can't bear!

RÖRLUND. You are stubborn, Dina.

DINA. Yes.

RÖRLUND. Why are you?

DINA. Because I am what I am.

RÖRLUND. Couldn't you try to be different?

DINA. No.

RÖRLUND. Why not?

DINA [*looking at him*]. Because I'm one of their moral delinquents!

RÖRLUND. Now, Dina!

DINA. My mother was also a moral delinquent.

RÖRLUND. Who's been talking to you about things like that?

DINA. Nobody. They never say anything. Why don't they? They all handle me so gingerly, as though I might break if . . . Oh, how I hate all this charity!

RÖRLUND. My dear Dina, I quite understand your feeling oppressed here, but . . .

DINA. Yes, if only I could get away from it all. I'd manage to get along all right, if only I didn't have to live among people who were so . . . so . . .

RÖRLUND. Well?

DINA. So respectable and so moral.

RÖRLUND. Dina, you can't really mean that?

DINA. You know very well what I mean! Every day along come Hilda and Netta to set me a good example. I can never be as nicely behaved as them. I don't *want* to be! Oh, if only I could get right away, I really would be a good girl.

RÖRLUND. But you *are* a good girl, Dina my dear.

DINA. What help is that to me here?

RÖRLUND. About this going away. . . . Are you thinking about it seriously?

DINA. If it wasn't for *you*, I wouldn't stay here a day longer.

RÖRLUND. Tell me, Dina . . . why do you like being with me?

DINA. Because you teach me all sorts of lovely things.

RÖRLUND. Lovely? You call the things I'm able to teach you 'lovely'?

DINA. Yes. Or rather . . . you don't in fact teach me anything. But I find myself seeing all sorts of lovely things, just listening to you talking.

RÖRLUND. What exactly do you understand by a 'lovely thing'?

DINA. I've never really thought about it.

RÖRLUND. Then think about it now. What do you understand by a 'lovely thing'?

DINA. A lovely thing is something big . . . and far away.

RÖRLUND. H'm. Dina, my dear. I am deeply concerned about you.

DINA. Is *that* all?

RÖRLUND. You know very well how unutterably dear you are to me.

DINA. If I happened to be Hilda or Netta, you wouldn't be afraid then of letting people see.

RÖRLUND. Oh, Dina, you have no conception of the thousand and one things that have to be borne in mind. . . . When a man is called to serve as a moral pillar of the society in which he lives, . . . one cannot be too careful. If only I could be sure that my motives would not be misinterpreted. . . . But there's nothing to be done about that. You *must* and *shall* be helped up. Dina, when I come . . . when circumstances permit me to come . . . and say, 'Here is my hand' . . . is it agreed that you will take it and be my wife? Do you promise me that, Dina?

DINA. Yes.

RÖRLUND. Thank you! Thank you! Because for my part, too . . . Oh, Dina, I am so very fond of you. . . . Hush! Somebody's coming. Dina, for my sake . . . go and join the others outside.

[*She goes out to the coffee table. That same moment,* RUMMEL, SAND-STAD *and* VIGELAND *come out from the room downstage left, followed by* BERNICK, *who carries in his hand a sheaf of papers.*]

BERNICK. Well, so that's settled then.

VIGELAND. Yes, thank God, let's hope so.

RUMMEL. It *is* settled, Bernick! A Norseman's word stands as firm as the rock of Dovrefjeld, you know that!

BERNICK. And nobody lets the side down, nobody backs out, no matter what opposition we meet!

RUMMEL. We stand or fall together, Bernick!

HILMAR TÖNNESEN [*who appears at the garden door*]. Fall? You'll forgive me, but don't you mean the railway's fallen through?

BERNICK. On the contrary. It's *going* through. . . .

RUMMEL. . . . Full steam ahead, Mr. Tönnesen!

HILMAR TÖNNESEN [*approaches*]. Oh?

RÖRLUND. How?

MRS. BERNICK [*at the garden door*]. Karsten dear, what's all this . . . ?

BERNICK. My dear Betty, what interest can this possibly have for *you*? [*To the three gentlemen.*] Now we must draw up the lists, and the sooner the better. Naturally, we four will subscribe first. The position we occupy in the community makes it incumbent on us to do our very utmost.

SANDSTAD. Naturally, Mr. Bernick.

RUMMEL. We'll do it, Bernick! We've given our word.

BERNICK. Oh yes, I am not the least anxious about the outcome. We must make a point of all doing our bit in our own circle; and once we can point to the fact that all sections of the community are showing a lively interest in the scheme, it automatically follows that the council will have to give it financial support.

MRS. BERNICK. But, Karsten, you must come out here and tell us. . . .

BERNICK. My dear Betty, it's not a thing for the ladies to worry their heads about.

HILMAR TÖNNESEN. Are you really going to give your backing to the railway after all?

BERNICK. Yes, of course.

RÖRLUND. But Mr. Bernick, last year . . . ?

BERNICK. Last year was quite a different matter. They were talking then about a line along the coast. . . .

VIGELAND. . . . Which would have been quite superfluous, Mr. Rörlund, seeing that we already have the steamer. . . .

SANDSTAD. . . . And which would have been preposterously expensive. . . .

RUMMEL. . . . And which moreover would have been detrimental to certain established interests in the town.

BERNICK. The main thing is that it wouldn't have benefited the community generally. That was why I opposed it; so then the cross-country route was adopted.

HILMAR TÖNNESEN. Yes, but it's not going to touch the towns around here.

BERNICK. It's going to touch *our* town, my dear Hilmar. Because we are going to build a branch line.

HILMAR TÖNNESEN. Aha! This is a new idea!

RUMMEL. Yes, isn't it a marvellous idea? Eh?

RÖRLUND. H'm. . . .

VIGELAND. It cannot be denied that Providence seems almost to have designed the lie of the land specially to suit a branch line.

RÖRLUND. You don't say so, Mr. Vigeland!

BERNICK. Yes, I must confess that I too see the hand of Providence at work. I had to take a business trip up there this spring, and I happened to find myself in a valley I'd never been in before. And, like a flash, it struck me that that was where we might be able to run a branch line down to us. I've had the land surveyed by an engineer; here I have provisional calculations and estimates. There's nothing to stop us.

MRS. BERNICK [*still at the garden door, along with the other ladies*]. But Karsten dear, fancy your keeping all this dark!

BERNICK. Oh, my dear Betty, you wouldn't really have understood the ramifications of the thing. Anyway, I haven't mentioned it to a single living soul until today. But now the crucial moment has arrived; the time for direct and forceful action has come! Yes, I shall see this thing through now, even if I have to throw in everything I've got.

RUMMEL. We are with you, Bernick! Depend on that!

RÖRLUND. Do you really expect so much from this undertaking, gentlemen?

BERNICK. Yes, I should say we do! Don't you see what a boost it will give to our whole community. Just think of the huge tracts of forest it will open up! Think of all those rich mineral deposits that can be worked! Think of the river, with one waterfall after another! What about the industrial development that could be made there!

RÖRLUND. And you have no misgivings that closer contact with the corruption of the outside world . . . ?

BERNICK. Oh no! Set your mind at rest about that, Mr. Rörlund! This bustling little town of ours rests nowadays, thank God, on sound moral foundations. All of us—if I may so put it—have helped to drain it clear; and we shall continue the process, each in our own way. You, Mr. Rörlund, will continue your wonderful work in school and in our homes. We, the practical men of business, will serve the community by bringing prosperity to as wide a circle as possible. And our women . . . yes, do come closer, ladies, I would like you to hear this . . . our women, I say, our wives and daughters —may you carry on undisturbed with your splendid social work, ladies, and may you also continue to be a help and a comfort to your nearest and dearest, as my dear Betty and Martha are to me and Olaf. . . . [*Looks round.*] Where is Olaf today?

MRS. BERNICK. Oh, in the holidays it's impossible to keep him in.

BERNICK. I bet he's down by the sea again! There'll be an accident there before he's finished, you'll see.

HILMAR TÖNNESEN. Puh! A bit of sport with the elements of nature. . . .

MRS. RUMMEL. How nice that you are so attached to your family, Mr. Bernick.

BERNICK. Well, after all, the family is the very nucleus of society. A good home, sincere and faithful friends, a small and intimate circle where no disruptive elements cast their shadow. . . .

[KRAP *comes in from the right with letters and newspapers.*]

KRAP. The foreign mail, Mr. Bernick . . . and a telegram from New York.

BERNICK [*takes it*]. Ah, from the owners of the *Indian Girl*.

RUMMEL. The post's in, eh? Well, if you'll excuse me. . . .

VIGELAND. Me, too.

SANDSTAD. Goodbye, Mr. Bernick.

BERNICK. Goodbye, goodbye, gentlemen. Don't forget we have another meeting at five o'clock this afternoon.

THE THREE MEN. Yes. Yes, indeed. Of course.

[*They go out, right.*]

BERNICK [*who has been reading the telegram*]. Well, isn't that just like the Americans! Absolutely outrageous!

MRS. BERNICK. Good heavens, Karsten, what is it?

BERNICK. Look at that, Mr. Krap! Read it!

KRAP [*reading*]. 'Do minimum possible repairs. Send *Indian Girl* as soon as she can be floated. Good season. In emergency, cargo will keep her afloat.' Well, I must say. . . .

BERNICK. Cargo keep her afloat! These gentlemen know very well that, with a cargo like that, the ship would go to the bottom like a stone if anything were to happen.

RÖRLUND. Ah, you see how things are in these much-vaunted big countries.

BERNICK. You are right. No respect for human life even, as soon as profit enters into it. [*To* KRAP.] Can the *Indian Girl* put to sea in four or five days?

KRAP. Yes, if Mr. Vigeland would agree to our stopping work on the *Palm Tree* in the meantime.

BERNICK. H'm, he won't do that. Well, look through the post, please, will you? By the way, you didn't see Olaf down at the quayside?

KRAP. No, Mr. Bernick.

[*He goes into the room, downstage left.*]

BERNICK [*looking again at the telegram*]. No scruples about gambling with the lives of eighteen men. . . .

HILMAR TÖNNESEN. Well, it's a sailor's job to defy the elements. That must be quite exhilarating, standing there with nothing but a thin plank between you and eternity. . . .

BERNICK. Ah, I'd like to see the shipowner here who would stoop to a thing like that! Not *one*, not a single *one*. . . . [*He catches sight of* OLAF.] Thank God, there he is, safe and sound.

[OLAF, *a fishing-line in his hand, comes running up the garden and in through the garden door.*]

OLAF [*still in the garden*]. Uncle Hilmar, I've been down to see the steamer.

BERNICK. Have you been down at the quayside again?

OLAF. No, I've only been out in a boat. D'you know what, Uncle Hilmar? A whole circus came ashore, with lots of horses and animals. And there were lots and lots of passengers, too.

MRS. RUMMEL. Well! We are not going to have a circus, are we?

RÖRLUND. We? I should hope not!

MRS. RUMMEL. Not *us*, of course, but . . .

DINA. I would like to see the circus.

OLAF. Me, too.

HILMAR TÖNNESEN. You are stupid! What's there to see in *that*? Just a few tricks they've been taught. Now, seeing the gaucho tearing across the pampas on his snorting mustang, that's something quite different. But, good God, in a little place like this. . . .

OLAF [*pulling at* MARTHA BERNICK]. Aunt Martha, look, look! They're coming!

MRS. HOLT. Yes, good heavens, there they are.

MRS. LYNGE. Ugh! What horrid people!

[*Several of the passengers and a whole crowd of townspeople are walking up the road.*]

MRS. RUMMEL. Yes, and a right set of rogues they look, too. Look at that woman in the grey skirt, Mrs. Holt, with that great bag over her shoulder.

MRS. HOLT. Look, she's carrying it by the handle of her umbrella! She must be the ringmaster's wife.

MRS. RUMMEL. And there's the ringmaster himself, the one with the beard. Really he just looks like a pirate. Don't look at him, Hilda!

MRS. HOLT. Or you either, Netta!

OLAF. Mother, the ringmaster's waving to us.

BERNICK. What's that?

MRS. BERNICK. What do you say, child?

MRS. RUMMEL. Good heavens, yes. And that woman's waving, too!

BERNICK. Really, this is too bad!

MARTHA BERNICK [*with an involuntary cry*]. Ah. . . !

MRS. BERNICK. What is it, Martha?

MARTHA BERNICK. Nothing! I just thought. . . .

OLAF [*shouting with joy*]. Look, look! There's the rest of them coming with the horses and the animals! And there are the Americans, too! All the sailors from the *Indian Girl*. . . .

[*The sound of 'Yankee Doodle' can be heard, accompanied by clarinet and drum.*]

HILMAR TÖNNESEN [*his hands to his ears*]. Ugh! Ugh!

RÖRLUND. I think we ought to withdraw just a little, ladies. This isn't anything for us. Let us go back to our work again.

MRS. BERNICK. Perhaps we ought to draw the curtains?

RÖRLUND. Just what I was thinking.

[*The ladies resume their seats at the table.* RÖRLUND *shuts the garden door, and draws the curtain across it and across the windows; the room is partly darkened.*]

OLAF [*peeping out*]. Mother, the ringmaster's wife has stopped by the pump and she's washing her face.

MRS. BERNICK. What! In the middle of the market place?

MRS. RUMMEL. In broad daylight!

HILMAR TÖNNESEN. Well, if I happened to be trekking across the desert and I stumbled upon a water-hole, I don't think I would hesitate either to . . . Ugh! That frightful clarinet!

RÖRLUND. There's really every justification for the police to intervene.

BERNICK. Oh, come! You mustn't be too severe on foreigners. After all, these people here have none of that deep-rooted sense of propriety that keeps *us* from overstepping the mark. Let them have their way. What does it matter to us? All this hooliganism, this defiance of established custom and decent manners . . . happily all this is completely foreign to our community, if I may say so. What's this!

[*The strange woman walks briskly in through the door, right.*]

THE LADIES [*in alarmed undertones*]. The circus woman! The ringmaster's wife.

MRS. BERNICK. Heavens! What does this mean!

MARTHA BERNICK [*leaps up*]. Ah. . . !

THE WOMAN. Good morning, Betty dear! Good morning, Martha! Good morning, brother-in-law!

MRS. BERNICK [*with a cry*]. Lona. . . !

BERNICK [*falling back a step*]. As I live and breathe. . . !

MRS. HOLT. But good gracious . . . !

MRS. RUMMEL. Surely it's not possible . . . !

HILMAR TÖNNESEN. Well! Ugh!

MRS. BERNICK. Lona . . . ! Is it really . . . ?

LONA HESSEL. Really me? You bet it is! Fall on my neck and kiss me, for that matter, if you like!

HILMAR TÖNNESEN. Ugh! Ugh!

MRS. BERNICK. Turning up here now as . . . ?

BERNICK. You aren't really going to perform. . . ?

LONA HESSEL. Perform? What do you mean, perform?

BERNICK. Well, I mean . . . with the circus . . . ?

LONA HESSEL. Ha! ha! Are you mad, Karsten? D'you think I'm with the circus? No! I know I've tried my hand at all sorts of things and made a clown of myself in many ways . . .

MRS. RUMMEL. H'm . . . !

LONA HESSEL. . . . but bare-back riding is a thing I've never tried.

BERNICK. So you're not . . . ?

MRS. BERNICK. Oh, thank God!

LONA HESSEL. No, we travelled across just like any other respectable people. . . . Second class, I admit, but we're used to that.

MRS. BERNICK. Did you say 'we'?

BERNICK [*takes a step forward*]. Who's 'we'?

LONA HESSEL. My little boy and me, of course.

THE LADIES [*with a cry*]. Your little boy!

HILMAR TÖNNESEN. What!

RÖRLUND. Well, I must say. . . .

LONA HESSEL. I mean John, of course. I haven't any other little boy but John, as far as I know . . . or Johan, as you used to call him.

MRS. BERNICK. Johan . . . !

MRS. RUMMEL [*to* MRS. LYNGE *in an undertone*]. The ne'er-do-well brother!

BERNICK [*hesitantly*]. Is Johan with you?

LONA HESSEL. Of course! Of course! I wouldn't come without him. But you all look so sad, sitting here in the dark sewing all these white things. There hasn't been a death in the family, has there?

RÖRLUND. My dear lady, you find yourself here in the Society for Moral Delinquents. . . .

LONA HESSEL [*in an undertone*]. What's that you say? You're not telling me all these nice quiet-looking ladies are . . . ?

MRS. RUMMEL. Well, really! I must say. . . !

LONA HESSEL. Oh, I see, I see. Well, I'll be damned if that isn't Mrs. Rummel. And there's Mrs. Holt, too. Ah, none of us have got any younger since we last met. What about letting the moral delinquents wait for one day, they'll not be any the worse for that. A joyful occasion like this . . . .

RÖRLUND. A home-coming is not always a joyful occasion.

LONA HESSEL. Oh? Is that the way you read your Bible, pastor?

RÖRLUND. I am not a pastor.

LONA HESSEL. You will be in time, sure enough. Puh, but all this moral linen smells bad . . . just like a shroud. I am used to the air of the prairies, I am.

BERNICK [*mopping his brow*]. Yes, it is a bit close in here.

LONA HESSEL. Wait, wait. We'll soon get ourselves out of this tomb. [*She draws the curtains aside.*] Clear daylight is what's needed here when the boy comes. Yes, then you'll see a fine clean-looking lad. . . .

HILMAR TÖNNESEN. Ugh!

LONA HESSEL [*opening doors and windows*]. At least that is when he *has* got himself cleaned up a bit . . . up at the hotel. He got as filthy as a pig on that boat.

HILMAR TÖNNESEN. Ugh! Ugh!

LONA HESSEL. Ugh? Well, if it isn't . . . ! [*Pointing to* HILMAR *and asking the others.*] Does he *still* come wandering round here saying 'Ugh' all the time?

HILMAR TÖNNESEN. I'm not wandering. I'm taking a walk for the sake of my health.

RÖRLUND. H'm! I don't think, ladies . . .

LONA HESSEL [*catching sight of* OLAF]. Is he *yours*, Betty? Give us your paw, lad! Or perhaps you're frightened of your ugly old aunt?

RÖRLUND [*putting his book under his arm*]. I don't think, ladies, that the mood is right for any further work today. But we'll be meeting again tomorrow?

LONA HESSEL [*as the visiting ladies get up to take their leave*]. Yes, let's do that. I'll be there.

RÖRLUND. *You*? You'll forgive me, madam, but what do *you* want in *our* society?

LONA HESSEL. I want to let in some fresh air, my dear pastor.

ACT TWO

The conservatory at BERNICK'S *house.* MRS. BERNICK *is sitting alone at a work-table with her sewing. After a moment or two,* CONSUL BERNICK *comes in, right, wearing hat and gloves and carrying a stick.*

MRS. BERNICK. Home already, Karsten?

BERNICK. Yes. I've got somebody coming to see me.

MRS. BERNICK [*with a sigh*]. Ah, yes. I suppose Johan is coming down here again.

BERNICK. It's one of the men, actually. [*He takes off his hat.*] Where are all the ladies today?

MRS. BERNICK. Mrs. Rummel and Hilda hadn't time.

BERNICK. Oh? Cried off?

MRS. BERNICK. Yes, they had such a lot to do in the house.

BERNICK. Naturally! And of course the others aren't coming either?

MRS. BERNICK. No, *they* had something on, too.

BERNICK. I could have told you that beforehand. Where's Olaf?

MRS. BERNICK. I let him go for a little walk with Dina.

BERNICK. H'm, Dina! Flighty little hussy! In no time, yesterday, she was all over Johan . . . !

MRS. BERNICK. But, Karsten dear, Dina has no idea. . . .

BERNICK. But Johan should at least have had the tact not to show her any attention. I could see Vigeland's eyes popping.

MRS. BERNICK [*her sewing in her lap*]. Karsten, can you understand what they've come home for?

BERNICK. H'm, there's that farm of his over there that doesn't seem to be doing particularly well. And *she* mentioned yesterday about their having had to travel second class. . . .

MRS. BERNICK. Yes, I'm afraid it must be something like that. But what brings *her* with him? Her! After the shocking way she insulted you. . . !

BERNICK. Oh, that's ancient history now! Stop thinking about it!

MRS. BERNICK. How can I help thinking about it, just now. He is my brother, after all. . . . Well, I'm not thinking so much of him as of all the unpleasantness it would involve *you* in, Karsten, I'm so dreadfully afraid that . . .

BERNICK. Afraid of what?

MRS. BERNICK. Mightn't they want to arrest him on account of that money of your mother's that was missing?

BERNICK. Rubbish! Who can prove that there was any money missing?

MRS. BERNICK. But, good Lord, I'm afraid the whole town knows. You said so yourself. . . .

BERNICK. I said nothing. The town knows nothing about this matter. The whole thing was just a wild rumour.

MRS. BERNICK. How magnanimous you are, Karsten!

BERNICK. Let's have no more of these reminiscences, please! You don't know how painful I find it when you go raking up all these things. [*He walks up and down; then he flings his stick away from him.*] Why did they have to come home just now . . . the very time when I need to appear in the best possible light, both in the town and in the press? There'll be reports in all the papers in the district. Regardless of whether I give them a warm reception or a cool one, it will all be discussed and turned inside out. They'll rake up all that old business again . . . just like *you* did! In a community such as ours. . . . [*He throws his gloves down on the table.*] And there isn't a single person here I can talk to, or turn to for support.

MRS. BERNICK. Nobody at all, Karsten?

BERNICK. Well, who *is* there? Why do they have to land on me at this time? They are sure to cause a scandal one way or another . . . especially her! What a blight it is, having people like that in the family!

MRS. BERNICK. Well, *I* can't help it if . . .

BERNICK. You can't help it if what? If they're your relations? No, that's very true.

MRS. BERNICK. And I didn't ask them to come home, either!

BERNICK. Ah, now we're off! 'I didn't ask them to come home. I didn't write for them to come. I didn't drag them home by the scruff of their necks.' I know the whole rigmarole off by heart.

MRS. BERNICK [*bursting into tears*]. You *are* unkind. . . !

BERNICK. Yes, that's right! Start crying, and give the town something *else* to gossip about. Stop this nonsense, Betty! Go and sit outside, somebody might come in. Do you want them to say they've seen you with your eyes all red? Ah, nice thing that would be if it got around that. . . ! I can hear somebody in the hall. [*There is a knock.*] Come in!

[MRS. BERNICK *goes on to the veranda with her sewing.* AUNE *comes in from the right.*]

AUNE. Good morning, Consul Bernick.

BERNICK. Good morning. Well, I suppose you can guess what I want you for?

AUNE. Mr. Krap said something yesterday about you not being very satisfied with . . .

BERNICK. I am most dissatisfied with the whole way the yard's being run, Aune. You are not getting on with those repair jobs at all. The *Palm Tree* should have been ready to sail long ago. I've had Mr. Vigeland coming along every day worrying me. He's a difficult man to have as a partner.

AUNE. The *Palm Tree* will be ready to sail the day after tomorrow.

BERNICK. At last! But what about the American boat, the *Indian Girl*? She's been lying for five weeks and . . .

AUNE. The American boat? I understood we were to concentrate on your own boat first.

BERNICK. Nothing I said should have given you that idea. You were supposed to press on as hard as possible with the American boat as well. But you haven't!

AUNE. That boat's hull is absolutely rotten, Mr. Bernick. The more we patch it, the worse it gets.

BERNICK. That's not what's at the bottom of all this. Mr. Krap has told me the real truth. You don't know how to work the new machinery I've installed—or more correctly, you don't *want* to.

AUNE. Mr. Bernick, I'm now turned fifty. Right from being a lad, I've been used to the old way of working. . . .

BERNICK. That won't do nowadays. You mustn't think, Aune, that it's just for the profits. Happily I'm not dependent on them. But I have to have some regard for the community in which I live, and for the business of which I am head. Progress must either come from me, or it will never come.

AUNE. I want progress too, Mr. Bernick.

BERNICK. Yes, but limited to your own kind, to the working class. Oh, I know all about you and your agitation . . . the speeches you make, the way you get the people all worked up. But as soon as something tangible in the way of progress presents itself—like now, with our machinery—you'll have nothing to do with it. You're afraid!

AUNE. That's right, I *am* afraid, Mr. Bernick. I'm afraid for all those who'll have the bread snatched from their mouths by these machines. You're always talking about having regard for society, Mr. Bernick, but I think society's got its obligations too. What business has science and capitalism got, bringing all these new inventions into the works, before society has produced a generation educated up to using them!

BERNICK. You read and think too much, Aune. It's not good for you. *That's* what makes you discontented with your position.

AUNE. It's not that, Mr. Bernick. But I can't stand seeing one good man after another being paid off and losing his job, on account of these machines.

BERNICK. H'm. When printing was invented, plenty of scribes lost their jobs.

AUNE. Would you have been all that pleased about it, Mr. Bernick, if you'd happened to be a scribe then?

BERNICK. I didn't ask you to come here to bandy words. I sent for you to tell you that the *Indian Girl* must be ready to sail the day after tomorrow.

AUNE. But, Mr. Bernick . . . !

BERNICK. The day after tomorrow, d'you hear! The same time as our own ship, not an hour later. I have good reason for wanting to hurry things up. Have you seen this morning's paper? Well then, you'll know that these Americans have been making a nuisance of themselves again. That gang of hooligans is turning the whole place upside down. Not a night passes but what there's some brawl somewhere, either in the public houses or in the streets. Not to speak of all the other disgusting things.

AUNE. Yes, it's quite clear they're a bad lot.

BERNICK. And who gets the blame for it all? Me! It all comes back to me. All these sly hints in the papers that we've been concentrating all our resources on the *Palm Tree*. Am I to let them throw this sort of thing in my face . . . I, whose job it is to set an example to my fellow citizens? I won't have it. I won't stand for having my name dragged through the mud like this.

AUNE. Oh, the name of Bernick is good enough to stand plenty of that, and more.

BERNICK. Not at this moment. At the present time I need all the respect and good-will my fellow citizens can give me. I have a big project in hand, as you've probably heard. And if any vindictive people managed to shake the unqualified confidence I enjoy, it could land me in the most serious difficulties. That's why I want to put a stop to these evil insinuations in the newspapers at any cost. And that's why I'm making it the day after tomorrow.

AUNE. You might as well make it this afternoon, Mr. Bernick.

BERNICK. You mean I'm demanding the impossible?

AUNE. Yes. With the labour force we have at present. . . .

BERNICK. All right! Then we'll have to look elsewhere.

AUNE. You aren't going to sack still more of the old hands?

BERNICK. No, that's not what I have in mind.

AUNE. Because I believe it would cause a lot of bad blood, both in the town and in the papers, if you did that.

BERNICK. That's not impossible. So we'll not do that. But if the *Indian Girl* isn't cleared by the day after tomorrow, *you're* sacked!

AUNE [*with a start*]. Me! [*He laughs.*] You are joking, Mr. Bernick.

BERNICK. I shouldn't rely on that!

AUNE. You would think of sacking *me*? Me, whose father and grandfather worked all their lives in the yard, just as I have . . .

BERNICK. Who's forcing me to do it?

AUNE. You're asking the impossible, Mr. Bernick.

BERNICK. Where there's a will there's a way. Yes, or no? I want a straight answer, or else I sack you here and now.

AUNE [*takes a step forward*]. Mr. Bernick, have you seriously thought what it means—giving an old workman the sack? You think he ought to look around for something else? Oh yes, I suppose he can. But is that the end of it? You ought to try being there sometimes, the night a workman comes home with the sack, and puts his toolchest behind the door.

BERNICK. Do you think I'm doing it lightly? Haven't I always been a reasonable employer?

AUNE. That's what makes it worse, Mr. Bernick. That's just why, when I get home, it won't be *you* they'll blame. They won't say anything to me, they won't dare. But they'll look at me when I'm not looking, and they'll think: he must have deserved it. And don't you see that's . . . that's something I can't bear. I may not count for very much, but I've always been used to being the head of the family. My modest little home is also a small community, Mr. Bernick . . . a small community I've been able to support and maintain, because my wife believed in me, and because my children believed in me. Now the whole lot's going to collapse.

BERNICK. Well, if there's nothing else for it, then the lesser must give way to the greater. The particular must, in God's name, be sacrificed to the general good. I can't say more than that, and that's the way of the world. You are a stubborn man, Aune! You are opposing me, not because you must, but because you don't want to admit the superiority of the machine over manual labour.

AUNE. You are sticking to that story, Mr. Bernick, because you know that, if you do kick me out, it will convince the press that you had only the best of intentions.

BERNICK. What if I am? I've told you what it means to me—either I get the entire press coming down on me, or else I win its approval —the very moment when I'm working on a big project for the common good. So what? Can I do anything other than what I *am* doing? I'll tell you where the crux lies here: it's either, as you put it, a question of upholding your home or of suppressing perhaps hundreds of new homes . . . hundreds of homes, that will never be built, never have a blazing hearth, unless I bring off what I'm working on. That's why I'm giving you this choice.

AUNE. In that case, I have nothing more to say.

BERNICK. H'm! My dear Aune, I am very sorry we are having to part.

AUNE. We're not parting, Mr. Bernick.

BERNICK. What do you mean?

AUNE. Even a common man has some things in this world he must preserve.

BERNICK. Indeed, indeed! So you think you can promise. . . ?

AUNE. The *Indian Girl* will be ready for clearance the day after tomorrow.

[*He bows and goes out, right.*]

BERNICK. Aha! That'll show him, the obstinate old . . . I regard that as a good omen.

[HILMAR TÖNNESEN, *a cigar in his mouth, comes in through the garden gate.*]

HILMAR TÖNNESEN [*on the veranda*]. Good morning, Betty! Good morning, Bernick!

MRS. BERNICK. Good morning.

HILMAR TÖNNESEN. You've been crying, I see. So you know?

MRS. BERNICK. Know what?

HILMAR TÖNNESEN. That the scandal is in full spate. Ugh!

BERNICK. What do you mean?

HILMAR TÖNNESEN [*coming in*]. Those two Americans are walking around town quite openly in the company of Dina Dorf.

MRS. BERNICK [*following him in*]. But Hilmar, is this possible. . . ?

HILMAR TÖNNESEN. I'm afraid it's absolutely true. Lona was even so tactless as to shout across to me, but naturally I pretended not to hear.

BERNICK. And I dare say all this has not gone unnoticed.

HILMAR TÖNNESEN. You're right, it hasn't. People stopped and stared at them. It seemed to run through the town like wild-fire . . . rather like a prairie fire out West. In every house there were people at the windows waiting for the procession to pass by, all with their heads together behind the curtains. . . . Ugh! You must excuse me, Betty, saying 'Ugh' . . . all this makes me so jumpy. If this goes on I'll have to think about taking a long holiday.

MRS. BERNICK. You should have spoken to him and pointed out . . .

HILMAR TÖNNESEN. There on the street! No thank you! How that man has the nerve to show himself at all in this town! We'll have to see if the newspapers can't put a stop to him. I'm sorry, Betty, but . . .

BERNICK. The newspapers, d'you say? Has there been any suggestion of that?

HILMAR TÖNNESEN. Oh yes, plenty! When I left here last night, I went for a little constitutional as far as the Club. I could tell from the silence that they'd been on about the two Americans. Then that editor chap, Hammer, comes across quite shamelessly and congratulates me in a loud voice on the return of my rich cousin.

BERNICK. Rich . . . ?

HILMAR TÖNNESEN. Yes, that's what he said. Of course, I just looked him up and down with the contempt he deserves and gave him to understand that I know nothing about Johan Tönnesen being rich. 'Oh?' he says, 'that's odd. In America people generally do pretty well for themselves if they've got a little bit to start with, and your cousin didn't exactly go over empty-handed, did he?'

BERNICK. H'm! Please do me a favour and . . .

MRS. BERNICK [*worried*]. You see, Karsten . . .

HILMAR TÖNNESEN. Anyway, it's given me a sleepless night, and all because of this person. There he goes, walking around the streets looking as if nothing was the matter. Why couldn't he go and disappear for good and all? It's absolutely intolerable, the way some people manage to survive.

MRS. BERNICK. Good heavens, Hilmar, what are you saying?

HILMAR TÖNNESEN. I'm not saying anything. But there he goes and escapes unscathed from railway disasters, and fights with Californian bears, and attacks by Blackfoot Indians. Didn't even get scalped! . . . Ugh! Here they come!

BERNICK [*looks up the road*]. Olaf is with them, too!

HILMAR TÖNNESEN. Of course! They want to remind people that they belong to the best family in town. Look at all those louts turning out of the drug store to stare at them, and passing remarks. Really, this is too much for my nerves! How any man can be expected to keep the flag of idealism flying in conditions like these . . . !

BERNICK. They're coming here. Listen to me now, Betty. It is my express wish that you show them every possible friendliness.

MRS. BERNICK. Is that what you want, Karsten?

BERNICK. Of course, of course. And you too, Hilmar. They probably won't stay long; and while we are with them, no pointed remarks! We mustn't offend them in any way.

MRS. BERNICK. Oh, Karsten, how magnanimous you are!

BERNICK. Now, now, never mind that!

MRS. BERNICK. But I must thank you! Forgive me for losing control of myself just now. Ah yes, you had every reason to . . .

BERNICK. Never mind, never mind, I said!

HILMAR TÖNNESEN. Ugh!

[JOHAN TÖNNESEN *and* DINA, *followed by* LONA HESSEL *and* OLAF *come up the garden.*]

LONA HESSEL. Good morning, good morning, my dear people.

JOHAN TÖNNESEN. We've been out looking at some of the old places, Karsten.

BERNICK. So I hear. Lots of changes, eh?

LONA HESSEL. Signs of Consul Bernick's great and splendid work everywhere! We've been up to the park you presented to the town. . . .

BERNICK. Ah, there!

LONA HESSEL. 'Presented by Karsten Bernick', as it says over the entrance. Yes, you are certainly the man who counts around here.

JOHAN TÖNNESEN. And some fine ships you've got, too. I met the captain of the *Palm Tree*, who used to be at school with me. . . .

LONA HESSEL. You've also built a new school-house. And I hear it's thanks to you there's both a gas works and a water works.

BERNICK. Well, one must do what one can for the community one lives in.

LONA HESSEL. Yes, that's a fine thing. But it's also nice to see how people appreciate you. I'm not vain I don't think, but I couldn't help reminding some of the people we talked to that we belonged to the family.

HILMAR TÖNNESEN. Ugh!

LONA HESSEL. Did you say 'Ugh'?

HILMAR TÖNNESEN. No, I said 'h'm'. . . .

LONA HESSEL. I think we might allow that, then, you poor old thing! But I see you're all alone today.

MRS. BERNICK. Yes, today we're all alone.

LONA HESSEL. Actually, we met a couple of your Moral What's-their-names up by the market place. They seemed very busy. But we still haven't had the chance of a proper talk together yet. Yesterday those three intrepid pioneers were here, and then we had that pastor. . . .

HILMAR TÖNNESEN. Schoolmaster.

LONA HESSEL. *I* call him the pastor. But what do you think of *my* work of these last fifteen years? Hasn't he turned out a grand lad? Whoever would recognize him now as that harum-scarum who ran away from home?

HILMAR TÖNNESEN. H'm . . . !

JOHAN TÖNNESEN. Oh, Lona, don't lay it on too thick.

LONA HESSEL. But it is something to be pretty proud of. Heaven knows, it's about the only thing I have achieved in this world. But it gives me a sort of right to exist. Yes, Johan, when I think how we two started over there, with only our four bare paws. . . .

HILMAR TÖNNESEN. Hands.

LONA HESSEL. *I* say paws. They were filthy enough . . .

HILMAR TÖNNESEN. Ugh!

LONA HESSEL. . . . *and* they were empty.

HILMAR TÖNNESEN. Empty? Well, I must say!

LONA HESSEL. What must you say?

BERNICK. H'm!

HILMAR TÖNNESEN. I must say. . . . Ugh!

[*He goes out on to the veranda.*]

LONA HESSEL. What's wrong with him?

BERNICK. Oh, don't worry about him. He's a bit jumpy at the moment. Wouldn't you like to take a little look at the garden? You haven't seen it properly yet, and I just happen to have the next hour free.

LONA HESSEL. Yes, I'd like to. Many's the time I've been with you here in this garden in my thoughts, believe me.

MRS. BERNICK. There have been big changes there too, as you'll see.

[BERNICK, MRS. BERNICK *and* LONA HESSEL *go into the garden, where during the following conversation they can occasionally be seen.*]

C

OLAF [*at the garden door*]. Uncle Hilmar, d'you know what Uncle Johan asked me? He asked me if I wanted to go with him to America.

HILMAR TÖNNESEN. You. . . ? Little fool! Running about here tied to your mother's apron strings. . . !

OLAF. Yes, but I don't want to any more. When I grow up you'll see. . . .

HILMAR TÖNNESEN. Fiddle-faddle! You haven't the guts to face up to things like . . .

[*Together they go into the garden.*]

JOHAN TÖNNESEN [*to* DINA, *who has taken off her hat and is standing by the door, right, shaking the dust off her skirt*]. Warm after your walk?

DINA. Yes, it was a lovely walk. I've never had such a lovely walk before.

JOHAN TÖNNESEN. Perhaps you don't often go out for walks in the morning?

DINA. Oh yes, but only with Olaf.

JOHAN TÖNNESEN. I see. . . . Perhaps you'd prefer to go out in the garden than stay here?

DINA. No, I'd prefer to stay here.

JOHAN TÖNNESEN. So would I. And it's all arranged then, that we go out for a walk like that every morning.

DINA. No, Mr Tönnesen, you mustn't do that.

JOHAN TÖNNESEN. Why mustn't I? You promised!

DINA. Yes, but on second thoughts . . . You mustn't go out with me.

JOHAN TÖNNESEN. Why not?

DINA. Of course, you're a stranger here. You don't understand. But I must tell you. . . .

JOHAN TÖNNESEN. Well?

DINA. No, I'd rather not talk about it.

JOHAN TÖNNESEN. Oh, of course you must! You can talk about anything you like to me.

DINA. Well, I must tell you, I'm not like the other girls. There's something . . . something about me. That's why you mustn't.

JOHAN TÖNNESEN. But I simply don't understand all this. You haven't done anything wrong, have you?

DINA. *I* haven't, no! But . . . No, I don't want to say any more about it. You'll hear about it soon enough from the others.

JOHAN TÖNNESEN. H'm.

DINA. But there was something else I wanted to ask you.

JOHAN TÖNNESEN. What was that?

DINA. They say that over in America it's easy to make good?

JOHAN TÖNNESEN. Well, it's not always so easy. Very often it's pretty tough going and plenty of hard work to begin with.

DINA. Ah, I wouldn't mind that. . . .

JOHAN TÖNNESEN. You?

DINA. I can work. I'm strong and healthy, and Aunt Martha has coached me in lots of things.

JOHAN TÖNNESEN. Why then, damn it, come along with us!

DINA. You're only joking. You said the same to Olaf. But what I wanted to know was: are the people terribly . . . terribly sort of *moral* over there?

JOHAN TÖNNESEN. Moral?

DINA. Yes. I mean, are they sort of . . . proper and respectable, like they are here?

JOHAN TÖNNESEN. At all events they're not as bad as the people here think they are. You needn't worry about that.

DINA. You don't understand. I was rather hoping they wouldn't be so terribly respectable and moral.

JOHAN TÖNNESEN. You were? And how would you like them to be, then?

DINA. I should like them to be natural.

JOHAN TÖNNESEN. Well, yes, that's perhaps exactly what they are.

DINA. In that case, it might be a good thing for me if I could get across.

JOHAN TÖNNESEN. I'm sure it would. That's why you must come with us.

DINA. No, I wouldn't go with you. I would have to go alone. Oh, I'd make the most of my chances. I'd make out all right. . . .

BERNICK [*at the foot of the garden steps with the two ladies*]. Wait there! I'll fetch it, Betty dear. You might catch cold.

[*He comes into the room, and looks for his wife's shawl.*]

MRS. BERNICK [*out in the garden*]. You must come along too, Johan. We're going down to the grotto.

BERNICK. No, Johan must stay here. Here, Dina! Take my wife's shawl, and you go along with them. Johan's staying here with me, Betty dear. I want to hear a bit about what things are like over there.

MRS. BERNICK. All right. But come along later. You know where to find us.

[MRS. BERNICK, LONA HESSEL *and* DINA *walk down the garden, left.*]

BERNICK [*watches them for a moment, walks across and shuts the door, upstage left, then goes over to* JOHAN, *seizes both his hands and clasps them*]. Johan, now we are alone. Please, now, let me thank you.

JOHAN TÖNNESEN. Oh, rubbish!

BERNICK. House and home, my family's happiness, my entire social position . . . I owe it all to you.

JOHAN TÖNNESEN. It's a pleasure, my dear Karsten. So some good did come of that stupid affair, after all.

BERNICK [*again clasps his hands*]. Thank you, thank you, all the same! Not one man in ten thousand would have done what you did for me that time.

JOHAN TÖNNESEN. Nonsense! Weren't we both young and a bit reckless? One of us had to take the blame.

BERNICK. But who more properly than the guilty one?

JOHAN TÖNNESEN. Stop! This time the *innocent* one was the proper one. There was I, free, footloose, no parents. It was sheer good luck to be able to get away from that awful office grind. You, on the other hand, still had your own mother living; and on top of that you'd only just got secretly engaged to Betty, and she was so very fond of you. How would she have taken it if she'd known. . . ?

BERNICK. True, true, true. But . . .

JOHAN TÖNNESEN. And wasn't it precisely for Betty's sake you broke off that little affair with Madam Dorf? The very reason you were up there with her that evening was to break things off. . . .

BERNICK. Yes, that wretched evening when that man came home, drunk . . . ! Yes, Johan, it was for Betty's sake. Still . . . it was very noble of you to draw suspicion on yourself and then leave. . . .

JOHAN TÖNNESEN. Don't fret, my dear Karsten. We agreed that was how it should be. You had to be saved, and you were my friend. Ah, how proud I was of that friendship! There was I, miserable little stick-in-the-mud still plodding along at home; then along you came, fine and elegant, just back from your grand foreign tour. You'd been to both Paris and London. Then you pick me as your special friend, even though I was four years younger than you. . . . Well, that was because you'd started courting Betty, I can see that *now*. But how proud I was! Who wouldn't have been? Who wouldn't have willingly sacrificed himself for you, especially when all it meant was a month's gossip, and then straight afterwards the chance of escaping into the great, wide world?

BERNICK. H'm! My dear Johan, to be quite honest I must tell you that the story isn't altogether forgotten.

JOHAN TÖNNESEN. It isn't? Well, what does it matter to me when I'm back over there again on my farm. . . .

BERNICK. So you are going back?

JOHAN TÖNNESEN. Of course.

BERNICK. But not too soon, I hope?

JOHAN TÖNNESEN. As soon as possible. The only reason I came across was I didn't want to disappoint Lona.

BERNICK. Oh? How d'you mean?

JOHAN TÖNNESEN. Well, you see, Lona isn't getting any younger, and lately she's been having pangs of homesickness—not that she'd ever admit it. [*Smiles.*] How could she risk leaving an irresponsible lot like me behind on his own, after what I'd got myself mixed up in as a nineteen-year-old. . . ?

BERNICK. So?

JOHAN TÖNNESEN. Karsten, I want to make a confession I'm rather ashamed of.

BERNICK. You didn't tell her the whole story, did you?

JOHAN TÖNNESEN. Yes, I did. It was wrong of me, but I couldn't do anything else. You can't imagine what Lona's been to me. You've never been able to stand her, but to me she's been like a mother. Those first years when things were so tight over there—how she worked! And when I was laid up sick for a long time, and couldn't go out to work, . . . I couldn't stop her, she went out singing in cafés . . . she gave lectures that people made fun of . . . then she wrote a book she's both laughed and cried over since. And all just to keep me alive. Last winter I couldn't stand by and watch her pining away, not after the way she'd slaved and sweated for me. No, I couldn't, Karsten. So I said: 'You go, Lona, and don't worry about *me*, I'm not as irresponsible as you think.' And then . . . she learnt it all.

BERNICK. And how did she take it?

JOHAN TÖNNESEN. Well, she said what was quite true: that since I knew I was innocent, I wouldn't mind taking a trip across with her. But don't worry, Lona won't give anything away. And I'll watch *I* don't open my big mouth another time.

BERNICK. Yes, I'm sure you won't.

JOHAN TÖNNESEN. Here's my hand. Now we'll let bygones be bygones. Fortunately it's the only bit of folly either of us has ever committed, I imagine. Now I really want to enjoy the few days I've got here. You wouldn't believe what a marvellous walk we had this morning. Who would have thought the little brat who used to run about here, and come on as a cherub in the theatre. . . ! But tell me . . . what happened afterwards about her parents?

BERNICK. Ah, Johan, I can't tell you any more than what I told you in that letter soon after you'd left. You got those two letters, I hope?

JOHAN TÖNNESEN. Yes, yes. I've got them both. That drunken sot went and left her, didn't he?

BERNICK. Then later he fell and broke his neck when he was dead drunk.

JOHAN TÖNNESEN. *She* died soon after, too, didn't she? But I suppose you did all you could for her, on the quiet?

BERNICK. She was proud. She didn't give anything away, but neither would she accept anything.

JOHAN TÖNNESEN. At any rate, you did the right thing in taking Dina into the house.

BERNICK. Yes, of course. Actually though, it was Martha who worked that.

JOHAN TÖNNESEN. It was Martha, was it? Ah, Martha . . . that's right. . . . Where's *she* today?

BERNICK. Oh, her! When she's not looking after the school, she's got her invalids.

JOHAN TÖNNESEN. So it was Martha who looked after her.

BERNICK. Yes, Martha's always had a great weakness for educating people. That's the reason she took a job at the council school. It was incredibly stupid of her.

JOHAN TÖNNESEN. Yes, she looked worn out yesterday. I'm worried in case her health isn't up to it.

BERNICK. Oh, her health could always stand up to it. But it's rather unpleasant for *me*. It looks as though her own brother weren't willing to support her.

JOHAN TÖNNESEN. Support her? But I thought she had sufficient means of her own to . . .

BERNICK. Not a penny. You remember how tight Mother was finding things just about the time you went away? She carried on for a time, with some assistance from me, but I didn't find that very satisfactory in the long run, so I arranged to go into the business with her. But that didn't work either. So I had to take over the whole concern. And when we went over the accounts, it became apparent that there was practically nothing left of Mother's share. So that when Mother died shortly afterwards, Martha was left pretty well high and dry, of course.

JOHAN TÖNNESEN. Poor Martha!

BERNICK. Poor? Why? You don't imagine I let her want for anything, do you? Oh no, I think I can say I'm a good brother to her. Of course, she lives with us, and eats at our table. Her teacher's salary is enough to keep her in clothes, and a single woman—what more does she need?

JOHAN TÖNNESEN. H'm! That's not the way we think in America.

BERNICK. No, I suppose not. Not in a hot-headed society like the American one. But in our little world here, where—thank God—corruption has as yet gained no foothold, here the women are content to assume a seemly, if modest status. Anyway, it's Martha's own fault. She could have been provided for long ago, if she'd wished.

JOHAN TÖNNESEN. You mean she could have married?

BERNICK. Yes, she could. And have been comfortably off, too. She's had several good offers, strangely enough. . . . A woman without means, no longer young, and rather insignificant.

JOHAN TÖNNESEN. Insignificant?

BERNICK. Well, I don't really hold it against her. I wouldn't really want her to be otherwise. You know . . . in a big house, like this . . . it's always good to have somebody steady about the place. Somebody who can cope with things as they crop up.

JOHAN TÖNNESEN. Yes, but what about *her*?

BERNICK. Her? What d'you mean? Oh, well *she* has plenty to interest her, of course. She's got me and Betty and Olaf and me. People should never think primarily of themselves, least of all women. We all have some sort of community, large or small, to support and work for. *I* do anyway. [*Pointing to* KRAP *who enters, right.*] Here comes proof of it. Do you think it's personal affairs that take up my time? Not at all. [*Quickly to* KRAP.] Well?

KRAP [*in a low voice, producing a sheaf of papers*]. All the conveyances are in order.

BERNICK. Splendid! Excellent! . . . Well, Johan, I must ask you to excuse me for a little while. [*Quietly and with a shake of the hand.*] Thank you, thank you, Johan. And rest assured that anything I can do for you . . . well, you know what I mean. Come along, Mr. Krap.

[*They go into* BERNICK'S *room.*]

JOHAN TÖNNESEN [*looking after him for a moment*]. H'm. . . ! [*He turns to go down into the garden. At that moment,* MARTHA BERNICK *comes in, right, with a little basket on her arm.*] Well, it's Martha!

MARTHA BERNICK. Ah . . . Johan! It's you!

JOHAN TÖNNESEN. Out and about so early!

MARTHA BERNICK. Yes. If you wait a moment, the others will be here directly.

[*She turns to go out, left.*]

JOHAN TÖNNESEN. I say, Martha! Are you always in such a hurry?

MARTHA BERNICK. Who, me?

JOHAN TÖNNESEN. All day yesterday you seemed to be keeping out of the way, and I never got a chance to talk to you. And today . . .

MARTHA BERNICK. Yes, but . . .

JOHAN TÖNNESEN. We were always together before . . . we two old playmates.

MARTHA BERNICK. Ah, Johan. That was many, many years ago.

JOHAN TÖNNESEN. Good Lord, it's fifteen years, neither more nor less. Do you think I've changed all that much?

MARTHA BERNICK. You? Oh yes, you too, although. . .

JOHAN TÖNNESEN. What do you mean?

MARTHA BERNICK. Oh, nothing.

JOHAN TÖNNESEN. You don't seem to be very excited to see me again.

MARTHA BERNICK. I have waited so long, Johan . . . too long.

JOHAN TÖNNESEN. Waited? For me to come?

MARTHA BERNICK. Yes.

JOHAN TÖNNESEN. And why did you think I would come?

MARTHA BERNICK. To atone for the wrong you did.

JOHAN TÖNNESEN. *I* did?

MARTHA BERNICK. Have you forgotten that a woman died in shame and poverty, and all because of you? Have you forgotten that, because of you, the best years of a young child's life were embittered?

JOHAN TÖNNESEN. And *you* can say this to me? Martha, did your brother never . . . ?

MARTHA BERNICK. What?

JOHAN TÖNNESEN. Did he never . . . ? I mean, did he never say anything at all in my defence . . . not a word?

MARTHA BERNICK. Ah, Johan, you know Karsten's strict principles.

JOHAN TÖNNESEN. H'm . . . of course, of course! I know all about my old friend Karsten's strict principles. But, really, this is . . . ! Well, I've just been talking to him. I think he has changed considerably.

MARTHA BERNICK. How can you say that? Karsten has always been a fine man.

JOHAN TÖNNESEN. That wasn't quite what I meant, but never mind. . . . H'm, I can see now what sort of light you must have seen me in. The prodigal's return, that's what you've been waiting for.

MARTHA BERNICK. Listen, Johan, and I'll tell you what sort of light I've seen you in. [*She points down into the garden.*] You see down there, that girl playing on the grass with Olaf? That's Dina. Do you remember that garbled letter you wrote to me when you left? You said I had to believe in you. I *did* believe in you, Johan. All those evil things we heard rumours about afterwards, they must have been done in a moment of aberration . . . thoughtless, impulsive things. . . .

JOHAN TÖNNESEN. What do you mean?

MARTHA BERNICK. You know very well what I mean . . . I won't say any more. Of course you had to get away . . . begin again . . . a new life. Look, Johan! I have stood in for you here at home . . . I, your old playmate. Those obligations you forgot to discharge here, or were unable to discharge, I discharged them for you. I'm telling you this so that you won't have *that* to reproach yourself with, too. I've been a mother to that poor, unfortunate child, brought her up as best I could. . . .

JOHAN TÖNNESEN. And wasted your whole life on it. . . .

MARTHA BERNICK. It hasn't been wasted. But you've been a long time, Johan.

JOHAN TÖNNESEN. Martha . . . if only I could tell you. . . . At any rate, let me thank you for your loyal friendship.

MARTHA BERNICK [*smiles sadly*]. H'm. . . ! Well, now we've had our say, Johan. Sh! Somebody's coming. Goodbye! I can't . . .

[*She goes out by the door, upstage left.* LONA HESSEL *comes in from the garden, followed by* MRS. BERNICK.]

MRS. BERNICK [*still in the garden*]. For heaven's sake, Lona, what can you be thinking of?

LONA HESSEL. Let me be, I tell you. I must and will talk to him.

MRS. BERNICK. But there would be the most frightful scandal! Ah, Johan, you still here?

LONA HESSEL. Out you go, lad! Don't hang around here indoors. Go down the garden and talk to Dina.

JOHAN TÖNNESEN. Just what I was thinking!

MRS. BERNICK. But . . .

LONA HESSEL. Listen, John! Have you ever taken a proper look at Dina?

JOHAN TÖNNESEN. Yes, I think so.

LONA HESSEL. Well, just you go and take a good long look at her, lad. She's the very thing for *you*!

MRS. BERNICK. But, Lona . . . !

JOHAN TÖNNESEN. For me?

LONA HESSEL. Yes. To look at, I mean. Go on!

JOHAN TÖNNESEN. All right, all right. Only too delighted!

[*He goes down into the garden.*]

MRS. BERNICK. Lona, you've got me quite petrified. You surely can't be serious?

LONA HESSEL. Indeed I am! Sound in wind and limb and mind, isn't she? Just the wife for John. He needs somebody like her over there ... somebody a bit different from his old step-sister.

MRS. BERNICK. Dina! Dina Dorf! But think. . . .

LONA HESSEL. I'm thinking first and foremost of the lad's happiness. But I'll have to push him a bit, he's not much of a hand at this kind of thing. He's never really bothered much about girls.

MRS. BERNICK. Him! Johan! I'd have thought we had plenty of evidence, unfortunately. . . .

LONA HESSEL. Oh, to hell with that stupid old story! Where's Karsten? I want to talk to him.

MRS. BERNICK. You shan't, Lona, I tell you.

LONA HESSEL. I will. If the lad likes her ... and she likes him ... then they shall have each other. Karsten can find some way out, seeing he's so clever. . . .

MRS. BERNICK. If you think these disgraceful American ways will be tolerated here ...

LONA HESSEL. Fiddle-faddle, Betty. . . .

MRS. BERNICK. . . . that a man like Karsten with his strict moral principles. . . .

LONA HESSEL. Puh! They're not so excessively strict as all that.

MRS. BERNICK. What's that you have the audacity to say?

LONA HESSEL. I have the audacity to say that Karsten's morals are not noticeably better than other men's.

MRS. BERNICK. So it's still there, this rooted hatred you have of him! What brings you here, if you've never been able to forget that. . . ? I can't understand how you even dare look him in the face after the shamefully insulting way you treated him that time.

LONA HESSEL. Yes, Betty. That time I forgot myself pretty badly.

MRS. BERNICK. And how generously he has forgiven you! He, who never did any wrong to anybody! He couldn't help it, that you went round building up your hopes. But since that time you have hated *me*, too. [*Bursts into tears.*] You've always grudged me my good luck. Now you come letting me in for all this . . . showing the whole town what sort of family I've brought Karsten into. Yes, I'm the one that has to suffer, and that's just what you want. Oh, it's horrid of you!

[*She goes out weeping by the door, upstage left.*]

LONA HESSEL [*looks after her*]. Poor Betty!

[*BERNICK comes out of his room.*]

BERNICK [*still in the doorway*]. Yes, yes, that's fine, Mr. Krap! That's excellent! Send 400 crowns to the poor-box. [*Turns.*] Lona! [*Comes closer.*] Are you alone? Isn't Betty coming?

LONA HESSEL. No. Shall I fetch her?

BERNICK. No, no, don't bother! Oh, Lona, you don't know how I've longed for the chance to talk freely to you . . . for the chance to beg your forgiveness.

LONA HESSEL. Look here, Karsten, let's not get all sentimental. It doesn't suit us.

BERNICK. You *must* listen to me, Lona. I know how appearances must be against me, now you know about Dina's mother. But I swear to you it was only a momentary infatuation. I really did love you once, honestly and truly.

LONA HESSEL. Why do you suppose I've come home?

BERNICK. Whatever you have in mind, I implore you not to do anything until I've had a chance to justify myself. I can, Lona! At least I can explain.

LONA HESSEL. Now you are afraid. . . . You loved me once, you said. Yes, you assured me of that plenty of times in your letters. It might even have been true . . . after a fashion . . . as long as you were living out there in the great, free world, a world that gave you the courage to think freely and generously yourself. You might even have found in me a bit more character and strength of mind and independence

than in most of the rest of them around here. Then again, it was a
secret between us two; nobody could make fun of your bad taste.

BERNICK. Lona, how can you possibly think. . . .

LONA HESSEL. But when you did come back, when you heard all the
ridicule they showered on me, when you heard the sniggers at what
they used to call my eccentricities. . . .

BERNICK. You *were* rather reckless in those days.

LONA HESSEL. Mostly to annoy all those petticoated prudes and trou-
sered ones too, we had prowling round the town. So that when you
met that glamorous young actress. . . .

BERNICK. That was just a bit of bravado, nothing more. I swear not a
tenth of all the rumour and gossip that went the rounds was true.

LONA HESSEL. Maybe not. But then when Betty came home . . . lovely
and radiant and idolized by everybody . . . and when it got out that
she was going to inherit all the aunt's money and I was to get
nothing. . . .

BERNICK. Ah, there we have it, Lona! Now listen and I won't pre-
varicate. I wasn't in love with Betty then. It wasn't any change of
heart that made me break things off with you. It was simply and
solely for the sake of the money. I had to do it. I had to make sure
of the money.

LONA HESSEL. You tell me this to my face!

BERNICK. Yes, I do. Listen, Lona. . . .

LONA HESSEL. Yet when you wrote to me, you said you had fallen
hopelessly in love with Betty; you appealed to my magnanimity,
implored me for Betty's sake to say nothing about what had been
between us. . . .

BERNICK. I had to, I tell you.

LONA HESSEL. Then, by God, I'm not sorry I forgot myself the way
I did that time!

BERNICK. Let me tell you, calmly and dispassionately, how things stood
in those days. As you remember, my mother was head of the firm;
but she had no sense for business whatever. I was called home from
Paris urgently, it was a critical time, and I was to put things on a

proper footing again. What did I find? I found—something that had to be kept a profound secret—that the firm was as good as ruined. Yes, as good as ruined, this old and respected house, which had stood for three generations. What could I do, the only son . . . but cast around for some means of salvation?

LONA HESSEL. So you saved the House of Bernick at a woman's expense!

BERNICK. You knew perfectly well that Betty loved me.

LONA HESSEL. But what about me?

BERNICK. Believe me, Lona . . . you would never have been happy with me.

LONA HESSEL. Was it concern for my happiness that made you drop me?

BERNICK. You don't think I acted as I did for selfish motives? If I had stood alone at that time, I should have been quite happy to start afresh from the beginning. But you have no idea how the life of a businessman gets caught up with the business he inherits, with all its tremendous responsibilities. Do you know that the welfare of hundreds . . . of thousands, even . . . depends on him? Don't you realize that this entire community—a community which both you and I call our home—would have suffered the most grievous consequences if the House of Bernick had collapsed?

LONA HESSEL. Was it also for the sake of this community that for fifteen years you have been living a lie?

BERNICK. A lie?

LONA HESSEL. What does Betty know of all these things that happened before her marriage to you?

BERNICK. Do you think I would want to hurt her by revealing these things—and all to no profit?

LONA HESSEL. To no profit you say? Ah, yes! You are a businessman, and you know all about profit. . . . But you listen to me, now, Karsten. Now *I'm* going to speak calmly and dispassionately. Tell me . . . are you really happy?

BERNICK. In my home, you mean?

LONA HESSEL. Yes.

BERNICK. I am, Lona. Ah, your sacrifices have not been in vain, my dear friend. I think I can say that I have become happier with every year that has passed. Betty is so good and adaptable. In the course of the years she has learnt to accommodate *her* nature to *my* way of life. . . .

LONA HESSEL. H'm!

BERNICK. To begin with, of course, she had a lot of rather hysterical ideas about love. She couldn't reconcile herself to the thought that it must gradually give way to a kind of gentle affection.

LONA HESSEL. But *now* she accepts that?

BERNICK. Completely. Daily contact with *me* has not been without some mellowing influence on her, you know. People have to learn to modify the demands they make on each other, if they are to do their best for the community they belong to. Betty also came to see that eventually, and that is why our house now stands as an example to our fellow citizens.

LONA HESSEL. But these fellow citizens know nothing about the lie?

BERNICK. The lie?

LONA HESSEL. Yes, the lie you've been living on now for fifteen years.

BERNICK. You call that . . . ?

LONA HESSEL. I call it a lie. A triple lie. First the lie to me, then the lie to Betty, and then the lie to Johan.

BERNICK. Betty has never demanded that I say anything.

LONA HESSEL. Because she didn't know anything.

BERNICK. And *you* won't ask me. . . . Out of consideration for her, you won't.

LONA HESSEL. Oh, no, I don't mind putting up with their guffaws. I've got a broad back.

BERNICK. And Johan won't ask me either. He's promised me.

LONA HESSEL. What about yourself, Karsten? Isn't there something in you that demands to be quit of that lie?

BERNICK. What, and wilfully sacrifice this happy home of mine, and my standing in society?

LONA HESSEL. What right have you to stand where you do stand?

BERNICK. Every day for fifteen years I have acquired a little more right . . . by my conduct and by what I have worked for and achieved.

LONA HESSEL. Yes, you have worked hard and achieved much, both for yourself and for others. You are the richest and most powerful man in town. They daren't do anything other than submit to you, all of them, because you have the reputation of being without stain or blemish. Your home is regarded as a model home, your life as a model life. But all this splendour, and you along with it . . . it's just as though it were built upon a shifting quagmire. A moment may come, a word can be spoken—and both you and all this splendour will collapse, if you don't take steps in time.

BERNICK. Lona . . . what are you after here?

LONA HESSEL. I want to help you to where you've firm ground under your feet, Karsten.

BERNICK. Revenge! You want to revenge yourself! I thought as much. But you won't succeed! There's only *one* person here who can speak with authority, and he is silent.

LONA HESSEL. Johan?

BERNICK. Yes, Johan. If anyone else accuses me, I'll deny everything. If they try to destroy me, I'll fight like grim death. But you'll never succeed, I tell you! The one man who can topple me down will keep silence . . . and he is leaving.

[RUMMEL *and* VIGELAND *come in from the right.*]

RUMMEL. Good morning, good morning, my dear Bernick! You must come up to the Chamber of Commerce with us. We have a meeting about the railway, you know.

BERNICK. I can't. Impossible just now.

VIGELAND. Really you must, Mr. Bernick. . . .

RUMMEL. You must, Bernick. Some people are opposing us. Mr. Hammer and all the others who favoured the coastal route are claiming that private interests are behind this new proposal.

BERNICK. Well then, explain to them. . . .

VIGELAND. It's no good *us* explaining, Mr. Bernick. . . .

RUMMEL. No, no, you must come yourself. Nobody will dare suspect you of anything like that.

LONA HESSEL. No, I should think not.

BERNICK. I can't, I tell you. I'm not well. . . . Oh, very well, wait a minute . . . let me collect myself.

[RÖRLUND *enters from the right.*]

RÖRLUND. Excuse me, Mr. Bernick, but here I am absolutely seething. . . .

BERNICK. What's the matter with you?

RÖRLUND. I've something I must ask you, Mr. Bernick. Is it with your consent that this young girl who has found shelter under your roof shows herself publicly in the street in the company of a person, who . . .

LONA HESSEL. Which person, pastor?

RÖRLUND. That person from whom, of all people in this world, she should be kept at the furthest remove.

LONA HESSEL. Ha! ha!

RÖRLUND. Is it with your consent, Mr. Bernick?

BERNICK [*looking for his hat and gloves*]. I know nothing at all about it. Excuse me, I'm in a hurry. I have to be at the Chamber of Commerce.

HILMAR TÖNNESEN [*comes in from the garden and walks over to the door, upstage left*]. Betty, Betty listen!

MRS. BERNICK [*in the doorway*]. What is it?

HILMAR TÖNNESEN. You'd better go down into the garden and put a stop to the hanky-panky going on between a certain person and that Dina Dorf. It's quite upset me to listen to it.

LONA HESSEL. Oh? And what did this person say?

HILMAR TÖNNESEN. Oh, only that he wanted her to go to America with him, that's all. Ugh!

RÖRLUND. Can this be possible?

MRS. BERNICK. What do you say?

LONA HESSEL. But that would be marvellous.

BERNICK. Impossible. You must have heard wrong.

HILMAR TÖNNESEN. Ask him yourself. Here's the pair of them. But let me keep out of it.

BERNICK [*to* RUMMEL *and* VIGELAND]. I'll follow you . . . just a minute. . . .

[RUMMEL *and* VIGELAND *go out right.* JOHAN TÖNNESEN *and* DINA *come from the garden.*]

JOHAN TÖNNESEN. Hurrah, Lona! She's coming with us!

MRS. BERNICK. But, Johan . . . you reckless . . . !

RÖRLUND. Is this true! This is an outrageous scandal. What seducer's tricks are these . . . ?

JOHAN TÖNNESEN. Now, now, man! Watch what you are saying!

RÖRLUND. Answer me, Dina! Is this your intention? Is this a completely voluntary decision?

DINA. I *must* get away from here.

RÖRLUND. But with *him* . . . with *him*!

DINA. Name me anyone else who would have had the courage to take me.

RÖRLUND. Well then, you shall also know who he is.

JOHAN TÖNNESEN. Be quiet!

BERNICK. Not another word!

RÖRLUND. How poorly in that case I should be serving the community, of whose standards and morals I am appointed guardian! And how indefensibly I should be acting towards this young girl in whose education I have played so considerable a part, and who to me is . . .

JOHAN TÖNNESEN. Take care what you are doing!

RÖRLUND. She *shall* know! Dina, this is the man who was the cause of your mother's shame and misfortune.

BERNICK. Mr. Rörlund. . . !

DINA. Him! [*To* JOHAN TÖNNESEN.] Is this true?

JOHAN TÖNNESEN. Karsten, you answer!

BERNICK. Not another word! Let's have no more of this today!

DINA. So it is true.

RÖRLUND. True, true. And more than that. This man you are putting your trust in did not run away empty-handed. . . . Old Mrs. Bernick's cash-box . . . Mr. Bernick can bear witness!

LONA HESSEL. Liar!

BERNICK. Ah. . . !

MRS. BERNICK. Oh, God! Oh, God!

JOHAN TÖNNESEN [*raising his fist to* RÖRLUND]. You dare . . . !

LONA HESSEL [*restraining*]. Don't hit him, Johan!

RÖRLUND. Yes, lay hands on me, if you like. But the truth will out, and that *is* the truth. Mr. Bernick said so himself, and the whole town knows. . . . Now, Dina, now you know him for what he is.

[*Short silence.*]

JOHAN TÖNNESEN [*in a low voice, seizing* BERNICK *by the arm*]. Karsten, Karsten, what have you done?

MRS. BERNICK [*softly and in tears*]. Oh, Karsten, that I should bring all this shame upon you.

SANDSTAD [*comes quickly in from the right and shouts, with his hand on the door handle*]. You must come now, Mr. Bernick! The whole railway's hanging by a thread.

BERNICK [*far away*]. What's that? What must I . . . ?

LONA HESSEL [*solemnly and with emphasis*]. You must go and be a pillar of society, Karsten.

JOHAN TÖNNESEN [*close by him*]. Karsten . . . we two will talk about this tomorrow.

[*He goes out through the garden.* BERNICK, *as though dazed, goes out to the right with* SANDSTAD.]

ACT THREE

The conservatory at BERNICK'S *house.* BERNICK, *with a cane in his hand, emerges in a violent temper from the rearmost room, left, leaving the door standing half-open behind him.*

BERNICK. There! For once I have shown that I meant it! He'll not forget a hiding like that in a hurry! [*To somebody inside the room.*] What do you say? ... And I say, you are being a stupid mother ... making excuses for him, encouraging him in all these idiotic tricks. ... Not idiotic? What do you call them, then? Sneaking out of the house at night, going right out to sea in a fishing boat, staying out nearly all day and putting the fear of death into me ... when I've got such a lot of other things to put up with! Then he has the nerve to threaten to run away, the scoundrel. Oh, just let him try! ... You wouldn't? No, that I can well believe. A fat lot you care about what happens to him! I do believe even if he were risking his life ... ! Oh? Yes, but I have my life's work to pass on. It doesn't suit my book at all to be left childless. ... Don't argue, Betty. It's to be as I've said, he's to stay in the house. ... [*Listens.*] Sh! Don't let anyone notice anything.

[KRAP *enters, right.*]

KRAP. Can you spare a moment, Mr. Bernick?

BERNICK [*throwing the cane down*]. Certainly, certainly. Have you been to the yard?

KRAP. Just come from there. H'm. ...

BERNICK. Well? Nothing wrong with the *Palm Tree*, is there?

KRAP. The *Palm Tree* can sail tomorrow, but ...

BERNICK. Then it's the *Indian Girl*? I might have guessed that that obstinate. ...

KRAP. The *Indian Girl* can also sail tomorrow. But ... it won't get very far.

BERNICK. What do you mean?

KRAP. Excuse me, Mr. Bernick, but that door's standing open, and I think there's somebody in there. . . .

BERNICK [*shutting the door*]. There. But what's all this that nobody must hear?

KRAP. Just that Aune intends to let the *Indian Girl* sink with all hands.

BERNICK. Good God! Whatever makes you think . . . ?

KRAP. I can't explain things any other way, Mr. Bernick.

BERNICK. Well, tell me as briefly as you can. . . .

KRAP. I will. You know yourself how slow things have been going down at the yard since we got the new machines and those new untrained men.

BERNICK. Yes, yes.

KRAP. Yet when I got down there this morning, I noticed that the repairs on the American ship were astonishingly far advanced. The big patch in the hull . . . you know, the bit that was rotten. . . .

BERNICK. Well, what about it?

KRAP. Completely repaired . . . to all appearances, at least. All boxed in. Just looked like new. I heard that Aune himself had been working down there all night by lamp-light.

BERNICK. Well, what then . . . ?

KRAP. Then I began wondering. The men had stopped for their break, so I took the opportunity of having a look round, inside and out, while nobody was looking. Had a job getting down into the hold when she was loaded. But I got what I was after. There's something funny going on, Mr. Bernick.

BERNICK. I can't believe it, Mr. Krap. I can't . . . I won't believe Aune could do a thing like that.

KRAP. I'm very sorry . . . but that's the honest truth. Something funny's going on, I tell you. Been no new timber put in at all, as far as I could judge. Just been plugged and caulked and patched with bits of plating and tarpaulin and that sort of thing. All faked up! The *Indian Girl* will never make New York. She'll go to the bottom like a leaky pot.

BERNICK. This is terrible! But what's made him do a thing like this, d'you think?

KRAP. Probably wants to discredit the machines. Wants to get his own back. Wants to have the old workmen taken on again.

BERNICK. And for that he's maybe sacrificing all those lives.

KRAP. The other day he said there weren't any men aboard the *Indian Girl*—only beasts.

BERNICK. Yes, yes, that's as may be. But doesn't he give any thought to the enormous capital that would be lost.

KRAP. Aune doesn't look very kindly on all this capital, Mr. Bernick.

BERNICK. True enough. He is a trouble-maker and an agitator. But anything as unscrupulous as this. . . ! Listen, Mr. Krap, this thing will have to be gone into again. Not a word to anybody about it. It does the yard no good to have people hearing about such things.

KRAP. Naturally, but . . .

BERNICK. You must get down there again during the dinner hour. I must have absolute proof.

KRAP. That you shall have, Mr. Bernick. But if you'll excuse me, what will you do then?

BERNICK. Report it, of course. We can't make ourselves parties to what is quite clearly a crime. I must have my conscience clear. Besides it will make a good impression both on the press and on the community generally, when I am seen to be putting all personal interest to one side and allowing justice to take its course.

KRAP. Very true, Mr. Bernick.

BERNICK. But first of all, absolute proof. And for the time being, absolute silence. . . .

KRAP. Not a word, Mr. Bernick. And proof you shall have.

[*He goes out through the garden and down the street.*]

BERNICK [*half aloud*]. Shocking! But no, it's impossible, of course . . . unthinkable!

[*He is about to go into his room when* HILMAR TÖNNESEN *comes from the right.*]

HILMAR TÖNNESEN. Good morning, Bernick! Let me congratulate you on your triumph in the Chamber of Commerce yesterday.

BERNICK. Thanks.

HILMAR TÖNNESEN. It was a brilliant victory, I hear, a triumph of intelligent public spirit over self-interest and prejudice ... a bit like the French raiding the Algerians. Strange after that unpleasant incident we had here, that you ...

BERNICK. Yes, yes, never mind that.

HILMAR TÖNNESEN. But the main battle is still to come, isn't it?

BERNICK. About the railway, you mean?

HILMAR TÖNNESEN. Yes. I suppose you know what our friend Hammer is cooking up?

BERNICK [tense]. No! What?

HILMAR TÖNNESEN. He's picked up this rumour that's going about, and he's going to run an article on it.

BERNICK. What rumour?

HILMAR TÖNNESEN. About these big property deals along the branch-line route, of course.

BERNICK. What's that you say? Is there such a rumour?

HILMAR TÖNNESEN. Yes, it's all over town. I heard it in the Club when I popped in there. One of the solicitors here is supposed to have been secretly commissioned to buy up all the forest land, all the mineral deposits, all the water rights. . . .

BERNICK. Do they say who for?

HILMAR TÖNNESEN. Up at the Club they thought it must have been some outside company that had got wind of what you were up to, and they were getting in quick before prices rose. . . . Isn't it contemptible? Ugh!

BERNICK. Contemptible?

HILMAR TÖNNESEN. Yes, for strangers to come barging in on our territory. And that one of our solicitors should lend himself to such a thing! Now a lot of outsiders are going to walk off with all the profit.

BERNICK. But this is just some wild rumour.

HILMAR TÖNNESEN. People believe it, anyway. And tomorrow or the day after our friend Hammer will have got it nailed down as a fact. Already up there, people were feeling generally rather bitter. I heard several of them say that if this rumour were confirmed, they would cross themselves off the list.

BERNICK. Impossible!

HILMAR TÖNNESEN. Oh? Why d'you suppose that tight-fisted lot were so ready to come in on your scheme? Don't you think they hadn't sniffed a chance themselves of . . . ?

BERNICK. Impossible, I tell you. At least in our community there's *that* much public spirit. . . .

HILMAR TÖNNESEN. Here? There speaks the optimist . . . judging people by yourself! But to any reasonably shrewd observer like myself. . . . There's not *one* person . . . present company excepted, of course . . . not *one* person I tell you, who tries to keep the flag of idealism flying. [*Moves upstage.*] Ugh, there they are!

BERNICK. Who?

HILMAR TÖNNESEN. The two Americans. [*Looking out, right.*] And who's that with them? Good Lord, isn't that the captain of the *Indian Girl*? Ugh!

BERNICK. What can they want with *him*?

HILMAR TÖNNESEN. Oh, they're fit company! They say he's been a slave trader or a pirate. And who knows what those other two have been up to all these years.

BERNICK. I tell you it's most unfair to think of them like that.

HILMAR TÖNNESEN. Ah, there speaks the optimist. But now we are going to be landed with them again, so while there's still time I'll just . . .

[*He walks over to the door, left.* LONA HESSEL *comes in from the right.*]

LONA HESSEL. Well, Hilmar, am I the one who is driving you away?

HILMAR TÖNNESEN. Not at all. I happened to be in a hurry. I wanted a word with Betty.

[*He goes into the rearmost room, left.*]

BERNICK [*after a short silence*]. Well, Lona?

LONA HESSEL. Yes?

BERNICK. How do I stand with you today?

LONA HESSEL. Same as yesterday. One lie more or less. . . .

BERNICK. I must explain. What's happened to Johan?

LONA HESSEL. He's coming. There was somebody he had to speak to.

BERNICK. After what you heard yesterday, you realize that my life will be ruined if the truth ever comes to light.

LONA HESSEL. I do realize.

BERNICK. Naturally you understand that *I* was not guilty of the crime those rumours were about.

LONA HESSEL. Of course, that's understood. But who was the thief?

BERNICK. There was no thief. No money was stolen. Not a penny was missing.

LONA HESSEL. What?

BERNICK. Not a penny, I tell you.

LONA HESSEL. But what about the rumours? How did that scandalous rumour get around that Johan . . . ?

BERNICK. Lona, I seem to be able to talk to you as I can to nobody else. I will conceal nothing from you. *I* was partly responsible for the rumour getting about.

LONA HESSEL. You? You could do that to the man who for your sake . . . !

BERNICK. You mustn't condemn me without recalling how things stood at the time. I was telling you about it yesterday. I came home and found my mother involved in a whole series of unwise undertakings. Then we had all kinds of bad luck. Disaster seemed to be threatening everywhere. Our firm was on the brink of ruin. There

I was, half reckless and half despairing. Lona, I think mostly it was to try to deaden my thoughts that I let myself get involved in that affair that led to Johan's going away.

LONA HESSEL. H'm!

BERNICK. You can imagine there were all sorts of rumours going about after you and he had left. This wasn't the first time he'd gone off the rails, people said. Some said Dorf had got a lot of money out of him to keep his mouth shut and push off. Others insisted *she'd* got it. At the same time, it couldn't be concealed that our firm was having difficulty in meeting its obligations. What was more natural than that the scandalmongers should put two and two together? When she stayed on here, obviously still poverty-stricken, then they claimed he'd taken the money with him to America, and rumour steadily went on making the amount bigger and bigger.

LONA HESSEL. And you, Karsten. . . ?

BERNICK. I clutched at the rumour like a drowning man at a straw.

LONA HESSEL. You helped to spread it?

BERNICK. I didn't deny it. Our creditors had begun to harry us. It was up to me to pacify them. The main thing was that nobody should suspect the solidarity of the firm. A temporary misfortune had struck us . . . as long as people didn't press us . . . just gave us time . . . everybody would get what was owing.

LONA HESSEL. And everybody did get it?

BERNICK. Yes, Lona, that rumour saved our firm, and made me what I am today.

LONA HESSEL. A lie, then, has made you what you are today.

BERNICK. What harm did it do anybody at the time? It was Johan's intention never to come back.

LONA HESSEL. You were asking what harm it did anybody. Look into your own heart and tell me whether you yourself haven't suffered some harm.

BERNICK. Look into any man's heart you like, and in every single case you will find *some* black spot he has to keep covered up.

LONA HESSEL. And you call yourselves pillars of society!

BERNICK. Society hasn't any better.

LONA HESSEL. And what does it matter whether a society like this is supported or not? What does count here? Lies and sham . . . nothing else. Here you are, the town's leading citizen, enjoying a splendid happy life, with all this power and glory . . . when you have branded an innocent man as a criminal.

BERNICK. Do you think I'm not deeply conscious of the wrong I've done him? And do you think I'm not ready to make it up to him again?

LONA HESSEL. How? By telling the truth?

BERNICK. You can't ask me to do that!

LONA HESSEL. What other way is there of righting that wrong?

BERNICK. I'm rich, Lona. Johan can ask whatever he likes. . . .

LONA HESSEL. Try offering him money, and you'll see what his answer will be.

BERNICK. What are his plans, do you know?

LONA HESSEL. No. Since yesterday, he hasn't said anything. It's as if all this business had made a mature man of him.

BERNICK. I must talk to him.

LONA HESSEL. There he is.

[JOHAN TÖNNESEN *enters, right.*]

BERNICK [*crossing towards him*]. Johan. . . !

JOHAN TÖNNESEN [*rebuffing him*]. *Me* first! Yesterday morning I gave you my word not to say anything.

BERNICK. You did.

JOHAN TÖNNESEN. But I didn't know then . . .

BERNICK. Johan, just a couple of words and I can explain the whole thing. . . .

JOHAN TÖNNESEN. No need. I understand the whole thing very well. The firm was in a bad way; and as I wasn't there, you had a defence-less name and reputation to do what you liked with. . . . Well, I don't blame you all that much, we were young and foolish in those days. But now I need the truth, and now you must speak.

BERNICK. And this is the very moment when I need all the moral credit I can get, and that's why I *cannot* say anything just now.

JOHAN TÖNNESEN. I'm not greatly worried about the tales you've spread about me. It's the other thing you've got to take the blame for. Dina's going to be my wife. And here, here in this town, I intend to set up home and live with her.

LONA HESSEL. You do?

BERNICK. With Dina! As your wife? Here in this town!

JOHAN TÖNNESEN. Yes, I'm staying right here. I'll show them what I think of them, these lying, back-biting . . . But before I can marry her, it's essential that you clear me.

BERNICK. You realize that immediately I admit one thing, it's as good as admitting the other as well? You might say I can prove from our books that there were no irregularities? But I can't. Our books weren't so meticulously kept in those days. And even if I could— what would be gained? Wouldn't I in any case be known as the man who once saved himself by an untruth, who for fifteen years let that untruth and all that went with it set hard without doing anything about it? You must have forgotten what this society of ours is like, or you would know that this would smash me completely.

JOHAN TÖNNESEN. I can only say that I mean to take Mrs. Dorf's daughter as my wife, and live with her here in this town.

BERNICK [*mopping the sweat off his brow*]. Listen to me, Johan . . . and you too, Lona. I'm in an unusually awkward situation just at this moment. The position is that if this blow is aimed at me, then you destroy me; and not only me but also the chance of a great and prosperous future for this township, which is after all your childhood home.

JOHAN TÖNNESEN. And if I don't strike this blow against you, then I destroy all my own future happiness.

LONA HESSEL. Go on, Karsten.

BERNICK. All right, listen. It's all tied up with the railway scheme, and that business isn't as simple as you think. No doubt you've heard that last year there were some negotiations about a coastal route? There was a lot of backing for it from influential people in the town and in the district, and particularly in the newspapers. But I got it stopped, because it would have been bad for our steamer trade along the coast.

LONA HESSEL. And are you interested yourself in the steamer trade?

BERNICK. Yes, but nobody dared suspect me on those grounds. My good name shielded me from that. For that matter, I could have stood the loss; but the town couldn't. So the cross-country route was decided on. Once that had been done, I secretly made sure that a branch line could be built down here.

LONA HESSEL. Why secretly, Karsten?

BERNICK. You've heard some talk about large property deals in forest land, and mines and waterfalls. . . ?

JOHAN TÖNNESEN. Yes, apparently some outside company. . . .

BERNICK. The way these properties now lie, they are worth practically nothing to their separate owners. So they have been sold comparatively cheap. If one had waited till the branch line had been discussed, the owners would have demanded quite exorbitant prices.

LONA HESSEL. Yes, yes. But so what?

BERNICK. Now comes the part that might be variously interpreted . . . something which, in our community, a man dare only risk if he has a good name and clear reputation to vouch for him.

LONA HESSEL. Well?

BERNICK. I am the one who bought everything up.

LONA HESSEL. You?

JOHAN TÖNNESEN. Out of your own pocket?

BERNICK. Out of my own pocket. If the branch line materializes, I am a millionaire. If it doesn't I am ruined.

LONA HESSEL. That was risky, Karsten.

BERNICK. I have staked everything I've got on this.

LONA HESSEL. I wasn't thinking of the money. But when it gets out that . . .

BERNICK. Yes, that's the whole point. With the clear reputation I have enjoyed up to now, I could take the whole thing on my shoulders and carry it through and then say to my fellow citizens: there, I have taken this risk for the benefit of the community.

LONA HESSEL. Of the community?

BERNICK. Yes. And not *one* will doubt my intentions.

LONA HESSEL. But some of the men here have acted more openly than you, with no ulterior motives, no private interests.

BERNICK. Who?

LONA HESSEL. Why, Rummel and Sandstad and Vigeland, of course.

BERNICK. To get their support, I had to let them in on it.

LONA HESSEL. Oh?

BERNICK. They stipulated a fifth share of the profits.

LONA HESSEL. Oh, these pillars of society!

BERNICK. Isn't it society itself that forces us into these devious ways? What would have happened here if I hadn't brought off those secret deals? Everybody would have jumped in on the scheme, split it up and shared it out, and made a complete hash of the whole thing. There isn't a single man in this town, apart from me, who knows how to run as big a concern as this one's going to be. In this country, the only people with any real capacity for big business are the immigrant families. This is why my conscience is clear in this case. In my hands alone is this property capable of bringing lasting benefit to the many people it will provide jobs for.

LONA HESSEL. I think you are right there, Karsten.

JOHAN TÖNNESEN. But I don't know any of these people, and my life's happiness is at stake.

BERNICK. The prosperity of your own birthplace is also at stake. If anything crops up now to cast a slur on my earlier conduct, all my

opponents will rise as one man and fall upon me. A youthful indiscretion is never wiped clean in this community of ours. People will
go over my entire life since that time, pick out a thousand little
incidents and interpret them in the light of the new disclosures.
They will crush me under the weight of their rumours and their
gossip. I shall be forced to withdraw from the railway scheme. And
if I let go of that, it's done for. And I shall be ruined financially as
well as finished socially.

LONA HESSEL. Johan, after what you've heard, you must leave and say
nothing.

BERNICK. Yes, yes, Johan, you must!

JOHAN TÖNNESEN. Well, I'll leave and say nothing. But I shall come
back, and then I shall speak.

BERNICK. Stay over there, Johan. Keep quiet about it, and I'm quite
ready to cut you in. . . .

JOHAN TÖNNESEN. Keep your money and give me back my name and
reputation.

BERNICK. And sacrifice my own!

JOHAN TÖNNESEN. That's for you and your community to work out
between you. I'm determined to have Dina for my wife. That's why
I'm sailing tomorrow in the *Indian Girl*. . . .

BERNICK. In the *Indian Girl*?

JOHAN TÖNNESEN. Yes. The captain has promised to take me. As I was
saying, I'm sailing across to sell my farm and clear up my affairs.
I'll be back again in two months.

BERNICK. And then you will tell?

JOHAN TÖNNESEN. Then the guilty party must take the blame
himself.

BERNICK. You are not forgetting I'll be blamed for something I'm *not*
guilty of!

JOHAN TÖNNESEN. Who was it who made the most of that shameful
rumour fifteen years ago?

BERNICK. You are driving me to desperation! But if you open your mouth, I'll deny everything! I'll say it's part of a plot against me . . . revenge . . . that you've come across here to blackmail me!

LONA HESSEL. For shame, Karsten!

BERNICK. I'm desperate, I tell you! And I'm fighting for my life. I'll deny everything, everything!

JOHAN TÖNNESEN. I have those two letters of yours. I found them in my trunk among my other papers. I read them through this morning. They're explicit enough.

BERNICK. You are going to produce them?

JOHAN TÖNNESEN. If it becomes necessary.

BERNICK. And you'll be back in two months?

JOHAN TÖNNESEN. I hope so. The wind is right. In three weeks I'll be in New York . . . as long as the *Indian Girl* doesn't sink.

BERNICK [*starts*]. Sink? Why should the *Indian Girl* sink?

JOHAN TÖNNESEN. Yes, why should she?

BERNICK [*scarcely audible*]. Sink?

JOHAN TÖNNESEN. Well, Bernick, now you know what to expect. Meanwhile, think it over. Goodbye! Give my regards to Betty, though she didn't exactly receive me like a loving sister. But Martha I want to see myself. She must tell Dina. . . . She must promise me. . . .

[*He goes out by the rearmost door, left.*]

BERNICK [*to himself*]. The *Indian Girl*. . . ? [*Quickly.*] Lona, you *must* stop this!

LONA HESSEL. You see yourself, Karsten. . . . I have no power over him any more. [*She goes after* JOHAN *into the room, left.*]

BERNICK [*uneasily*]. Sink . . . ?

[AUNE *comes in, right.*]

AUNE. Excuse me, Mr. Bernick, is it convenient . . . ?

BERNICK [*turning angrily*]. What do you want?

D

AUNE. I wondered if I might ask you a question, Mr. Bernick.

BERNICK. All right, hurry up! What do you want to ask?

AUNE. I wanted to ask if it's final . . . absolutely final . . . that I'll be sacked from the yard if the *Indian Girl* isn't able to sail tomorrow.

BERNICK. What's this? The boat *will* be ready to sail.

AUNE. Yes, it will. But supposing it wasn't . . . would I get the sack?

BERNICK. Why ask pointless questions?

AUNE. I just wanted to know, Mr. Bernick. Just answer me this: would I get the sack?

BERNICK. Do I generally keep my word or not?

AUNE. So tomorrow I'd have lost any standing I ever had in my own home and among my own folk . . . lost all my influence among the workers . . . lost any chance of helping the poor and the under-privileged.

BERNICK. Aune, we've already been through all that.

AUNE. Then let the *Indian Girl* sail.

[*Short silence.*]

BERNICK. Listen to me. I can't have my eyes everywhere. I can't be responsible for everything . . . I suppose you are prepared to assure me that the repairs have been satisfactorily carried out?

AUNE. You gave me very little time, Mr. Bernick.

BERNICK. But the repairs have been properly done, you would say?

AUNE. It's mid-summer, and the weather is good.

[*Another silence.*]

BERNICK. Was there anything else you wanted to ask me?

AUNE. I can't think of anything.

BERNICK. Well then, the *Indian Girl* sails. . . .

AUNE. Tomorrow?

BERNICK. Yes.

AUNE. Very well.

[*He bows and goes out.* CONSUL BERNICK *stands a moment, undecided; then he comes quickly to the door as though he wanted to call* AUNE *back, but stops uncertainly with his hand on the doorknob. At that moment the door is opened from outside and* KRAP *comes in.*]

KRAP [*in a low voice*]. Aha! He's been here. Has he confessed?

BERNICK. H'm. . . . Did you find anything?

KRAP. Was there any need to? Couldn't you see by the look in his eyes he had a bad conscience, Mr. Bernick?

BERNICK. Come now . . . you can't see that sort of thing. I asked you if you'd discovered anything.

KRAP. Couldn't get in. Too late. They were already hauling the ship out of the dock. But the very fact they were in such a hurry clearly proves that. . .

BERNICK. Proves nothing. They've had the inspection, haven't they?

KRAP. Of course, but . . .

BERNICK. There you are. And no cause for complaint was found, of course?

KRAP. Mr. Bernick, you know very well how these inspections are carried out, especially in a shipyard with a reputation like ours.

BERNICK. Makes no difference. We are covered.

KRAP. Mr. Bernick, could you really not tell by looking at Aune that . . . ?

BERNICK. I must tell you that Aune has entirely satisfied me.

KRAP. And I tell you I'm virtually convinced that . . .

BERNICK. Where does that get us, Mr. Krap? I know very well you've got your knife into this man. But if you are thinking of picking a quarrel with him, I must ask you to choose some other occasion. You know how essential it is for me . . . or rather for the company . . . that the *Indian Girl* should sail tomorrow.

KRAP. Very well. So be it. But when we'll ever hear again of *that* ship . . . h'm!

[VIGELAND *comes in, right.*]

VIGELAND. Good morning, Consul! Have you a moment to spare?

BERNICK. At your service, Mr. Vigeland.

VIGELAND. Well, I just wanted to know whether you also agree that the *Palm Tree* should sail tomorrow?

BERNICK. Yes, I do. Surely that was decided?

VIGELAND. But the captain's just been to see me to say there's a gale warning.

KRAP. The barometer has fallen a lot since this morning.

BERNICK. Oh? So we're expecting gales?

VIGELAND. A stiff breeze, at any rate. But no head winds. On the contrary. . . .

BERNICK. H'm. Well, what do you say?

VIGELAND. I say what I said to the captain: that the *Palm Tree* is in the hands of Providence. And anyway, she's only crossing the North Sea to start with. And freight prices are pretty high in England at the moment, so . . .

BERNICK. Yes, it would probably mean a loss for us if we waited.

VIGELAND. And it's a good sturdy ship, and fully insured, moreover. Now, with the *Indian Girl* it's a much more risky business. . . .

BERNICK. How do you mean?

VIGELAND. She's also sailing tomorrow.

BERNICK. Yes, the owners asked for the job to be done urgently, and anyway . . .

VIGELAND. Well, if that old tub dare put out . . . and with a crew like that . . . it would be a scandal if we couldn't . . .

BERNICK. All right. I presume you have the ship's papers with you?

VIGELAND. Yes, here.

BERNICK. Good. If you wouldn't mind stepping in with Mr. Krap, then?

KRAP. This way, please. Soon deal with that.

VIGELAND. Thank you. And we leave things in the hands of the Almighty, Mr. Bernick.

[*He and* KRAP *go into the room downstage left.* RÖRLUND *comes through the garden.*]

RÖRLUND. Ah, do I find you at home at this time of day, Mr. Bernick?

BERNICK [*lost in thought*]. As you see.

RÖRLUND. Actually it was your wife I looked in to see. I thought she might be in need of a few words of comfort.

BERNICK. She probably is. But *I* would like a word with you, too.

RÖRLUND. With pleasure, Mr. Bernick. Is anything wrong? You look quite pale and upset.

BERNICK. Oh? Do I? Well, it's only what one might expect . . . with everything piling up on top of me at the moment. All the firm's business . . . and the matter of the railway. . . . Tell me something, Mr. Rörlund. I want to ask you a question.

RÖRLUND. Gladly, Mr. Bernick.

BERNICK. About a thought that's occurred to me. Suppose one is contemplating a course of action so vast in its implications that it promises to benefit many thousands of people. . . . And if this were then to demand a single sacrifice. . . ?

RÖRLUND. How do you mean?

BERNICK. Suppose, for example, a man were thinking of building a big factory. He knows for certain . . . for experience has taught him this . . . that sooner or later while the factory is operating, some human life will be lost.

RÖRLUND. Yes, that is only too probable.

BERNICK. Or take somebody who starts a mine. He employs both family men and healthy young fellows. Can't it be said with certainty that not all these will escape with their lives?

RÖRLUND. I'm afraid that's very true.

BERNICK. Well, then. That man knows in advance that the scheme he is starting will inevitably at some time take its toll of human life. But it's a scheme that operates for the common good. For every human life it costs, it will just as inevitably benefit hundreds of people.

RÖRLUND. Aha, you are thinking of the railway . . . of all the dangers of blasting and excavating and so on. . . .

BERNICK. Well, yes, I am thinking of the railway. Besides, the railway will result in both factories and mines being built. But still don't you think . . . ?

RÖRLUND. My dear Consul, you are almost too scrupulous. I think that if you place the matter in the hands of Providence . . .

BERNICK. Yes, of course, Providence. . . .

RÖRLUND. . . . then no blame attaches to you. Build your railway and don't worry.

BERNICK. Yes, but now let me take a particular case. Suppose there is blasting to be done at some specially dangerous point; and unless that blasting is done, the railway can't be built. Supposing the engineer knows it will cost the life of the workman who does the detonating. Yet it must be detonated, and it is the engineer's duty to send a workman to do it.

RÖRLUND. H'm.

BERNICK. I know what you will say. It would be a splendid thing if the engineer himself went and ignited the fuse. But that kind of thing isn't done. So he must sacrifice a workman.

RÖRLUND. None of *our* engineers would ever do that.

BERNICK. No engineer in the bigger countries would think twice before doing it.

RÖRLUND. In the bigger countries? No, that I can quite believe. In those corrupt and unscrupulous communities. . . .

BERNICK. Oh, there are plenty of good things about *those* communities.

RÖRLUND. You can say that? When you yourself . . . ?

BERNICK. At least in these bigger countries there's room to develop useful enterprises; and they have courage when it comes to making sacrifices in a great cause. But here you're tied hand and foot by all sorts of petty considerations.

RÖRLUND. Is human life a petty consideration?

BERNICK. When that human life threatens the welfare of thousands.

RÖRLUND. But you are postulating quite unthinkable situations, Mr. Bernick! I simply don't understand you today. Then you go referring to those larger communities. Ah, in those places . . . what does a human life count *there*? They calculate in human lives as they do capital assets. But I think I can say that *we* take an entirely different moral point of view. Look at our admirable shipowners! Name me a single one of them who, for miserable profit, would think of sacrificing human life! And think of those scoundrels in the bigger countries who, for the sake of their bank balances, send out one unseaworthy ship after another. . . .

BERNICK. I'm not talking about unseaworthy ships!

RÖRLUND. But I am, Mr. Bernick.

BERNICK. Yes, but where's all this leading? It's got nothing to do with it. . . . Oh, these petty, little considerations. If one of our generals were to lead his men under fire so they got shot, he would have sleepless nights ever after. That's not how things are in other places. You should hear him in there, when he starts talking. . . .

RÖRLUND. Him? Who? The American. . . ?

BERNICK. Yes, indeed. You should hear how people in America . . .

RÖRLUND. He's in there? And you didn't tell me? I'm going straight in to . . .

BERNICK. It won't do you any good. You'll get nowhere with him.

RÖRLUND. We'll see about that. Ah, here he comes.

[JOHAN TÖNNESEN *comes out of the room, left.*]

JOHAN TÖNNESEN [*speaking back through the open door*]. All right, Dina, let's leave it at that! But I'm not going to let you go, all the same. I'm coming back, and then everything's going to be all right between us.

RÖRLUND. Excuse me, but what are you implying by these words? What is it you want?

JOHAN TÖNNESEN. I want the girl, in whose eyes you maligned me yesterday, to be my wife.

RÖRLUND. Your . . . ? You think you can . . . ?

JOHAN TÖNNESEN. I mean to have her for my wife.

RÖRLUND. Well then, there's something you must know. . . . [*Goes across to the half-open door.*] Mrs. Bernick, will you be so kind as to be a witness. . . . And you too, Miss Martha. And tell Dina to come in. [*He sees* LONA HESSEL.] Ah, you here too?

LONA HESSEL [*in the doorway*]. Am I to come too?

RÖRLUND. As many as you like . . . the more the better.

BERNICK. What are you going to do?

[LONA HESSEL, MRS. BERNICK, MARTHA BERNICK, DINA *and* HILMAR TÖNNESEN *come out of the room.*]

MRS. BERNICK. Mr. Rörlund, with the best will in the world I haven't been able to prevent him. . . .

RÖRLUND. I shall prevent him, Mrs. Bernick. . . . Dina, you are a thoughtless girl. But I don't blame you so very much. Too long you have been without the moral support you should have had to sustain you. I blame myself for not providing you with that support before.

DINA. You mustn't say anything now.

MRS. BERNICK. But what is it?

RÖRLUND. The time has come when I must speak, Dina, although your conduct yesterday and today makes it ten times more difficult for me. But to save you, all other considerations must give way. You remember the promise I gave you? You remember what you promised to answer when I felt the time had come. Now I mustn't hesitate any longer, and so . . . [*To* JOHAN TÖNNESEN.] This young girl you are pursuing is my fiancée.

MRS. BERNICK. What's that you say?

BERNICK. Dina!

JOHAN TÖNNESEN. She is! Your . . . ?

MARTHA BERNICK. No, no, Dina!

LONA HESSEL. Lies!

JOHAN TÖNNESEN. Dina . . . is this man speaking the truth?

DINA [*after a short pause*]. Yes.

RÖRLUND. This, I trust, will mean the defeat of all your seducer's tricks. This step, which I have decided upon for Dina's good, can now be announced to our entire community. I trust and hope it will not be misinterpreted. But now, Mrs. Bernick. I think we had better take her away from here and try to restore her peace of mind and a sense of proportion.

MRS. BERNICK. Yes, come along. Oh, Dina, what a lucky girl you are!

[*She leads* DINA *out, left;* RÖRLUND *accompanies them.*]

MARTHA BERNICK. Goodbye, Johan!

[*She goes.*]

HILMAR TÖNNESEN [*at the door into the garden*]. H'm . . . .Really, I must say. . . .

LONA HESSEL [*who has followed* DINA *with her eyes*]. Keep your chin up, lad. I'll stay here and keep an eye on the pastor.

[*She goes out, right.*]

BERNICK. Johan, now you won't be sailing on the *Indian Girl*!

JOHAN TÖNNESEN. Now I will!

BERNICK. Then you won't be coming back?

JOHAN TÖNNESEN. I'll be back!

BERNICK. After this? What will you do here after this?

JOHAN TÖNNESEN. Get my own back on the whole lot of you. Smash as many of you as I can.

[*He goes out, right.* VIGELAND *and* KRAP *come out of* BERNICK'S *room.*]

VIGELAND. There we are, now the papers are in order, Mr. Bernick.

BERNICK. Good, good. . . .

KRAP [*in a low voice*]. And it's settled that the *Indian Girl* sails tomorrow?

BERNICK. She sails.

[*He goes into his room.* VIGELAND *and* KRAP *go out, right.* HILMAR TÖNNESEN *is about to follow them; but that same moment* OLAF *cautiously puts his head round the door, left.*]

OLAF. Uncle! Uncle Hilmar!

HILMAR TÖNNESEN. Ugh, is that you? Why don't you stay upstairs? You know you are confined to your room.

OLAF [*takes a step forward*]. Sh! Uncle Hilmar, do you know something?

HILMAR TÖNNESEN. Yes, I know you got a good hiding today.

OLAF [*looks defiantly towards his father's room*]. He won't hit me any more. But do you know Uncle Johan's sailing with the Americans tomorrow?

HILMAR TÖNNESEN. What's that got to do with you? Get yourself back again upstairs.

OLAF. Perhaps I might get myself on a buffalo hunt yet, Uncle.

HILMAR TÖNNESEN. Rubbish! A little milksop like you. . . .

OLAF. Just you wait. You'll be hearing something in the morning.

HILMAR TÖNNESEN. Idiot!

[*He goes out through the garden.* OLAF *runs back into the room again when he sees* KRAP *coming in, right.*]

KRAP [*walks across to* BERNICK'S *door and half opens it*]. Excuse me coming again, Mr. Bernick, but there's a tremendous storm blowing up. [*He waits a moment; there is no answer.*] Is the *Indian Girl* to sail just the same?

[*A short pause.*]

BERNICK [*answering from inside his room*]. The *Indian Girl* sails just the same.

[KRAP *shuts the door and goes out again, right.*]

ACT FOUR

The conservatory at BERNICK's *house. The work-table has been removed. It is a stormy afternoon, and already growing dark; it gets darker as the scene progresses. A servant is lighting the chandelier; two maids bring in pots of flowers, lamps and candles and place them on the table, and on stands along the wall.* RUMMEL, *in evening dress, with gloves and a white cravat, is standing in the room, giving instructions.*

RUMMEL [*to the servant*]. Only every other candle, Jacob. It mustn't look too grand, it's meant to come as a surprise, you know. And all these flowers . . . ? Oh, well, might as well let them stay. It might look as though they always . . .

[BERNICK *comes out of his room.*]

BERNICK [*in the doorway*]. What's going on here?

RUMMEL. Oh dear, is that you? [*To the servants.*] All right, you can go now, that's all for the time being.

[*The servants and the maids go out by the door, upstage left.*]

BERNICK [*approaching*]. But, Rummel, what is the meaning of all this?

RUMMEL. It means that your proudest moment has arrived. The whole town is marching here in procession this evening to do honour to its leading citizen.

BERNICK. What do you say?

RUMMEL. A procession, with banners and a band! We were supposed to be having torches as well, but we didn't feel like risking it in this wind. Still, we'll be having some illuminations. And I imagine that will sound pretty good when it gets into the newspapers.

BERNICK. Listen, Rummel, I won't have it.

RUMMEL. Ah, but it's too late now. Half an hour, and they'll be here.

BERNICK. Why didn't you tell me about it before?

RUMMEL. Precisely because I was afraid you'd raise objections. But I did approach your wife. She gave me permission to make one or two arrangements, and she's offered to look after the refreshments.

BERNICK [*listening*]. What's that? Are they coming already? I thought I could hear singing.

RUMMEL [*at the garden door*]. Singing? Oh, that's just the Americans. They're hauling the *Indian Girl* out to the buoy.

BERNICK. Hauling her out! Ah. . . . No, I can't face this tonight, Rummel. I'm not well.

RUMMEL. Yes, you do look pretty rotten. But you must pull yourself together. Damn it, man, you must pull yourself together! Sandstad and Vigeland and I, we all felt it was of the utmost importance to get this thing arranged. The weight of public opinion must be so overwhelming as to crush all possible opposition. Rumours in town are increasing. Some announcement about buying up that property can't be delayed very much longer. In fact it's imperative you tell them about it tonight. . . . Amid the songs and the speeches and the clink of glasses, in other words when the party spirit is at its height, you must break the news of what you have risked for the sake of the community. When this party spirit, as I just called it, is on them, it's extraordinary what a lot can be done with the people here. But you've got to have *that*, otherwise it won't work.

BERNICK. Yes, yes, yes.

RUMMEL. Especially when it's such a delicate and ticklish business as this. Well, thank God you've got a reputation that can carry it off, Bernick. But listen, now; we ought to plan things a bit. Hilmar Tönnesen has written a song in your honour. It begins quite delightfully with the words: 'Raise the ideal's banner high'. And Mr. Rörlund has been given the job of making the speech. You must reply to it, of course.

BERNICK. I can't face it tonight, Rummel. Couldn't *you* . . . ?

RUMMEL. Impossible, much as I would like to. As you might expect, the speech is addressed particularly to you. Well, perhaps a word or two about the rest of us. I have talked to Vigeland and Sandstad about it. We thought you might reply with a toast to the prosperity of the community. Sandstad will say a few words about the harmony that reigns among the different sections of the community; Vigeland will say something about how desirable it is that the new enterprise should not disturb the present moral foundations on which we stand; and I'm thinking of addressing a few chosen words to the women, whose more modest contribution to our affairs is nevertheless not without some significance for our society. But you're not listening. . . .

BERNICK. Yes . . . yes, I am. But tell me, do you think that's a very heavy sea running out there?

RUMMEL. You worried about the *Palm Tree*? It's well insured.

BERNICK. Insured, yes. But . . .

RUMMEL. And in good repair. And that's the main thing.

BERNICK. H'm. . . . If anything does happen to a vessel, it doesn't necessarily mean that lives will be lost. The ship and the cargo might be lost . . . people might lose their luggage and their papers. . . .

RUMMEL. Damn it, luggage and papers don't matter.

BERNICK. They don't? No, no, all I meant was. . . . Sh! They're singing again.

RUMMEL. That's on board the *Palm Tree*.

[VIGELAND *comes in from the right.*]

VIGELAND. Yes, they're hauling the *Palm Tree* out now. Good evening, Mr. Bernick.

BERNICK. And as a seafaring man you still maintain . . .

VIGELAND. I maintain my trust in Providence, Mr. Bernick, that's what I do. Besides, I've just been aboard myself and handed out a few short tracts which I hope will be of some benefit.

[SANDSTAD *and* KRAP *enter from the right.*]

SANDSTAD [*still in the doorway*]. Well, if *that* makes it, anything can. Ah, good evening, good evening!

BERNICK. Anything happening, Mr. Krap?

KRAP. I'd rather not say anything, Mr. Bernick.

SANDSTAD. The crew of the *Indian Girl* is drunk, every one of them. If that pack ever gets out of this alive, I'm a Dutchman.

[LONA HESSEL *comes from the right.*]

LONA HESSEL [*to* BERNICK]. He asked me to say goodbye for him.

BERNICK. Already aboard?

LONA HESSEL. Soon will be, at any rate. I left him outside the hotel.

BERNICK. And his mind's made up?

LONA HESSEL. Firm as a rock.

RUMMEL [*over by the window*]. Damn these new-fangled gadgets. I can't get the curtains to come down.

LONA HESSEL. You want them down? I thought on the contrary. . . .

RUMMEL. Down to begin with, Miss Hessel. You know what's going on, don't you?

LONA HESSEL. Of course. Let me help. [*Takes hold of the cords.*] I shall lower the curtain on my brother-in-law . . . though I'd rather it went up.

RUMMEL. That you can do later. When the garden is filled with a surging throng, then the curtains go up, revealing within a surprised and happy family. . . . A man's home ought to be like a show-case. [BERNICK *seems about to say something, but turns quickly and goes into his room.*] Well, let's have a final conference. You come along as well, Mr. Krap. You must help us to get a few of our facts right.

[*All the men go into* BERNICK'S *room.* LONA HESSEL *has drawn all the curtains over the windows, and is just about to do the same with the curtain on the open glass door, when* OLAF *jumps down on to the veranda from above. He has a plaid over his shoulders, and a bundle in his hand.*]

LONA HESSEL. Good Lord, lad, what a start you gave me!

OLAF [*hiding the bundle*]. Hush, Aunt Lona!

LONA HESSEL. What are you doing, jumping out of the window? Where are you going?

OLAF. Sh! Don't say anything. I want to see Uncle Johan . . . just down to the quayside, you know . . . just to say goodbye. Goodnight, Aunt Lona!

[*He runs out through the garden.*]

LONA HESSEL. No, stop. Olaf . . . Olaf!

[JOHAN TÖNNESEN, *dressed for travelling, with a bag slung over his shoulder, comes warily in through the door on the right.*]

JOHAN TÖNNESEN. Lona!

LONA HESSEL [*turning*]. What! You're back?

JOHAN TÖNNESEN. There's still a few minutes left. I must see her just once more. We can't part like this.

[MARTHA BERNICK *and* DINA, *both wearing coats, and the latter with a small hold-all in her hand, come in through the rearmost door, left.*]

DINA. I must see him. I must see him.

MARTHA BERNICK. And so you shall, Dina!

DINA. There he is!

JOHAN TÖNNESEN. Dina!

DINA. Take me with you!

JOHAN TÖNNESEN. What . . . !

LONA HESSEL. Is that what you want?

DINA. Yes, take me with you! That man's written me a letter saying he's going to make a public announcement tonight. . . .

JOHAN TÖNNESEN. Dina . . . you don't love him?

DINA. I've never loved that man. I'll throw myself into the fjord if I've got to be engaged to him! Oh, he treated me like dirt yesterday, him with all his high and mighty talk! He felt he was lowering himself, taking up with a poor creature like me—and didn't he let me know it! I'm not going to be treated that way any longer. I'm leaving. Please may I come with you?

JOHAN TÖNNESEN. Yes, yes . . . oh, a thousand times yes!

DINA. I'll not be a burden to you for long. Just help me to get across. Help me to find my feet at the beginning. . . .

JOHAN TÖNNESEN. Hurrah! We'll manage that all right, Dina!

LONA HESSEL [*pointing to* BERNICK'S *door*]. Hush! Not so loud, not so loud!

JOHAN TÖNNESEN. Dina, I shall take good care of you!

DINA. I won't let you. I want to take care of myself. And over there I can. If only I get away from here. Oh, these women . . . you just don't know . . . they've also written to me today; they tell me I ought to count myself very lucky . . . point out how magnanimous he's being. Tomorrow and every day they'll be watching and watching to see if I'm proving myself worthy of it all. I'm terrified of all this respectability.

JOHAN TÖNNESEN. Tell me, Dina, is that the only reason you are leaving? Do I mean nothing to you?

DINA. Oh yes, Johan. You mean more to me than anyone.

JOHAN TÖNNESEN. Oh, Dina. . . !

DINA. Everybody here tells me I ought to hate and detest you. That it's my duty to. But I don't understand all this about duty. I'll never understand.

LONA HESSEL. You don't have to, either, child.

MARTHA BERNICK. No, you don't have to. That's why you shall go with him as his wife.

JOHAN TÖNNESEN. Yes, yes!

LONA HESSEL. What? Come here and let me kiss you, Martha! *This* is something I never expected from *you*!

MARTHA BERNICK. No, I suppose not. I hadn't expected it myself. But I was bound to break out sometime. Oh, the tyranny of all this convention, doing the right thing, how we are made to suffer under it here! Resist it, Dina! Be his wife. Let's see somebody kick over the traces for once.

JOHAN TÖNNESEN. What do you say, Dina?

DINA. Yes, I will be your wife.

JOHAN TÖNNESEN. Dina!

DINA. But first I want to work . . . and make something of my life, as you have done. I don't just want to be a thing, there for the taking.

LONA HESSEL. Fine! That's as it should be!

JOHAN TÖNNESEN. Very well. I shall wait and hope. . . .

LONA HESSEL. . . . and win, lad! But now, on board with you!

JOHAN TÖNNESEN. Yes, on board! Ah, Lona, my dear sister, just one word. Listen . . .

[*He takes her to the back of the room and talks rapidly to her.*]

MARTHA BERNICK. Dina, you lucky girl . . . let me look at you. Let me kiss you once more . . . the last time.

DINA. Not the last time, dear Aunt Martha. No, we'll be seeing each other again.

MARTHA BERNICK. Never! Promise me, Dina, don't ever come back. [*She seizes both her hands and looks at her.*] Go now and be happy, my darling . . . across the sea. Oh, how often I've sat in the schoolroom and longed to be over there! It must be beautiful out there . . . a larger sky, clouds higher than here . . . and the wind freer about your head. . . .

DINA. Oh, Aunt Martha, some day you'll come and join us.

MARTHA BERNICK. Me? Never, never. I have my work here, and now I think I can achieve what I'm capable of achieving.

DINA. I can't imagine having to part from you.

MARTHA BERNICK. Oh, people can be parted from lots of things, Dina. [*Kisses her.*] But let's hope you never have to try, my sweet. Promise me you'll make him happy.

DINA. I won't promise anything. I hate promises. Things must take their course.

MARTHA BERNICK. Yes, yes, they must. Just you stay as you are— faithful and true to yourself.

DINA. I will, Aunt Martha.

LONA HESSEL [*puts some papers* JOHAN *has given her into her pocket*]. Fine, fine, my dear boy. But away with you now.

JOHAN TÖNNESEN. Yes, now there's no time to lose. Goodbye, Lona! Thank you for all your love. Goodbye, Martha, and thank you, too, for being such a true friend.

MARTHA BERNICK. Goodbye, Johan! Goodbye, Dina! And good luck be with you always.

[*She and* LONA HESSEL *urge them towards the door at the back.* JOHAN TÖNNESEN *and* DINA *go quickly out through the garden.* LONA HESSEL *shuts the door and draws the curtain.*]

LONA HESSEL. Now we're alone, Martha. You've lost her and I've lost him.

MARTHA BERNICK. You . . . him?

LONA HESSEL. Oh, I'd already half lost him over there. The lad was longing to stand on his own feet. That's why I let him think I was homesick.

MARTHA BERNICK. So that was why? Yes, I can see now why you came. But he'll want you back, Lona.

LONA HESSEL. An old step-sister . . . what'll he want with her now? . . . Men tear to shreds so many of the things about them in their pursuit of happiness.

MARTHA BERNICK. That often happens.

LONA HESSEL. But we will stick together, Martha.

MARTHA BERNICK. Can I be anything to you?

LONA HESSEL. Who more? A couple of foster-mothers like us . . . haven't we both lost our children? Now we are alone.

MARTHA BERNICK. Yes, alone. That's why I want you to know, too . . . that I loved him more than anything else in the world.

LONA HESSEL. Mártha! [*Grips her arm.*] Is this the truth?

MARTHA BERNICK. My whole life is contained in those words. I loved him and waited for him. Every summer I waited for him to come. Then he came . . . but he didn't see me.

LONA HESSEL. Loved him! Yet it was you who handed him his happiness.

MARTHA BERNICK. Why shouldn't I give him his happiness, seeing that I loved him. Yes, I loved him. My whole life has been lived for him, ever since he went away. You are wondering what grounds I had for hope? Oh, I do think I had some grounds. But when he did come back . . . it was just as if everything had been wiped out of his memory. He simply didn't see me.

LONA HESSEL. It was Dina who overshadowed you, Martha.

MARTHA BERNICK. Just as well she did. When he went away, we were about the same age. When I saw him again . . . oh, that terrible moment . . . I realized I was now ten years older than him. He'd been living out there in the bright sparkling sunlight, drinking in youth and health with every breath he took. And meanwhile I sat in here, spinning and spinning . . .

LONA HESSEL. . . . spinning the threads of his happiness, Martha.

MARTHA BERNICK. Yes, it was gold I spun. No bitterness! Lona, we have been two good sisters to him, haven't we?

LONA HESSEL [*putting her arms round her*]. Martha!

[BERNICK *comes out of his room.*]

BERNICK [*to the men within*]. All right, make what arrangements you like. When the time comes, I suppose I'll . . . [*He shuts the door.*] Ah, you here? Look Martha, you'd better smarten yourself up a bit. And tell Betty to do the same. I don't want anything fancy, of course, just something nice and homely. But you must hurry.

LONA HESSEL. And see you look joyful and happy, Martha! It's meant to be a pleasant surprise to you both, you know.

BERNICK. Olaf must come downstairs, too. I want him to be beside me.

LONA HESSEL. H'm. . . . Olaf. . . .

MARTHA BERNICK. I'll go and tell Betty.

[*She goes out through the door, upstage left.*]

LONA HESSEL. Well, so now the great and solemn hour has arrived.

BERNICK [*walks restlessly up and down*]. Yes, it has.

LONA HESSEL. A man must feel proud and happy at such a time, I imagine.

BERNICK [*looking at her*]. H'm!

LONA HESSEL. The whole town is to be lit up, I hear.

BERNICK. Yes, they've got something like that in mind.

LONA HESSEL. All the local groups are turning out with their banners. Your name will be written in letters of fire. Tonight, telegrams will be sent to every corner of the land: 'Surrounded by the happy members of his family, Consul Bernick received the congratulations of his fellow citizens as one of the pillars of their society.'

BERNICK. Quite so. And outside they'll call for three cheers, and the crowd will shout until I appear at that door there, and I'll have to bow and thank them.

LONA HESSEL. *Have* to. . . ?

BERNICK. Do you think I shall feel happy at that moment?

LONA HESSEL. No, *I* don't think you can feel particularly happy.

BERNICK. Lona, you despise me.

LONA HESSEL. Not yet.

BERNICK. You have no right to. Not to *despise* me! . . . Lona, you can't imagine how unutterably lonely I am here, in this shrivelled stunted little community. . . . How I've been forced year after year to whittle down any hopes I might have had of living a full and satisfying life. What in fact *have* I achieved, however much it may seem? Bits and pieces . . . trivialities. But here they won't tolerate anything else . . . or anything more. If I wanted to take one step in advance of the current views and opinions of the day, that would put paid to any power I have. Do you know what we are . . . those of us who count as pillars of society? We are society's tools, neither more nor less.

LONA HESSEL. Why has it taken you till now to see this?

BERNICK. Because I've been doing a lot of thinking lately . . . since you came back . . . especially this evening. . . . Oh, Lona, why didn't I know you properly then . . . in the old days?

LONA HESSEL. And if you had?

BERNICK. I'd never have let you go. And if I had had you, I wouldn't be where I am now.

LONA HESSEL. Do you never think what *she* might have been to you . . . she, whom you chose instead of me?

BERNICK. All I know is she's never been any of the things I needed.

LONA HESSEL. Because you never shared your interests with her. Because you've never been open or frank with her in any of your dealings. Because you let her go on suffering under the shame you unburdened on her family.

BERNICK. Yes, yes, yes. It all comes from this lying and pretence.

LONA HESSEL. Then why not have done with all this lying and pretence?

BERNICK. Now? It's too late now, Lona.

LONA HESSEL. Karsten, tell me what satisfaction does this pretence and deception give you?

BERNICK. It doesn't give me any. I must go to the wall, like all the rest of this hashed-up society. But there's a generation growing up after us. It's my son I'm working for. It's *him* I'm making a career for. The time will come when truth begins to establish itself in our social life; and on this he will, I hope, build a happier life than his father's.

LONA HESSEL. With a lie as its foundation? Think what it is you are giving your son for his inheritance.

BERNICK [*with suppressed despair*]. The inheritance I give him is a thousand times worse than you think. Yet some day surely the curse must be lifted. And yet . . . nevertheless. . . . [*Bursts out.*] How could you bring all this down on my head! But it's done now! I must go on. I'm not going to let myself be crushed by you!

[HILMAR TÖNNESEN *comes rushing in from the right, distracted and with an open letter in his hand.*]

HILMAR TÖNNESEN. But this is . . . Betty! Betty!

BERNICK. What's this? Are they coming already?

HILMAR TÖNNESEN. No, no. But I simply must speak to somebody. . . .

[*He goes out by the upstage door, left.*]

LONA HESSEL. Karsten, you keep saying we came to crush you. Let me just tell you what sort of stuff he's made of . . . this prodigal son your highly-moral community has been avoiding like the plague. He can manage quite well without you lot, because now he's gone.

BERNICK. But he was going to come back. . . .

LONA HESSEL. Johan will never come back. He's gone for good, and Dina's gone with him.

BERNICK. Not coming back? And Dina's gone with him?

LONA HESSEL. Yes, to be his wife. That's their way of slapping your smug little community in the face, just as I once . . . Ah, well!

BERNICK. Gone. . . ! She too . . . on the *Indian Girl*!

LONA HESSEL. No. He didn't dare trust such a precious cargo to that depraved crowd. Johan and Dina sailed on the *Palm Tree*.

BERNICK. Ah! So it's all been . . . in vain. . . . [*Walks quickly across, tears open the door to his room and shouts in.*] Krap, stop the *Indian Girl*. She mustn't sail tonight!

KRAP [*within*]. The *Indian Girl* has already put out to sea, Mr. Bernick.

BERNICK [*shuts the door and says dully*]. Too late . . . and all to no purpose. . . .

LONA HESSEL. What do you mean?

BERNICK. Nothing, nothing. Get away from me. . . !

LONA HESSEL. H'm! Look here, Karsten. Johan wants you to know he's entrusted me with the fair name and reputation he once lent you, along with that other thing you stole from him while he was away. Johan will say nothing, and I can please myself what I do, or don't do. I've got both your letters in my hand here.

BERNICK. You've got them! And now . . . now you want . . . perhaps tonight when the procession. . . .

LONA HESSEL. I didn't come here to expose you. I wanted to give you such a shaking that you were ready to speak up of your own accord. It hasn't succeeded. So you'll just have to stay there, stuck fast in your lies. Look here, I'm tearing up those two letters of yours. Take the bits, there you are. There's no evidence against you now. You are safe now. And now be happy too . . . if you can.

BERNICK [*greatly moved*]. Lona . . . why didn't you do that before? Now it's too late. I've thrown away my whole life now. I can't go on living after today.

LONA HESSEL. What's happened?

BERNICK. Don't ask me. . . . Yet I *must* live! I will live . . . for Olaf's sake. He'll put everything right . . . make amends. . . .

LONA HESSEL. Karsten. . . !

[HILMAR TÖNNESEN *comes hurrying back in.*]

HILMAR TÖNNESEN. Nobody there! Gone! No Betty either!

BERNICK. What's the matter with you?

HILMAR TÖNNESEN. I daren't tell you.

BERNICK. What is it? Tell me! You must tell me!

HILMAR TÖNNESEN. Very well. Olaf has run away on the *Indian Girl*.

BERNICK [*staggers back*]. Olaf . . . on the *Indian Girl*! No! No!

LONA HESSEL. Yes, he has! Now I understand. I saw him jump out of the window.

BERNICK [*at the door of his room, shouting distractedly*]. Krap, stop the *Indian Girl* at any cost!

KRAP [*comes out*]. Impossible, Mr. Bernick. How do you suppose . . . ?

BERNICK. We *must* stop her! Olaf is on board!

KRAP. What's that you say!

RUMMEL [*comes out*]. Olaf's run away? Impossible!

SANDSTAD [*coming too*]. He'll be sent back with the pilot, Mr. Bernick.

HILMAR TÖNNESEN. No, no! He's left a note for me. [*Showing the note.*] He says he's going to hide among the cargo till they've reached the open sea.

BERNICK. I'll never see him again!

RUMMEL. Oh nonsense. A good, strong ship, only just repaired . . .

VIGELAND [*who has also come out*]. . . . in your own yard, Mr. Bernick!

BERNICK. I'll never see him again, I tell you. I've lost him, Lona, and . . . I see it now . . . he was never really mine. [*Listens.*] What is that?

RUMMEL. Music. The procession's coming.

BERNICK. I can't. I won't see anybody.

RUMMEL. What are you thinking about? You can't do this.

SANDSTAD. Impossible, Mr. Bernick. Remember what you've got at stake.

BERNICK. What do I care about all that now! Who've I got to work for now?

RUMMEL. How can you say such a thing? You've got us, and the community.

VIGELAND. Ah, that's very true.

SANDSTAD. And you're not forgetting, are you, Mr. Bernick, that . . . ?

[*MARTHA BERNICK enters by the upstage door, left. The music can be faintly heard, down on the street.*]

MARTHA BERNICK. The procession's coming. But Betty isn't in the house. I can't imagine where . . .

BERNICK. Not in the house! There you are, you see, Lona. No support from her, either in joy or in sorrow.

RUMMEL. Pull the curtains! Come and help me, Mr. Krap. You as well, Mr. Sandstad. Dreadful pity the family's scattered all over the place at a moment like this! This wasn't on the programme at all.

[*The curtains are drawn back from the windows and the door. The whole street can be seen lit up. On the house opposite is a large illuminated sign with the words: 'Long live Karsten Bernick, Pillar of our Society!'*]

BERNICK [*shrinking back*]. Take it away! I don't want to see it! Put it out! Put it out!

RUMMEL. Forgive me for asking, but are you quite right in the head?

MARTHA BERNICK. What's wrong with him, Lona?

LONA HESSEL. Sh!

[*She says something to her in a low voice.*]

BERNICK. Take that sign away, I tell you! It's all a mockery. Don't you see all those lights sticking their tongues out at us?

RUMMEL. Well, I must say. . . .

BERNICK. Oh, how can you understand. . . . But I . . . I . . . Candles in a death chamber, that's what they are!

KRAP. H'm. . . .

RUMMEL. Really, you know . . . you are taking it all much too seriously.

SANDSTAD. The lad will get himself a trip across the Atlantic, and then you'll have him back again.

VIGELAND. Just have faith in the hand of the Almighty, Mr. Bernick.

RUMMEL. And in the ship, Bernick. It's hardly likely to sink, surely.

KRAP. H'm. . . .

RUMMEL. Now if she'd been one of those floating coffins you hear about in the bigger countries. . . .

BERNICK. I'm sure my hair must be turning grey at this moment.

[MRS. BERNICK, *with a large shawl over her head, enters by the garden door.*]

MRS. BERNICK. Karsten, Karsten, do you know . . . ?

BERNICK. Yes, I know. . . . As for you . . . you never see anything. . . . Can't even keep a proper eye on him, his own mother . . . !

MRS. BERNICK. Oh, please do listen. . . !

BERNICK. Why didn't you watch him? Now I've lost him. Give him back to me, if you can!

MRS. BERNICK. Yes, I can! I've got him!

BERNICK. You've got him!

THE MEN. Ah!

HILMAR TÖNNESEN. Ah, I thought as much.

MARTHA BERNICK. You've got him back, Karsten!

LONA HESSEL. Now you must make him really yours.

BERNICK. You've got him! Is it true what you say? Where is he?

MRS. BERNICK. I'm not telling you till you've forgiven him.

BERNICK. Forgiven . . . ! But how did you find out. . . ?

MRS. BERNICK. Do you think a mother doesn't see things? I was scared to death you'd find out. A couple of words he let slip yesterday. . . . Then when his room was empty, and his rucksack and his clothes had gone. . . .

BERNICK. Yes, yes. . . ?

MRS. BERNICK. I ran and got hold of Aune. We went out in his sailing boat. The American ship was just about to sail. But thank God, we got there just in time . . . got on board . . . searched the hold . . . and found him. Oh, Karsten, please, you mustn't punish him!

BERNICK. Betty!

MRS. BERNICK. Nor Aune, either!

BERNICK. Aune? What do you know about him? Is the *Indian Girl* under sail again?

MRS. BERNICK. No, that's just it. . . .

BERNICK. Go on! Go on!

MRS. BERNICK. Aune was just as shaken as I was. The search took time, it was getting dark, and the pilot was beginning to object. So Aune took it upon himself . . . in your name . . .

BERNICK. Well?

MRS. BERNICK. . . . to hold the ship till tomorrow.

KRAP. H'm. . . .

BERNICK. Oh, how incredibly lucky!

MRS. BERNICK. You are not angry?

BERNICK. Oh, what stupendous good luck, Betty!

RUMMEL. Oh, you take things far too much to heart.

HILMAR TÖNNESEN. As soon as there's any question of a bit of a tussle with the elements . . . ugh!

KRAP [*by the windows*]. The procession's just come in the garden gate, Mr. Bernick.

BERNICK. Yes, let them come now.

RUMMEL. The whole garden is filling up with people.

SANDSTAD. The whole street is jammed.

RUMMEL. The whole town's turned out, Bernick. This really is an inspiring moment.

VIGELAND. Let us take things in a spirit of humility, Mr. Rummel.

RUMMEL. All the flags are out. What a procession! And there is the organizing committee, with Mr. Rörlund at its head.

BERNICK. Let them come, I said!

RUMMEL. But, I say, aren't you rather worked up. . . ?

BERNICK. Well?

RUMMEL. I wouldn't be averse to saying a few words on your behalf.

BERNICK. No, thank you. Tonight I want to speak myself.

RUMMEL. You know what you are supposed to say?

BERNICK. Don't worry, Rummel. . . . I know what I've got to say.

[*Meantime the music has ceased. The veranda door is thrown open. RÖRLUND enters at the head of the committee, accompanied by two hired servants carrying a covered basket. After them come all manner of townspeople, as many as the room can hold. An immense crowd carrying banners and flags can be seen outside in the garden and in the street.*]

RÖRLUND. Consul Bernick! I see by the expression of surprise on your countenance that we come as unexpected guests, intruding ourselves upon you as you sit in the bosom of your family, by your own peaceful fireside in the company of distinguished and influential friends and fellow citizens. But it is in obedience to a heartfelt desire that we come to pay you our homage. This is not the first time that this has happened, but never before on such a grand scale. Many is the time we have expressed to you our gratitude for the firm moral foundation on which, as it were, you have built up our community. This time it is more specifically the fellow citizen we honour, indefatigable and selfless, a man whose vision and readiness to put himself last has led him to seize the initiative in an enterprise which—in the opinion of experts—will give a tremendous boost to the material well-being and prosperity of our community.

VOICES IN THE CROWD. Bravo, bravo!

RÖRLUND. Consul Bernick! You have for many years now set our town a shining example. I am referring here not to your exemplary domestic life, nor yet to the spotless record of your personal conduct in general. Such things belong to more intimate occasions, and not to a formal address! I want to speak rather of your public service, something that is there for all to see. Magnificent ships sail from your yard to carry the flag to distant seas. Your workmen—a large and happy body of men—look up to you as a father. By launching new enterprises, you have assured the welfare of many hundreds of families. In other words . . . you are, in the fullest sense of the term, the very corner-stone of our community.

VOICES. Hear, hear! Bravo!

RÖRLUND. Above all it is this quality of selflessness, which colours everything you do, that makes your influence the immensely beneficial thing it is, especially in times like the present. You are now engaged in acquiring for us—and I use, bluntly and without hesitation, the common word—a railway.

MANY VOICES. Bravo! Bravo!

RÖRLUND. But this enterprise appears to have encountered a number of difficulties, largely dictated by narrow self-interest.

VOICES. Hear, hear!

RÖRLUND. It has not escaped our knowledge that certain individuals—not being members of our community—have stolen a march on the hard-working citizens of this place, and acquired certain advantages which by rights ought to have benefited our own town.

VOICES. Yes, yes! Hear, hear!

RÖRLUND. This distressing information has, of course, also come to your knowledge, Mr. Bernick. But this in no way diminishes the resolution with which you continue to pursue your objective, knowing full well that a patriotic citizen must always take into account more than merely parochial interests.

VARIOUS VOICES. H'm! No, no! Yes, yes!

RÖRLUND. Thus, what we are gathered here together to honour tonight in your person, is the citizen and the patriot—the man, as ideally he ought to be. May your endeavours bring real and lasting benefit to our community. It is true that the railway may expose us to the risk of admitting elements of corruption from without; yet it could equally be a quick way of getting rid of them. Even as it is now, we cannot always stop undesirable elements coming in from outside. But the fact that, from what rumour says, we have fortunately succeeded—rather more rapidly than we expected—in getting rid of certain elements of this kind in time for tonight's celebrations . . .

VOICES. Sh! sh!

RÖRLUND. . . . this I regard as a happy omen for the enterprise. The fact that I touch on this point *here* is an indication that we find ourselves in a house where ethical considerations rank higher than family ties.

VOICES. Hear, hear! Bravo!

BERNICK [*simultaneously*]. Allow me . . .

RÖRLUND. Just a few words more, Mr. Bernick. What you have done for this place, you have clearly not done with any ulterior thought of material advantage for yourself. But you would not wish to refuse some modest token of the appreciation of your fellow citizens, least of all at this auspicious moment when we—so we are assured by practical men of affairs—stand on the threshold of a new era.

MANY VOICES. Bravo! Hear, hear!

[RÖRLUND *signs to the servants, who carry the basket forward. During the following speech, the members of the organizing committee take out and present the articles, to which reference is made.*]

RÖRLUND. And now, Mr. Bernick, we have pleasure in presenting you with this silver coffee service. May it grace your table when, in the future as so often in the past, we have the pleasure of forgathering in this most hospitable house. And you too, gentlemen, who have given such loyal support to our leading citizen, we beg you to accept some small memento of the occasion. For you, Mr. Rummel, this silver goblet. Many is the time you have, with great eloquence amidst the clink of glasses, fought for the civic interests of our community; may you find many more occasions worthy of raising and emptying this goblet. To you, Mr. Sandstad, I present this album with photographs of your fellow citizens. So well-known and so widely acknowledged is your altruism that you are in the happy position of having friends in all sections of the community. And to you Mr. Vigeland, to grace your own inner sanctum, this volume of sermons, printed on vellum and luxuriously bound. Mellowed by the passing of the years, you have arrived at a grave and wise philosophy of life; the part you have played in our daily affairs throughout the years has been purified and ennobled by thoughts of higher and holier things. [*He turns to the crowd.*] And with that, my friends, long live Mr. Bernick and his comrades! Three cheers for the Pillars of Society!

THE WHOLE CROWD. Consul Bernick! The Pillars of Society! Hurrah! hurrah! hurrah!

LONA HESSEL. Congratulations, Karsten!

[*Expectant silence.*]

BERNICK [*beginning earnestly and slowly*]. Fellow citizens! Your spokesman has said this evening that we are standing on the threshold of a new era ... and I hope that will indeed prove to be the case. But for this to be so, we must first have possession of the truth ... the truth which until tonight has been a complete and utter outcast from our community. [*Surprise among the audience.*] So I must begin by rejecting those flattering phrases with which you, Mr. Rörlund—as is customary on such occasions—have overwhelmed me. I do not deserve them. Because until today I have not by any means been a disinterested man. Even if I have not always striven for monetary gain, it is nevertheless clear to me now that a lust for power, a craving for influence and for position has been the driving force behind most of my actions.

RUMMEL [*under his breath*]. Now what?

BERNICK. To my fellow citizens I say: I do not reproach myself for this. For I still believe I may count myself as one of the more capable men of this town.

MANY VOICES. Yes, yes, yes!

BERNICK. But what I do charge myself with is this: that I have often been weak enough to follow somewhat devious ways, simply because I recognized and feared the way our society is inclined to impute base motives to whatever a man does. And now I come to a case in point.

RUMMEL [*uneasily*]. H'm! h'm!

BERNICK. There have been rumours of large purchases of land up-country. This land I have bought . . . all of it . . . I alone.

SUBDUED VOICES. What does he say? Bernick? Consul Bernick?

BERNICK. It is for the present in my hands. Of course, I have taken my colleagues into my confidence, Mr. Rummel, Mr. Vigeland and Mr. Sandstad, and we are agreed that . . .

RUMMEL. That's not true! Proof! Proof!

VIGELAND. We didn't agree to anything.

SANDSTAD. Well, I must say. . . .

BERNICK. That is quite right. We haven't reached agreement yet on what I was going to mention. But I feel sure these three gentlemen will back me up when I tell you that tonight I decided in my own mind these properties should be run by a public company. Anybody who wants to can buy shares in it.

MANY VOICES. Hurrah! Three cheers for Consul Bernick!

RUMMEL [*in a low voice to* BERNICK]. What a dirty fraud. . . !

SANDSTAD [*similarly*]. Fooled us, eh!

VIGELAND. The devil take . . . good Lord, what am I saying?

THE CROWD [*outside*]. Hurrah! hurrah! hurrah!

BERNICK. Silence, gentlemen, please. I have no right to this applause. Because what I have now decided was not my original intention. That intention was to keep the whole thing for myself; and I still am of the opinion that these properties can best be exploited by remaining concentrated in the hands of one man. But it is for you to choose. If you wish it, I am willing to administer them to the best of my ability.

VOICES. Yes! yes! yes!

BERNICK. But first, my friends, you must know me for what I really am. Then let each of us scrutinize himself; and then let it be that from tonight we start a new era. The old one with its veneer, its hypocrisy and its sham, with its pretence of respectability and its fawning ways, can stand as a kind of museum for us, open for our edification. And to this museum we shall present—shall we not, gentlemen?—the coffee service and the goblet and the album and the sermons printed on vellum and luxuriously bound.

RUMMEL. Yes, of course.

VIGELAND [*mumbling*]. If you've taken all the rest, then . . .

SANDSTAD. Do, please.

BERNICK. And now for the chief item in my account with the community. It has been said that certain undesirable elements had left us this evening. I can add something that isn't generally known: the man referred to did not go alone. With him, to become his wife, went . . .

LONA HESSEL [*loudly*]. Dina Dorf!

RÖRLUND. What!

MRS. BERNICK. What do you say?

[*Great commotion.*]

RÖRLUND. Gone? Run away . . . with *him*! Impossible!

BERNICK. To become his wife, Mr. Rörlund. And I'll add something more. [*In a low voice.*] Betty, hold on for what's coming. [*Aloud.*] I say 'Hats off to that man', for he nobly took upon himself another man's guilt. My friends, I'm sick of this lying. It's all but poisoned every fibre in me. You shall know everything. Fifteen years ago, *I* was the guilty one.

MRS. BERNICK [*in a low trembling voice*]. Karsten!

MARTHA BERNICK [*similarly*]. Ah, Johan. . . !

LONA HESSEL. Victory over yourself at last!

[*Speechless amazement among those present.*]

BERNICK. Yes, my friends, I was the guilty one, and he went away. Those evil lying rumours which later got about—it is no longer humanly possible to disprove them. Not that I should be the one to complain about that. Fifteen years ago I rose to the top on these rumours. Whether I am now to fall by them, is for each one of you to decide for himself.

RÖRLUND. What a thunderbolt! The leading man in the town. . . ! [*In a low voice to* MRS. BERNICK.] Oh, how I pity you, Mrs. Bernick.

HILMAR TÖNNESEN. What a confession! Well, I must say . . . !

BERNICK. But let us not decide anything tonight. I ask each one of you to go to his home . . . to compose himself . . . to look into his heart. And when we have all calmed down, it will be seen whether I have lost or gained by speaking out. Goodbye! I still have much . . . very much . . . to repent of, but that concerns my own conscience alone. Good night! Away with all this show. We all feel it is rather out of place here.

RÖRLUND. It certainly is. [*In a low voice to* MRS. BERNICK.] Run away! So in fact she was completely unworthy of me, after all. [*Louder, to the organizing committee.*] Yes, gentlemen, after this I think we had better quietly remove ourselves.

HILMAR TÖNNESEN. How anybody can be expected to keep the flag of idealism flying after this. . . . Ugh!

[*In the meantime, the news has been whispered from mouth to mouth. All those taking part in the procession go out by the garden.* RUMMEL, SANDSTAD *and* VIGELAND, *arguing violently with each other in low*

E

voices, also go. HILMAR TÖNNESEN *sneaks out, right. Remaining behind in the room in silence are* BERNICK, MRS. BERNICK, MARTHA BERNICK, LONA HESSEL *and* KRAP.]

BERNICK. Betty, can you forgive me?

MRS. BERNICK [*looks at him and smiles*]. You know, Karsten, you've made the outlook seem brighter than it's been for years!

BERNICK. How?

MRS. BERNICK. For years I've thought that you'd once been mine and that I'd lost you. Now I know that you never really were mine; but now I shall make you mine.

BERNICK [*putting his arms round her*]. Oh, Betty, you *have* made me yours. It was through Lona I first got to know the real you. But let Olaf come in now.

MRS. BERNICK. Yes, you shall have him now. Mr. Krap. . . !

[*She speaks to him in an undertone at the back of the room. He goes out through the garden door. During what follows, all the illuminated signs and all the lights in the houses go out one after the other.*]

BERNICK [*in a low voice*]. Thank you, Lona, you have saved what was best in me . . . and for me.

LONA HESSEL. What else do you suppose it was I wanted?

BERNICK. Ah, was it? Or wasn't it? I can't quite make you out.

LONA HESSEL. H'm. . . .

BERNICK. So it wasn't hatred? Wasn't revenge? Why did you come back, then?

LONA HESSEL. Old friendship doesn't go rusty.

BERNICK. Lona!

LONA HESSEL. When Johan told me all that about the lie, I swore to myself: my girlhood hero shall win through to truth and freedom.

BERNICK. Oh, I don't deserve all this of you—miserable creature that I am!

LONA HESSEL. Ah, once we women began asking who deserved what, Karsten. . . !

[AUNE *comes in with* OLAF *from the garden.*]

BERNICK [*going to him*]. Olaf!

OLAF. Father, I promise you I'll never again . . .

BERNICK. Run away?

OLAF. Yes, yes, I promise, Father.

BERNICK. And I promise you'll never have reason to. From now on you can grow up, not as someone destined to inherit *my* life, but as one with his own life to live.

OLAF. And can I also be what I want?

BERNICK. Yes, you can.

OLAF. Thank you. Then I don't want to be a pillar of society.

BERNICK. Oh? Why not?

OLAF. Well, I think it must be so boring.

BERNICK. You shall be yourself, Olaf. The rest can take care of itself. . . . And you, Aune. . . .

AUNE. I know, Mr. Bernick. I'm sacked.

BERNICK. We stick together, Aune. And forgive me. . . .

AUNE. What d'you mean? The ship didn't sail tonight.

BERNICK. And she's not sailing tomorrow, either. I didn't give you enough time. She needs a more thorough going-over.

AUNE. She will get it, Mr. Bernick. *And* with the new machines!

BERNICK. That's fine! But properly and thoroughly. A lot of things here could do with a proper, thorough overhaul. Well, goodnight, Aune.

AUNE. Goodnight, Mr. Bernick. And thank you, thank you!

[*He goes out, right.*]

MRS. BERNICK. Now they've all gone.

BERNICK. And we are alone. My name is no longer up in lights. And all the lamps in the windows have gone out.

LONA HESSEL. Would you want them lit again?

BERNICK. Not at any price! Where have I been? It would horrify you to know. I feel as though I were just coming round after being poisoned. But I *do* feel I can be young and strong again. Oh, come closer . . . all round me. Come along, Betty! Come along, Olaf, my boy. And you, Martha . . . it seems as though I hadn't seen you all these years.

LONA HESSEL. No, I can well believe it. This society of yours is like a lot of old bachelors: you never see the women.

BERNICK. True, true! And that's just why—yes, it's all settled, Lona— you mustn't leave Betty and me.

MRS. BERNICK. No, Lona, you mustn't.

LONA HESSEL. What possible excuse could I have for going away and leaving you two young people, just when you are beginning to set up home together. A foster-mother like me! You and I, Martha, we two old aunts. . . . What are you looking at?

MARTHA BERNICK. The sky is clearing. It's brightening over the sea. Good luck is with the *Palm Tree*.

LONA HESSEL. And good luck with those on board.

BERNICK. As for us . . . we have a long and hard day's work ahead of us. Particularly me. But let it come. Just as long as my two loyal and true-hearted women stand by me. That's something else I've learnt these last few days: it's you women who are the pillars of society.

LONA HESSEL. That's a pretty feeble piece of wisdom you've learnt, Karsten. [*Placing her hand firmly on his shoulder.*] No, my friend, the spirit of truth and the spirit of freedom—*these* are the pillars of society.

A DOLL'S HOUSE
[Et dukkehjem]

PLAY IN THREE ACTS
(1879)

CHARACTERS

TORVALD HELMER, a lawyer

NORA, his wife

DR. RANK

MRS. KRISTINE LINDE

NILS KROGSTAD

ANNE MARIE, the nursemaid

HELENE, the maid

The Helmers' three children

A porter

The action takes place in the Helmers' flat.

ACT ONE

A pleasant room, tastefully but not expensively furnished. On the back wall, one door on the right leads to the entrance hall, a second door on the left leads to HELMER's *study. Between these two doors, a piano. In the middle of the left wall, a door; and downstage from it, a window. Near the window a round table with armchairs and a small sofa. In the right wall, upstage, a door; and on the same wall downstage, a porcelain stove with a couple of armchairs and a rocking-chair. Between the stove and the door a small table. Etchings on the walls. A whatnot with china and other small objets d'art; a small bookcase with books in handsome bindings. Carpet on the floor; a fire burns in the stove. A winter's day.*

The front door-bell rings in the hall; a moment later, there is the sound of the front door being opened. NORA *comes into the room, happily humming to herself. She is dressed in her outdoor things, and is carrying lots of parcels which she then puts down on the table, right. She leaves the door into the hall standing open; a* PORTER *can be seen outside holding a Christmas tree and a basket; he hands them to the* MAID *who has opened the door for them.*

NORA. Hide the Christmas tree away carefully, Helene. The children mustn't see it till this evening when it's decorated. [*To the* PORTER, *taking out her purse.*] How much?

PORTER. Fifty öre.

NORA. There's a crown. Keep the change.

[*The* PORTER *thanks her and goes.* NORA *shuts the door. She continues to laugh quietly and happily to herself as she takes off her things. She takes a bag of macaroons out of her pocket and eats one or two; then she walks stealthily across and listens at her husband's door.*]

NORA. Yes, he's in.

[*She begins humming again as she walks over to the table, right.*]

HELMER [*in his study*]. Is that my little sky-lark chirruping out there?

NORA [*busy opening some of the parcels*]. Yes, it is.

HELMER. Is that my little squirrel frisking about?

NORA. Yes!

HELMER. When did my little squirrel get home?

NORA. Just this minute. [*She stuffs the bag of macaroons in her pocket and wipes her mouth.*] Come on out, Torvald, and see what I've bought.

HELMER. I don't want to be disturbed! [*A moment later, he opens the door and looks out, his pen in his hand.*] 'Bought', did you say? All that? Has my little spendthrift been out squandering money again?

NORA. But, Torvald, surely this year we can spread ourselves just a little. This is the first Christmas we haven't had to go carefully.

HELMER. Ah, but that doesn't mean we can afford to be extravagant, you know.

NORA. Oh yes, Torvald, surely we can afford to be just a little bit extravagant now, can't we? Just a teeny-weeny bit. You are getting quite a good salary now, and you are going to earn lots and lots of money.

HELMER. Yes, after the New Year. But it's going to be three whole months before the first pay cheque comes in.

NORA. Pooh! We can always borrow in the meantime.

HELMER. Nora! [*Crosses to her and takes her playfully by the ear.*] Here we go again, you and your frivolous ideas! Suppose I went and borrowed a thousand crowns today, and you went and spent it all over Christmas, then on New Year's Eve a slate fell and hit me on the head and there I was. . . .

NORA [*putting her hand over his mouth*]. Sh! Don't say such horrid things.

HELMER. Yes, but supposing something like that did happen . . . what then?

NORA. If anything as awful as that did happen, I wouldn't care if I owed anybody anything or not.

HELMER. Yes, but what about the people I'd borrowed from?

NORA. Them? Who cares about them! They are only strangers!

HELMER. Nora, Nora! Just like a woman! Seriously though, Nora, you know what I think about these things. No debts! Never borrow! There's always something inhibited, something unpleasant, about a home built on credit and borrowed money. We two have managed to stick it out so far, and that's the way we'll go on for the little time that remains.

NORA [*walks over to the stove*]. Very well, just as you say, Torvald.

HELMER [*following her*]. There, there! My little singing bird mustn't go drooping her wings, eh? Has it got the sulks, that little squirrel of mine? [*Takes out his wallet.*] Nora, what do you think I've got here?

NORA [*quickly turning round*]. Money!

HELMER. There! [*He hands her some notes*]. Good heavens, I know only too well how Christmas runs away with the housekeeping.

NORA [*counts*]. Ten, twenty, thirty, forty. Oh, thank you, thank you, Torvald! This will see me quite a long way.

HELMER. Yes, it'll have to.

NORA. Yes, yes, I'll see that it does. But come over here, I want to show you all the things I've bought. And so cheap! Look, some new clothes for Ivar . . . and a little sword. There's a horse and a trumpet for Bob. And a doll and a doll's cot for Emmy. They are not very grand but she'll have them all broken before long anyway. And I've got some dress material and some handkerchiefs for the maids. Though, really, dear old Anne Marie should have had something better.

HELMER. And what's in this parcel here?

NORA [*shrieking*]. No, Torvald! You mustn't see that till tonight!

HELMER. All right. But tell me now, what did my little spendthrift fancy for herself?

NORA. For me? Puh, I don't really want anything.

HELMER. Of course you do. Anything reasonable that you think you might like, just tell me.

NORA. Well, I don't really know. As a matter of fact, though, Torvald . . .

HELMER. Well?

NORA [*toying with his coat buttons, and without looking at him*]. If you did want to give me something, you could . . . you could always . . .

HELMER. Well, well, out with it!

NORA [*quickly*]. You could always give me money, Torvald. Only what you think you could spare. And then I could buy myself something with it later on.

HELMER. But Nora. . . .

NORA. Oh, please, Torvald dear! Please! I beg you. Then I'd wrap the money up in some pretty gilt paper and hang it on the Christmas tree. Wouldn't that be fun?

HELMER. What do we call my pretty little pet when it runs away with all the money?

NORA. I know, I know, we call it a spendthrift. But please let's do what I said, Torvald. Then I'll have a bit of time to think about what I need most. Isn't that awfully sensible, now, eh?

HELMER [*smiling*]. Yes, it is indeed—that is, if only you really could hold on to the money I gave you, and really did buy something for yourself with it. But it just gets mixed up with the housekeeping and frittered away on all sorts of useless things, and then I have to dig into my pocket all over again.

NORA. Oh but, Torvald. . . .

HELMER. You can't deny it, Nora dear. [*Puts his arm round her waist.*] My pretty little pet is very sweet, but it runs away with an awful lot of money. It's incredible how expensive it is for a man to keep such a pet.

NORA. For shame! How can you say such a thing? As a matter of fact I save everything I can.

HELMER [*laughs*]. Yes, you are right there. Everything you *can*. But you simply can't.

NORA [*hums and smiles quietly and happily*]. Ah, if you only knew how many expenses the likes of us sky-larks and squirrels have, Torvald!

HELMER. What a funny little one you are! Just like your father. Always on the look-out for money, wherever you can lay your hands on it; but as soon as you've got it, it just seems to slip through your fingers. You never seem to know what you've done with it. Well, one must accept you as you are. It's in the blood. Oh yes, it is, Nora. That sort of thing is hereditary.

NORA. Oh, I only wish I'd inherited a few more of Daddy's qualities.

HELMER. And I wouldn't want my pretty little song-bird to be the least bit different from what she is now. But come to think of it, you look rather . . . rather . . . how shall I put it? . . . rather guilty today. . . .

NORA. Do I?

HELMER. Yes, you do indeed. Look me straight in the eye.

NORA [*looks at him*]. Well?

HELMER [*wagging his finger at her*]. My little sweet-tooth surely didn't forget herself in town today?

NORA. No, whatever makes you think that?

HELMER. She didn't just pop into the confectioner's for a moment?

NORA. No, I assure you, Torvald. . . !

HELMER. Didn't try sampling the preserves?

NORA. No, really I didn't.

HELMER. Didn't go nibbling a macaroon or two?

NORA. No, Torvald, honestly, you must believe me. . . !

HELMER. All right then! It's really just my little joke. . . .

NORA [*crosses to the table*]. I would never dream of doing anything you didn't want me to.

HELMER. Of course not, I know that. And then you've given me your word. . . . [*Crosses to her.*] Well then, Nora dearest, you shall keep your little Christmas secrets. They'll all come out tonight, I dare say, when we light the tree.

NORA. Did you remember to invite Dr. Rank?

HELMER. No. But there's really no need. Of course he'll come and have dinner with us. Anyway, I can ask him when he looks in this morning. I've ordered some good wine. Nora, you can't imagine how I am looking forward to this evening.

NORA. So am I. And won't the children enjoy it, Torvald!

HELMER. Oh, what a glorious feeling it is, knowing you've got a nice, safe job, and a good fat income. Don't you agree? Isn't it wonderful, just thinking about it?

NORA. Oh, it's marvellous!

HELMER. Do you remember last Christmas? Three whole weeks beforehand you shut yourself up every evening till after midnight making flowers for the Christmas tree and all the other splendid things you wanted to surprise us with. Ugh, I never felt so bored in all my life.

NORA. I wasn't the least bit bored.

HELMER [*smiling*]. But it turned out a bit of an anticlimax, Nora.

NORA. Oh, you are not going to tease me about that again! How was I to know the cat would get in and pull everything to bits?

HELMER. No, of course you weren't. Poor little Nora! All you wanted was for us to have a nice time—and it's the thought behind it that counts, after all. All the same, it's a good thing we've seen the back of those lean times.

NORA. Yes, really it's marvellous.

HELMER. Now there's no need for me to sit here all on my own, bored to tears. And you don't have to strain your dear little eyes, and work those dainty little fingers to the bone. . . .

NORA [*clapping her hands*]. No, Torvald, I don't, do I? Not any more. Oh, how marvellous it is to hear that! [*Takes his arm.*] Now I want to tell you how I've been thinking we might arrange things, Torvald. As soon as Christmas is over. . . . [*The door-bell rings in the hall.*] Oh, there's the bell. [*Tidies one or two things in the room.*] It's probably a visitor. What a nuisance!

HELMER. Remember I'm not at home to callers.

MAID [*in the doorway*]. There's a lady to see you, ma'am.

NORA. Show her in, please.

MAID [*to* HELMER]. And the doctor's just arrived, too, sir.

HELMER. Did he go straight into my room?

MAID. Yes, he did, sir.

> [HELMER *goes into his study. The* MAID *shows in* MRS. LINDE, *who is in travelling clothes, and closes the door after her.*]

MRS. LINDE [*subdued and rather hesitantly*]. How do you do, Nora?

NORA [*uncertainly*]. How do you do?

MRS. LINDE. I'm afraid you don't recognize me.

NORA. No, I don't think I . . . And yet I seem to. . . . [*Bursts out suddenly.*] Why! Kristine! Is it really you?

MRS. LINDE. Yes, it's me.

NORA. Kristine! Fancy not recognizing you again! But how was I to, when . . . [*Gently.*] How you've changed, Kristine!

MRS. LINDE. I dare say I have. In nine . . . ten years. . . .

NORA. Is it so long since we last saw each other? Yes, it must be. Oh, believe me these last eight years have been such a happy time. And now you've come up to town, too? All that long journey in wintertime. That took courage.

MRS. LINDE. I just arrived this morning on the steamer.

NORA. To enjoy yourself over Christmas, of course. How lovely! Oh, we'll have such fun, you'll see. Do take off your things. You are not cold, are you? [*Helps her.*] There now! Now let's sit down here in comfort beside the stove. No, here, you take the armchair, I'll sit here on the rocking-chair. [*Takes her hands.*] Ah, now you look a bit more like your old self again. It was just that when I first saw you. . . . But you are a little paler, Kristine . . . and perhaps even a bit thinner!

MRS. LINDE. And much, much older, Nora.

NORA. Yes, perhaps a little older . . . very, very little, not really very much. [*Stops suddenly and looks serious.*] Oh, what a thoughtless creature I am, sitting here chattering on like this! Dear, sweet Kristine, can you forgive me?

MRS. LINDE. What do you mean, Nora?

NORA [*gently*]. Poor Kristine, of course you're a widow now.

MRS. LINDE. Yes, my husband died three years ago.

NORA. Oh, I remember now. I read about it in the papers. Oh, Kristine, believe me I often thought at the time of writing to you. But I kept putting it off, something always seemed to crop up.

MRS. LINDE. My dear Nora, I understand so well.

NORA. No, it wasn't very nice of me, Kristine. Oh, you poor thing, what you must have gone through. And didn't he leave you anything?

MRS. LINDE. No.

NORA. And no children?

MRS. LINDE. No.

NORA. Absolutely nothing?

MRS. LINDE. Nothing at all . . . not even a broken heart to grieve over.

NORA [*looks at her incredulously*]. But, Kristine, is that possible?

MRS. LINDE [*smiles sadly and strokes* NORA's *hair*]. Oh, it sometimes happens, Nora.

NORA. So utterly alone. How terribly sad that must be for you. I have three lovely children. You can't see them for the moment, because they're out with their nanny. But now you must tell me all about yourself. . . .

MRS. LINDE. No, no, I want to hear about you.

NORA. No, you start. I won't be selfish today. I must think only about your affairs today. But there's just one thing I really must tell you. Have you heard about the great stroke of luck we've had in the last few days?

MRS. LINDE. No. What is it?

NORA. What do you think? My husband has just been made Bank Manager!

MRS. LINDE. Your husband? How splendid!

NORA. Isn't it tremendous! It's not a very steady way of making a living, you know, being a lawyer, especially if he refuses to take on anything that's the least bit shady—which of course is what Torvald does, and I think he's quite right. You can imagine how pleased we are! He starts at the Bank straight after New Year, and he's getting a big salary and lots of commission. From now on we'll be able to live quite differently . . . we'll do just what we want. Oh, Kristine, I'm so happy and relieved. I must say it's lovely to have plenty of money and not have to worry. Isn't it?

MRS. LINDE. Yes. It must be nice to have enough, at any rate.

NORA. No, not just enough, but pots and pots of money.

MRS. LINDE [*smiles*]. Nora, Nora, haven't you learned any sense yet? At school you used to be an awful spendthrift.

NORA. Yes, Torvald still says I am. [*Wags her finger.*] But little Nora isn't as stupid as everybody thinks. Oh, we haven't really been in a position where I could afford to spend a lot of money. We've both had to work.

MRS. LINDE. You too?

NORA. Yes, odd jobs—sewing, crochet-work, embroidery and things like that. [*Casually.*] And one or two other things, besides. I suppose you know that Torvald left the Ministry when we got married. There weren't any prospects of promotion in his department, and of course he needed to earn more money than he had before. But the first year he wore himself out completely. He had to take on all kinds of extra jobs, you know, and he found himself working all hours of the day and night. But he couldn't go on like that; and he became seriously ill. The doctors said it was essential for him to go South.

MRS. LINDE. Yes, I believe you spent a whole year in Italy, didn't you?

NORA. That's right. It wasn't easy to get away, I can tell you. It was just after I'd had Ivar. But of course we had to go. Oh, it was an absolutely marvellous trip. And it saved Torvald's life. But it cost an awful lot of money, Kristine.

MRS. LINDE. That I can well imagine.

NORA. Twelve hundred dollars. Four thousand eight hundred crowns. That's a lot of money, Kristine.

MRS. LINDE. Yes, but in such circumstances, one is very lucky if one has it.

NORA. Well, we got it from Daddy, you see.

MRS. LINDE. Ah, that was it. It was just about then your father died, I believe, wasn't it?

NORA. Yes, Kristine, just about then. And do you know, I couldn't even go and look after him. Here was I expecting Ivar any day. And I also had poor Torvald, gravely ill, on my hands. Dear, kind Daddy! I never saw him again, Kristine. Oh, that's the saddest thing that has happened to me in all my married life.

MRS. LINDE. I know you were very fond of him. But after that you left for Italy?

NORA. Yes, we had the money then, and the doctors said it was urgent. We left a month later.

MRS. LINDE. And your husband came back completely cured?

NORA. Fit as a fiddle!

MRS. LINDE. But . . . what about the doctor?

NORA. How do you mean?

MRS. LINDE. I thought the maid said something about the gentleman who came at the same time as me being a doctor.

NORA. Yes, that was Dr. Rank. But this isn't a professional visit. He's our best friend and he always looks in at least once a day. No, Torvald has never had a day's illness since. And the children are fit and healthy, and so am I. [*Jumps up and claps her hands.*] Oh God, oh God, isn't it marvellous to be alive, and to be happy, Kristine! . . . Oh, but I ought to be ashamed of myself . . . Here I go on talking about nothing but myself. [*She sits on a low stool near* MRS. LINDE *and lays her arms on her lap.*] Oh, please, you mustn't be angry with me!

Tell me, is it really true that you didn't love your husband? What made you marry him, then?

MRS. LINDE. My mother was still alive; she was bedridden and helpless. And then I had my two young brothers to look after as well. I didn't think I would be justified in refusing him.

NORA. No, I dare say you are right. I suppose he was fairly wealthy then?

MRS. LINDE. He was quite well off, I believe. But the business was shaky. When he died, it went all to pieces, and there just wasn't anything left.

NORA. What then?

MRS. LINDE. Well, I had to fend for myself, opening a little shop, running a little school, anything I could turn my hand to. These last three years have been one long relentless drudge. But now it's finished, Nora. My poor dear mother doesn't need me any more, she's passed away. Nor the boys either; they're at work now, they can look after themselves.

NORA. What a relief you must find it. . . .

MRS. LINDE. No, Nora! Just unutterably empty. Nobody to live for any more. [*Stands up restlessly.*] That's why I couldn't stand it any longer being cut off up there. Surely it must be a bit easier here to find something to occupy your mind. If only I could manage to find a steady job of some kind, in an office perhaps. . . .

NORA. But, Kristine, that's terribly exhausting; and you look so worn out even before you start. The best thing for you would be a little holiday at some quiet little resort.

MRS. LINDE [*crosses to the window*]. I haven't any father I can fall back on for the money, Nora.

NORA [*rises*]. Oh, please, you mustn't be angry with me!

MRS. LINDE [*goes to her*]. My dear Nora, you mustn't be angry with me either. That's the worst thing about people in my position, they become so bitter. One has nobody to work for, yet one has to be on the look-out all the time. Life has to go on, and one starts thinking only of oneself. Believe it or not, when you told me the good news about your step up, I was pleased not so much for your sake as for mine.

NORA. How do you mean? Ah, I see. You think Torvald might be able to do something for you.

MRS. LINDE. Yes, that's exactly what I thought.

NORA. And so he shall, Kristine. Just leave things to me. I'll bring it up so cleverly . . . I'll think up something to put him in a good mood. Oh, I do so much want to help you.

MRS. LINDE. It is awfully kind of you, Nora, offering to do all this for me, particularly in your case, where you haven't known much trouble or hardship in your own life.

NORA. When I . . . ? I haven't known much . . . ?

MRS. LINDE [*smiling*]. Well, good heavens, a little bit of sewing to do and a few things like that. What a child you are, Nora!

NORA [*tosses her head and walks across the room*]. I wouldn't be too sure of that, if I were you.

MRS. LINDE. Oh?

NORA. You're just like the rest of them. You all think I'm useless when it comes to anything really serious. . . .

MRS. LINDE. Come, come. . . .

NORA. You think I've never had anything much to contend with in this hard world.

MRS. LINDE. Nora dear, you've only just been telling me all the things you've had to put up with.

NORA. Pooh! They were just trivialities! [*Softly.*] I haven't told you about the really big thing.

MRS. LINDE. What big thing? What do you mean?

NORA. I know you rather tend to look down on me, Kristine. But you shouldn't, you know. You are proud of having worked so hard and so long for your mother.

MRS. LINDE. I'm sure I don't look down on anybody. But it's true what you say: I am both proud and happy when I think of how I was able to make Mother's life a little easier towards the end.

NORA. And you are proud when you think of what you have done for your brothers, too.

MRS. LINDE. I think I have every right to be.

NORA. I think so too. But now I'm going to tell you something, Kristine. I too have something to be proud and happy about.

MRS. LINDE. I don't doubt that. But what is it you mean?

NORA. Not so loud. Imagine if Torvald were to hear! He must never on any account . . . nobody must know about it, Kristine, nobody but you.

MRS. LINDE. But what is it?

NORA. Come over here. [*She pulls her down on the sofa beside her.*] Yes, Kristine, I too have something to be proud and happy about. I was the one who saved Torvald's life.

MRS. LINDE. Saved . . . ? How . . . ?

NORA. I told you about our trip to Italy. Torvald would never have recovered but for that. . . .

MRS. LINDE. Well? Your father gave you what money was necessary. . . .

NORA [*smiles*]. That's what Torvald thinks, and everybody else. But . . .

MRS. LINDE. But . . . ?

NORA. Daddy never gave us a penny. I was the one who raised the money.

MRS. LINDE. You? All that money?

NORA. Twelve hundred dollars. Four thousand eight hundred crowns. What do you say to that!

MRS. LINDE. But, Nora, how was it possible? Had you won a sweepstake or something?

NORA [*contemptuously*]. A sweepstake? Pooh! There would have been nothing to it then.

MRS. LINDE. Where did you get it from, then?

NORA [*hums and smiles secretively*]. H'm, tra-la-la!

MRS. LINDE. Because what you couldn't do was borrow it.

NORA. Oh? Why not?

MRS. LINDE. Well, a wife can't borrow without her husband's consent.

NORA [*tossing her head*]. Ah, but when it happens to be a wife with a bit of a sense for business . . . a wife who knows her way about things, then. . . .

MRS. LINDE. But, Nora, I just don't understand. . . .

NORA. You don't have to. I haven't said I did borrow the money. I might have got it some other way. [*Throws herself back on the sofa.*] I might even have got it from some admirer. Anyone as reasonably attractive as I am. . . .

MRS. LINDE. Don't be so silly!

NORA. Now you must be dying of curiosity, Kristine.

MRS. LINDE. Listen to me now, Nora dear—you haven't done anything rash, have you?

NORA [*sitting up again*]. Is it rash to save your husband's life?

MRS. LINDE. I think it was rash to do anything without telling him. . . .

NORA. But the whole point was that he mustn't know anything. Good heavens, can't you see! He wasn't even supposed to know how desperately ill he was. It was me the doctors came and told his life was in danger, that the only way to save him was to go South for a while. Do you think I didn't try talking him into it first? I began dropping hints about how nice it would be if I could be taken on a little trip abroad, like other young wives. I wept, I pleaded. I told him he ought to show some consideration for my condition, and let me have a bit of my own way. And then I suggested he might take out a loan. But at that he nearly lost his temper, Kristine. He said I was being frivolous, that it was his duty as a husband not to give in to all these whims and fancies of mine—as I do believe he called them. All right, I thought, somehow you've got to be saved. And it was then I found a way. . . .

MRS. LINDE. Did your husband never find out from your father that the money hadn't come from him?

NORA. No, never. It was just about the time Daddy died. I'd intended letting him into the secret and asking him not to give me away. But when he was so ill . . . I'm sorry to say it never became necessary.

MRS. LINDE. And you never confided in your husband?

NORA. Good heavens, how could you ever imagine such a thing! When he's so strict about such matters! Besides, Torvald is a man with a good deal of pride—it would be terribly embarrassing and humiliating for him if he thought he owed anything to me. It would spoil everything between us; this happy home of ours would never be the same again.

MRS. LINDE. Are you never going to tell him?

NORA [*reflectively, half-smiling*]. Oh yes, some day perhaps . . . in many years time, when I'm no longer as pretty as I am now. You mustn't laugh! What I mean of course is when Torvald isn't quite so much in love with me as he is now, when he's lost interest in watching me dance, or get dressed up, or recite. Then it might be a good thing to have something in reserve. . . . [*Breaks off.*] What nonsense! That day will never come. Well, what have you got to say to my big secret, Kristine? Still think I'm not much good for anything? One thing, though, it's meant a lot of worry for me, I can tell you. It hasn't always been easy to meet my obligations when the time came. You know in business there is something called quarterly interest, and other things called instalments, and these are always terribly difficult things to cope with. So what I've had to do is save a little here and there, you see, wherever I could. I couldn't really save anything out of the housekeeping, because Torvald has to live in decent style. I couldn't let the children go about badly dressed either—I felt any money I got for them had to go on them alone. Such sweet little things!

MRS. LINDE. Poor Nora! So it had to come out of your own allowance?

NORA. Of course. After all, I was the one it concerned most. Whenever Torvald gave me money for new clothes and such-like, I never spent more than half. And always I bought the simplest and cheapest things. It's a blessing most things look well on me, so Torvald never noticed anything. But sometimes I did feel it was a bit hard, Kristine, because it is nice to be well dressed, isn't it?

MRS. LINDE. Yes, I suppose it is.

NORA. I have had some other sources of income, of course. Last winter I was lucky enough to get quite a bit of copying to do. So I shut myself up every night and sat and wrote through to the small hours of the morning. Oh, sometimes I was so tired, so tired. But it was tremendous fun all the same, sitting there working and earning money like that. It was almost like being a man.

MRS. LINDE. And how much have you been able to pay off like this?

NORA. Well, I can't tell exactly. It's not easy to know where you are with transactions of this kind, you understand. All I know is I've paid off just as much as I could scrape together. Many's the time I was at my wit's end. [*Smiles.*] Then I used to sit here and pretend that some rich old gentleman had fallen in love with me. . . .

MRS. LINDE. What! What gentleman?

NORA. Oh, rubbish! . . . and that now he had died, and when they opened his will, there in big letters were the words: 'My entire fortune is to be paid over, immediately and in cash, to charming Mrs. Nora Helmer.'

MRS. LINDE. But my dear Nora—who *is* this man?

NORA. Good heavens, don't you understand? There never was any old gentleman; it was just something I used to sit here pretending, time and time again, when I didn't know where to turn next for money. But it doesn't make very much difference; as far as I'm concerned, the old boy can do what he likes, I'm tired of him; I can't be bothered any more with him or his will. Because now all my worries are over. [*Jumping up.*] Oh God, what a glorious thought, Kristine! No more worries! Just think of being without a care in the world . . . being able to romp with the children, and making the house nice and attractive, and having things just as Torvald likes to have them! And then spring will soon be here, and blue skies. And maybe we can go away somewhere. I might even see something of the sea again. Oh yes! When you're happy, life is a wonderful thing!

[*The door-bell is heard in the hall.*]

MRS. LINDE [*gets up*]. There's the bell. Perhaps I'd better go.

NORA. No, do stay, please. I don't suppose it's for me; it's probably somebody for Torvald. . . .

MAID [*in the doorway*]. Excuse me, ma'am, but there's a gentleman here wants to see Mr. Helmer, and I didn't quite know . . . because the Doctor is in there. . . .

NORA. Who is the gentleman?

KROGSTAD [*in the doorway*]. It's me, Mrs. Helmer.

[MRS. LINDE *starts, then turns away to the window.*]

NORA [*tense, takes a step towards him and speaks in a low voice*]. You? What is it? What do you want to talk to my husband about?

KROGSTAD. Bank matters . . . in a manner of speaking. I work at the bank, and I hear your husband is to be the new manager. . . .

NORA. So it's . . .

KROGSTAD. Just routine business matters, Mrs. Helmer. Absolutely nothing else.

NORA. Well then, please go into his study.

[*She nods impassively and shuts the hall door behind him; then she walks across and sees to the stove.*]

MRS. LINDE. Nora . . . who was that man?

NORA. His name is Krogstad.

MRS. LINDE. So it really was him.

NORA. Do you know the man?

MRS. LINDE. I used to know him . . . a good many years ago. He was a solicitor's clerk in our district for a while.

NORA. Yes, so he was.

MRS. LINDE. How he's changed!

NORA. His marriage wasn't a very happy one, I believe.

MRS. LINDE. He's a widower now, isn't he?

NORA. With a lot of children. There, it'll burn better now.

[*She closes the stove door and moves the rocking chair a little to one side.*]

MRS. LINDE. He does a certain amount of business on the side, they say?

NORA. Oh? Yes, it's always possible. I just don't know. . . . But let's not think about business . . . it's all so dull.

[DR. RANK *comes in from* HELMER'S *study.*]

DR. RANK [*still in the doorway*]. No, no, Torvald, I won't intrude. I'll just look in on your wife for a moment. [*Shuts the door and notices* MRS. LINDE.] Oh, I beg your pardon. I'm afraid I'm intruding here as well.

NORA. No, not at all! [*Introduces them.*] Dr. Rank . . . Mrs. Linde.

RANK. Ah! A name I've often heard mentioned in this house. I believe I came past you on the stairs as I came in.

MRS. LINDE. I have to take things slowly going upstairs. I find it rather a trial.

RANK. Ah, some little disability somewhere, eh?

MRS. LINDE. Just a bit run down, I think, actually.

RANK. Is that all? Then I suppose you've come to town for a good rest —doing the rounds of the parties?

MRS. LINDE. I have come to look for work.

RANK. Is that supposed to be some kind of sovereign remedy for being run down?

MRS. LINDE. One must live, Doctor.

RANK. Yes, it's generally thought to be necessary.

NORA. Come, come, Dr. Rank. You are quite as keen to live as anybody.

RANK. Quite keen, yes. Miserable as I am, I'm quite ready to let things drag on as long as possible. All my patients are the same. Even those with a moral affliction are no different. As a matter of fact, there's a bad case of that kind in talking with Helmer at this very moment. . . .

MRS. LINDE [*softly*]. Ah!

NORA. Whom do you mean?

RANK. A person called Krogstad—nobody you would know. He's rotten to the core. But even he began talking about having to *live*, as though it were something terribly important.

NORA. Oh? And what did he want to talk to Torvald about?

RANK. I honestly don't know. All I heard was something about the Bank.

NORA. I didn't know that Krog . . . that this Mr. Krogstad had anything to do with the Bank.

RANK. Oh yes, he's got some kind of job down there. [*To* MRS. LINDE.] I wonder if you've got people in your part of the country too who go rushing round sniffing out cases of moral corruption, and then installing the individuals concerned in nice, well-paid jobs where they can keep them under observation. Sound, decent people have to be content to stay out in the cold.

MRS. LINDE. Yet surely it's the sick who most need to be brought in.

RANK [*shrugs his shoulders*]. Well, there we have it. It's that attitude that's turning society into a clinic.

[NORA, *lost in her own thoughts, breaks into smothered laughter and claps her hands.*]

RANK. Why are you laughing at that? Do you know in fact what society is?

NORA. What do I care about your silly old society? I was laughing about something quite different . . . something frightfully funny. Tell me, Dr. Rank, are all the people who work at the Bank dependent on Torvald now?

RANK. Is *that* what you find so frightfully funny?

NORA [*smiles and hums*]. Never you mind! Never you mind! [*Walks about the room.*] Yes, it really is terribly amusing to think that we . . . that Torvald now has power over so many people. [*She takes the bag out of her pocket.*] Dr. Rank, what about a little macaroon?

RANK. Look at this, eh? Macaroons. I thought they were forbidden here.

NORA. Yes, but these are some Kristine gave me.

MRS. LINDE. What? I . . . ?

NORA. Now, now, you needn't be alarmed. You weren't to know that Torvald had forbidden them. He's worried in case they ruin my teeth, you know. Still . . . what's it matter once in a while! Don't you think so, Dr. Rank? Here! [*She pops a macaroon into his mouth.*] And you too, Kristine. And I shall have one as well; just a little one . . . or two at the most. [*She walks about the room again.*] Really I am so happy. There's just one little thing I'd love to do now.

RANK. What's that?

NORA. Something I'd love to say in front of Torvald.

RANK. Then why can't you?

NORA. No, I daren't. It's not very nice.

MRS. LINDE. Not very nice?

RANK. Well, in that case it might not be wise. But to us, I don't see why. . . . What is this you would love to say in front of Helmer?

NORA. I would simply love to say: 'Damn'.

RANK. Are you mad!

MRS. LINDE. Good gracious, Nora. . . !

RANK. Say it! Here he is!

NORA [*hiding the bag of macaroons*]. Sh! Sh!

[HELMER *comes out of his room, his overcoat over his arm and his hat in his hand.*]

NORA [*going over to him*]. Well, Torvald dear, did you get rid of him?

HELMER. Yes, he's just gone.

NORA. Let me introduce you. This is Kristine, who has just arrived in town. . . .

HELMER. Kristine. . . ? You must forgive me, but I don't think I know. . .

NORA. Mrs. Linde, Torvald dear. Kristine Linde.

HELMER. Ah, indeed. A school-friend of my wife's, presumably.

MRS. LINDE. Yes, we were girls together.

NORA. Fancy, Torvald, she's come all this long way just to have a word with you.

HELMER. How is that?

MRS. LINDE. Well, it wasn't really. . . .

NORA. The thing is, Kristine is terribly clever at office work, and she's frightfully keen on finding a job with some efficient man, so that she can learn even more. . . .

HELMER. Very sensible, Mrs. Linde.

NORA. And then when she heard you'd been made Bank Manager—there was a bit in the paper about it—she set off at once. Torvald please! You *will* try and do something for Kristine, won't you? For my sake?

HELMER. Well, that's not altogether impossible. You are a widow, I presume?

MRS. LINDE. Yes.

HELMER. And you've had some experience in business?

MRS. LINDE. A fair amount.

HELMER. Well, it's quite probable I can find you a job, I think. . . .

NORA [*clapping her hands*]. There, you see!

HELMER. You have come at a fortunate moment, Mrs. Linde. . . .

MRS. LINDE. Oh, how can I ever thank you. . . ?

HELMER. Not a bit. [*He puts on his overcoat.*] But for the present I must ask you to excuse me. . . .

RANK. Wait. I'm coming with you.

[*He fetches his fur coat from the hall and warms it at the stove.*]

NORA. Don't be long, Torvald dear.

HELMER. Not more than an hour, that's all.

NORA. Are you leaving too, Kristine?

MRS. LINDE [*putting on her things*]. Yes, I must go and see if I can't find myself a room.

HELMER. Perhaps we can all walk down the road together.

NORA [*helping her*]. What a nuisance we are so limited for space here. I'm afraid it just isn't possible. . . .

MRS. LINDE. Oh, you mustn't dream of it! Goodbye, Nora dear, and thanks for everything.

NORA. Goodbye for the present. But . . . you'll be coming back this evening, of course. And you too, Dr. Rank? What's that? If you are up to it? Of course you'll be up to it. Just wrap yourself up well.

[*They go out, talking, into the hall; children's voices can be heard on the stairs.*]

NORA. Here they are! Here they are! [*She runs to the front door and opens it.* ANNE MARIE, *the nursemaid, enters with the children.*] Come in! Come in! [*She bends down and kisses them.*] Ah! my sweet little darlings. . . . You see them, Kristine? Aren't they lovely!

RANK. Don't stand here chattering in this draught!

HELMER. Come along, Mrs. Linde. The place now becomes unbearable for anybody except mothers.

[DR. RANK, HELMER *and* MRS. LINDE *go down the stairs: the* NURSEMAID *comes into the room with the children, then* NORA, *shutting the door behind her.*]

NORA. How fresh and bright you look! My, what red cheeks you've got! Like apples and roses. [*During the following, the children keep chattering away to her.*] Have you had a nice time? That's splendid. And you gave Emmy and Bob a ride on your sledge? Did you now! Both together! Fancy that! There's a clever boy, Ivar. Oh, let me take her a little while, Anne Marie. There's my sweet little baby-doll! [*She takes the youngest of the children from the nursemaid and dances with her.*] All right, Mummy will dance with Bobby too. What? You've been throwing snowballs? Oh, I wish I'd been there. No, don't bother, Anne Marie, I'll help them off with their things. No, please, let me—I like doing it. You go on in, you look frozen. You'll find some hot coffee on the stove. [*The nursemaid goes into the room, left.* NORA *takes off the children's coats and hats and throws them down anywhere, while the children all talk at once.*] Really! A great big dog came running after you? But he didn't bite. No, the doggies wouldn't bite my pretty little dollies. You mustn't touch the parcels, Ivar! What are they? Wouldn't you like to know! No, no, that's nasty. Now? Shall we play something? What shall we play? Hide and seek? Yes, let's play hide and seek. Bob can hide first. Me first? All right, let me hide first.

[*She and the children play, laughing and shrieking, in this room and in the adjacent room on the right. Finally* NORA *hides under the table; the children come rushing in to look for her but cannot find her; they hear her stifled laughter, rush to the table, lift up the tablecloth and find her. Tremendous shouts of delight. She creeps out and pretends to frighten them. More shouts. Meanwhile there has been a knock at the front door, which nobody has heard. The door half opens, and* KROGSTAD *can be seen. He waits a little; the game continues.*]

KROGSTAD. I beg your pardon, Mrs. Helmer. . . .

NORA [*turns with a stifled cry and half jumps up*]. Ah! What do you want?

KROGSTAD. Excuse me. The front door was standing open. Somebody must have forgotten to shut it. . . .

NORA [*standing up*]. My husband isn't at home, Mr. Krogstad.

KROGSTAD. I know.

NORA. Well . . . what are you doing here?

KROGSTAD. I want a word with you.

NORA. With . . . ? [*Quietly, to the children.*] Go to Anne Marie. What? No, the strange man won't do anything to Mummy. When he's gone we'll have another game. [*She leads the children into the room, left, and shuts the door after them; tense and uneasy.*] You want to speak to me?

KROGSTAD. Yes, I do.

NORA. Today? But it isn't the first of the month yet. . . .

KROGSTAD. No, it's Christmas Eve. It depends entirely on you what sort of Christmas you have.

NORA. What do you want? Today I can't possibly . . .

KROGSTAD. Let's not talk about that for the moment. It's something else. You've got a moment to spare?

NORA. Yes, I suppose so, though . . .

KROGSTAD. Good. I was sitting in Olsen's café, and I saw your husband go down the road. . .

NORA. Did you?

KROGSTAD. . . . with a lady.

NORA. Well?

KROGSTAD. May I be so bold as to ask whether that lady was a Mrs. Linde?

NORA. Yes.

KROGSTAD. Just arrived in town?

NORA. Yes, today.

KROGSTAD. And she's a good friend of yours?

NORA. Yes, she is. But I can't see . . .

KROGSTAD. I also knew her once.

NORA. I know.

KROGSTAD. Oh? So you know all about it. I thought as much. Well, I want to ask you straight: is Mrs. Linde getting a job in the Bank?

NORA. How dare you cross-examine me like this, Mr. Krogstad? You, one of my husband's subordinates? But since you've asked me, I'll tell you. Yes, Mrs. Linde *has* got a job. And I'm the one who got it for her, Mr. Krogstad. Now you know.

KROGSTAD. So my guess was right.

NORA [*walking up and down*]. Oh, I think I can say that some of us have a little influence now and again. Just because one happens to be a woman, that doesn't mean. . . . People in subordinate positions, ought to take care they don't offend anybody . . . who . . . hm . . .

KROGSTAD. . . . has influence?

NORA. Exactly.

KROGSTAD [*changing his tone*]. Mrs. Helmer, will you have the goodness to use your influence on my behalf?

NORA. What? What do you mean?

KROGSTAD. Will you be so good as to see that I keep my modest little job at the Bank?

NORA. What do you mean? Who wants to take it away from you?

KROGSTAD. Oh, you needn't try and pretend to me you don't know. I can quite see that this friend of yours isn't particularly anxious to bump up against me. And I can also see now whom I can thank for being given the sack.

NORA. But I assure you. . . .

KROGSTAD. All right, all right. But to come to the point: there's still time. And I advise you to use your influence to stop it.

NORA. But, Mr. Krogstad, I *have* no influence.

KROGSTAD. Haven't you? I thought just now you said yourself . . .

NORA. I didn't mean it that way, of course. Me? What makes you think I've got any influence of that kind over my husband?

KROGSTAD. I know your husband from our student days. I don't suppose he is any more steadfast than other married men.

NORA. You speak disrespectfully of my husband like that and I'll show you the door.

KROGSTAD. So the lady's got courage.

NORA. I'm not frightened of you any more. After New Year I'll soon be finished with the whole business.

KROGSTAD [*controlling himself*]. Listen to me, Mrs. Helmer. If necessary I shall fight for my little job in the Bank as if I were fighting for my life.

NORA. So it seems.

KROGSTAD. It's not just for the money, that's the last thing I care about. There's something else . . . well, I might as well out with it. You see it's like this. You know as well as anybody that some years ago I got myself mixed up in a bit of trouble.

NORA. I believe I've heard something of the sort.

KROGSTAD. It never got as far as the courts; but immediately it was as if all paths were barred to me. So I started going in for the sort of

business you know about. I had to do something, and I think I can
say I haven't been one of the worst. But now I have to get out of it.
My sons are growing up; for their sake I must try and win back
what respectability I can. That job in the Bank was like the first
step on the ladder for me. And now your husband wants to kick me
off the ladder again, back into the mud.

NORA. But in God's name, Mr. Krogstad, it's quite beyond my power
to help you.

KROGSTAD. That's because you haven't the will to help me. But I have
ways of making you.

NORA. You wouldn't go and tell my husband I owe you money?

KROGSTAD. Suppose I did tell him?

NORA. It would be a rotten shame. [*Half choking with tears.*] That secret
is all my pride and joy—why should he have to hear about it in this
nasty, horrid way . . . hear about it from *you*. You would make
things horribly unpleasant for me. . . .

KROGSTAD. Merely unpleasant?

NORA [*vehemently*]. Go on, do it then! It'll be all the worse for you.
Because then my husband will see for himself what a bad man you
are, and then you certainly won't be able to keep your job.

KROGSTAD. I asked whether it was only a bit of domestic unpleasantness you were afraid of?

NORA. If my husband gets to know about it, he'll pay off what's owing
at' once. And then we'd have nothing more to do with you.

KROGSTAD [*taking a pace towards her*]. Listen, Mrs. Helmer, either you
haven't a very good memory, or else you don't understand much
about business. I'd better make the position a little bit clearer for you.

NORA. How do you mean?

KROGSTAD. When your husband was ill, you came to me for the loan
of twelve hundred dollars.

NORA. I didn't know of anybody else.

KROGSTAD. I promised to find you the money. . . .

NORA. And you did find it.

KROGSTAD. I promised to find you the money on certain conditions. At the time you were so concerned about your husband's illness, and so anxious to get the money for going away with, that I don't think you paid very much attention to all the incidentals. So there is perhaps some point in reminding you of them. Well, I promised to find you the money against an IOU which I drew up for you.

NORA. Yes, and which I signed.

KROGSTAD. Very good. But below that I added a few lines, by which your father was to stand security. This your father was to sign.

NORA. Was to . . . ? He did sign it.

KROGSTAD. I had left the date blank. The idea was that your father was to add the date himself when he signed it. Remember?

NORA. Yes, I think. . . .

KROGSTAD. I then gave you the IOU to post to your father. Wasn't that so?

NORA. Yes.

KROGSTAD. Which of course you did at once. Because only about five or six days later you brought it back to me with your father's signature. I then paid out the money.

NORA. Well? Haven't I paid the instalments regularly?

KROGSTAD. Yes, fairly. But . . . coming back to what we were talking about . . . that was a pretty bad period you were going through then, Mrs. Helmer.

NORA. Yes, it was.

KROGSTAD. Your father was seriously ill, I believe.

NORA. He was very near the end.

KROGSTAD. And died shortly afterwards?

NORA. Yes.

KROGSTAD. Tell me, Mrs. Helmer, do you happen to remember which day your father died? The exact date, I mean.

NORA. Daddy died on 29 September.

F

KROGSTAD. Quite correct. I made some inquiries. Which brings up a rather curious point [*takes out a paper*] which I simply cannot explain.

NORA. Curious . . . ? I don't know . . .

KROGSTAD. The curious thing is, Mrs. Helmer, that your father signed this document three days after his death.

NORA. What? I don't understand. . . .

KROGSTAD. Your father died on 29 September. But look here. Your father has dated his signature 2 October. Isn't that rather curious, Mrs. Helmer? [NORA *remains silent.*] It's also remarkable that the words '2 October' and the year are not in your father's handwriting, but in a handwriting I rather think I recognize. Well, perhaps that could be explained. Your father might have forgotten to date his signature, and then somebody else might have made a guess at the date later, before the fact of your father's death was known. There is nothing wrong in that. What really matters is the signature. And *that* is of course genuine, Mrs. Helmer? It really was your father who wrote his name here?

NORA [*after a moment's silence, throws her head back and looks at him defiantly*]. No, it wasn't. It was me who signed father's name.

KROGSTAD. Listen to me. I suppose you realize that that is a very dangerous confession?

NORA. Why? You'll soon have all your money back.

KROGSTAD. Let me ask you a question: why didn't you send that document to your father?

NORA. It was impossible. Daddy was ill. If I'd asked him for his signature, I'd have had to tell him what the money was for. Don't you see, when he was as ill as that I couldn't go and tell him that my husband's life was in danger. It was simply impossible.

KROGSTAD. It would have been better for you if you had abandoned the whole trip.

NORA. No, that was impossible. This was the thing that was to save my husband's life. I couldn't give it up.

KROGSTAD. But did it never strike you that this was fraudulent. . . ?

NORA. That wouldn't have meant anything to me. Why should I worry about you? I couldn't stand you, not when you insisted on going through with all those cold-blooded formalities, knowing all the time what a critical state my husband was in.

KROGSTAD. Mrs. Helmer, it's quite clear you still haven't the faintest idea what it is you've committed. But let me tell you, my own offence was no more and no worse than that, and it ruined my entire reputation.

NORA. You? Are you trying to tell me that you once risked everything to save your wife's life?

KROGSTAD. The law takes no account of motives.

NORA. Then they must be very bad laws.

KROGSTAD. Bad or not, if I produce this document in court, you'll be condemned according to them.

NORA. I don't believe it. Isn't a daughter entitled to try and save her father from worry and anxiety on his deathbed? Isn't a wife entitled to save her husband's life? I might not know very much about the law, but I feel sure of one thing: it must say somewhere that things like this are allowed. You mean to say you don't know that—you, when it's your job? You must be a rotten lawyer, Mr. Krogstad.

KROGSTAD. That may be. But when it comes to business transactions— like the sort between us two—perhaps you'll admit I know something about *them*? Good. Now you must please yourself. But I tell you this: if I'm pitched out a second time, you are going to keep me company.

[*He bows and goes out through the hall.*]

NORA [*stands thoughtfully for a moment, then tosses her head*]. Rubbish! He's just trying to scare me. I'm not such a fool as all that. [*Begins gathering up the children's clothes; after a moment she stops.*] Yet . . . ? No, it's impossible! I did it for love, didn't I?

THE CHILDREN [*in the doorway, left*]. Mummy, the gentleman's just gone out of the gate.

NORA. Yes, I know. But you mustn't say anything to anybody about that gentleman. You hear? Not even to Daddy!

THE CHILDREN. All right, Mummy. Are you going to play again?

NORA. No, not just now.

THE CHILDREN. But Mummy, you promised!

NORA. Yes, but I can't just now. Off you go now, I have a lot to do. Off you go, my darlings. [*She herds them carefully into the other room and shuts the door behind them. She sits down on the sofa, picks up her embroidery and works a few stitches, but soon stops.*] No! [*She flings her work down, stands up, goes to the hall door and calls out.*] Helene! Fetch the tree in for me, please. [*She walks across to the table, left, and opens the drawer; again pauses.*] No, really, it's quite impossible!

MAID [*with the Christmas tree*]. Where shall I put it, ma'am?

NORA. On the floor there, in the middle.

MAID. Anything else you want me to bring?

NORA. No, thank you. I've got what I want.

[*The maid has put the tree down and goes out.*]

NORA [*busy decorating the tree*]. Candles here . . . and flowers here.— Revolting man! It's all nonsense! There's nothing to worry about. We'll have a lovely Christmas tree. And I'll do anything you want me to, Torvald; I'll sing for you, dance for you. . . .

[HELMER, *with a bundle of documents under his arm, comes in by the hall door.*]

NORA. Ah, back again already?

HELMER. Yes. Anybody been?

NORA. Here? No.

HELMER. That's funny. I just saw Krogstad leave the house.

NORA. Oh? O yes, that's right. Krogstad was here a minute.

HELMER. Nora, I can tell by your face he's been asking you to put a good word in for him.

NORA. Yes.

HELMER. And you were to pretend it was your own idea? You were to keep quiet about his having been here. He asked you to do that as well, didn't he?

NORA. Yes, Torvald. But . . .

HELMER. Nora, Nora, what possessed you to do a thing like that? Talking to a person like him, making him promises? And then on top of everything, to tell me a lie!

NORA. A lie. . . ?

HELMER. Didn't you say that nobody had been here? [*Wagging his finger at her.*] Never again must my little song-bird do a thing like that! Little song-birds must keep their pretty little beaks out of mischief; no chirruping out of tune! [*Puts his arm round her waist.*] Isn't that the way we want things to be? Yes, of course it is. [*Lets her go.*] So let's say no more about it. [*Sits down by the stove.*] Ah, nice and cosy here!

[*He glances through his papers.*]

NORA [*busy with the Christmas tree, after a short pause*]. Torvald!

HELMAR. Yes.

NORA. I'm so looking forward to the fancy dress ball at the Stenborgs on Boxing Day.

HELMER. And I'm terribly curious to see what sort of surprise you've got for me.

NORA. Oh, it's too silly.

HELMER. Oh?

NORA. I just can't think of anything suitable. Everything seems so absurd, so pointless.

HELMER. Has my little Nora come to *that* conclusion?

NORA [*behind his chair, her arms on the chairback*]. Are you very busy, Torvald?

HELMER. Oh. . . .

NORA. What are all those papers?

HELMER. Bank matters.

NORA. Already?

HELMER. I have persuaded the retiring manager to give me authority to make any changes in organization or personnel I think necessary. I have to work on it over the Christmas week. I want everything straight by the New Year.

NORA. So that was why that poor Krogstad. . . .

HELMER. Hm!

NORA [*still leaning against the back of the chair, running her fingers through his hair*]. If you hadn't been so busy, Torvald, I'd have asked you to do me an awfully big favour.

HELMER. Let me hear it. What's it to be?

NORA. Nobody's got such good taste as you. And the thing is I do so want to look my best at the fancy dress ball. Torvald, couldn't you give me some advice and tell me what you think I ought to go as, and how I should arrange my costume?

HELMER. Aha! So my impulsive little woman is asking for somebody to come to her rescue, eh?

NORA. Please, Torvald, I never get anywhere without your help.

HELMER. Very well, I'll think about it. We'll find something.

NORA. That's sweet of you. [*She goes across to the tree again; pause.*] How pretty these red flowers look.—Tell me, was it really something terribly wrong this man Krogstad did?

HELMER. Forgery. Have you any idea what that means?

NORA. Perhaps circumstances left him no choice?

HELMER. Maybe. Or perhaps, like so many others, he just didn't think. I am not so heartless that I would necessarily want to condemn a man for a single mistake like that.

NORA. Oh no, Torvald, of course not!

HELMER. Many a man might be able to redeem himself, if he honestly confessed his guilt and took his punishment.

NORA. Punishment?

HELMER. But that wasn't the way Krogstad chose. He dodged what was due to him by a cunning trick. And that's what has been the cause of his corruption.

NORA. Do you think it would . . . ?

HELMER. Just think how a man with a thing like that on his conscience will always be having to lie and cheat and dissemble; he can never drop the mask, not even with his own wife and children. And the children—*that's* the most terrible part of it, Nora.

NORA. Why?

HELMER. A fog of lies like that in a household, and it spreads disease and infection to every part of it. Every breath the children take in that kind of house is reeking with evil germs.

NORA [*closer behind him*]. Are you sure of that?

HELMER. My dear Nora, as a lawyer I know what I'm talking about. Practically all juvenile delinquents come from homes where the mother is dishonest.

NORA. Why mothers particularly?

HELMER. It's generally traceable to the mothers, but of course fathers can have the same influence. Every lawyer knows that only too well. And yet there's Krogstad been poisoning his own children for years with lies and deceit. That's the reason I call him morally depraved. [*Holds out his hands to her.*] That's why my sweet little Nora must promise me not to try putting in any more good words for him. Shake hands on it. Well? What's this? Give me your hand. There now! That's settled. I assure you I would have found it impossible to work with him. I quite literally feel physically sick in the presence of such people.

NORA [*draws her hand away and walks over to the other side of the Christmas tree*]. How hot it is in here! And I still have such a lot to do.

HELMER [*stands up and collects his papers together*]. Yes, I'd better think of getting some of this read before dinner. I must also think about your costume. And I might even be able to lay my hands on some-thing to wrap in gold paper and hang on the Christmas tree. [*He lays his hand on her head.*] My precious little singing bird.

[*He goes into his study and shuts the door behind him.*]

NORA [*quietly, after a pause*]. Nonsense! It can't be. It's impossible. It *must* be impossible.

MAID [*in the doorway, left*]. The children keep asking so nicely if they can come in and see Mummy.

NORA. No, no, don't let them in! You stay with them, Anne Marie.

MAID. Very well, ma'am.

[*She shuts the door.*]

NORA [*pale with terror*]. Corrupt my children. . . ! Poison my home? [*Short pause; she throws back her head.*] It's not true! It could never, never be true!

ACT TWO

The same room. In the corner beside the piano stands the Christmas tree, stripped, bedraggled and with its candles burnt out. Nora's outdoor things lie on the sofa. NORA, *alone there, walks about restlessly; at last she stops by the sofa and picks up her coat.*

NORA [*putting her coat down again*]. Somebody's coming! [*Crosses to the door, listens.*] No, it's nobody. Nobody will come today, of course, Christmas Day—nor tomorrow, either. But perhaps. . . . [*She opens the door and looks out.*] No, nothing in the letter box; quite empty. [*Comes forward.*] Oh, nonsense! He didn't mean it seriously. Things like that *can't* happen. It's impossible. Why, I have three small children.

[THE NURSEMAID *comes from the room, left, carrying a big cardboard box.*]

NURSEMAID. I finally found it, the box with the fancy dress costumes.

NORA. Thank you. Put it on the table, please.

NURSEMAID [*does this*]. But I'm afraid they are in an awful mess.

NORA. Oh, if only I could rip them up into a thousand pieces!

NURSEMAID. Good heavens, they can be mended all right, with a bit of patience.

NORA. Yes, I'll go over and get Mrs. Linde to help me.

NURSEMAID. Out again? In this terrible weather? You'll catch your death of cold, Ma'am.

NORA. Oh, worse things might happen.—How are the children?

NURSEMAID. Playing with their Christmas presents, poor little things, but . . .

NORA. Do they keep asking for me?

NURSEMAID. They are so used to being with their Mummy.

NORA. Yes, Anne Marie, from now on I can't be with them as often as I was before.

NURSEMAID. Ah well, children get used to anything in time.

NORA. Do you think so? Do you think they would forget their Mummy if she went away for good?

NURSEMAID. Good gracious—for good?

NORA. Tell me, Anne Marie—I've often wondered—how on earth could you bear to hand your child over to strangers?

NURSEMAID. Well, there was nothing else for it when I had to come and nurse my little Nora.

NORA. Yes but . . . how could you *bring* yourself to do it?

NURSEMAID. When I had the chance of such a good place? When a poor girl's been in trouble she must make the best of things. Because *he* didn't help, the rotter.

NORA. But your daughter will have forgotten you.

NURSEMAID. Oh no, she hasn't. She wrote to me when she got confirmed, and again when she got married.

NORA [*putting her arms round her neck*]. Dear old Anne Marie, you were a good mother to me when I was little.

NURSEMAID. My poor little Nora never had any other mother but me.

NORA. And if my little ones only had you, I know you would. . . . Oh, what am I talking about! [*She opens the box.*] Go in to them. I must . . . Tomorrow I'll let you see how pretty I am going to look.

NURSEMAID. Ah, there'll be nobody at the ball as pretty as my Nora.

[*She goes into the room, left.*]

NORA [*begins unpacking the box, but soon throws it down*]. Oh, if only I dare go out. If only I could be sure nobody would come. And that nothing would happen in the meantime here at home. Rubbish—nobody's going to come. I mustn't think about it. Brush this muff. Pretty gloves, pretty gloves! I'll put it right out of my mind. One, two, three, four, five, six. . . . [*Screams.*] Ah, they are coming. . . . [*She starts towards the door, but stops irresolute.* MRS. LINDE *comes from the hall, where she has taken off her things.*] Oh, it's you, Kristine. There's nobody else out there, is there? I'm so glad you've come.

MRS. LINDE. I heard you'd been over looking for me.

NORA. Yes, I was just passing. There's something you must help me with. Come and sit beside me on the sofa here. You see, the Stenborgs are having a fancy dress party upstairs tomorrow evening, and now Torvald wants me to go as a Neapolitan fisher lass and dance the tarantella. I learned it in Capri, you know.

MRS. LINDE. Well, well! So you are going to do a party piece?

NORA. Torvald says I should. Look, here's the costume, Torvald had it made for me down there. But it's got all torn and I simply don't know. . . .

MRS. LINDE. We'll soon have that put right. It's only the trimming come away here and there. Got a needle and thread? Ah, here's what we are after.

NORA. It's awfully kind of you.

MRS. LINDE. So you are going to be all dressed up tomorrow, Nora? Tell you what—I'll pop over for a minute to see you in all your finery. But I'm quite forgetting to thank you for the pleasant time we had last night.

NORA [*gets up and walks across the room*]. Somehow I didn't think yesterday was as nice as things generally are.—You should have come to town a little earlier, Kristine.—Yes, Torvald certainly knows how to make things pleasant about the place.

MRS. LINDE. You too, I should say. You are not your father's daughter for nothing. But tell me, is Dr. Rank always as depressed as he was last night?

NORA. No, last night it was rather obvious. He's got something seriously wrong with him, you know. Tuberculosis of the spine, poor fellow. His father was a horrible man, who used to have mistresses and things like that. That's why the son was always ailing, right from being a child.

MRS. LINDE [*lowering her sewing*]. But my dear Nora, how do you come to know about things like that?

NORA [*walking about the room*]. Huh! When you've got three children, you get these visits from . . . women who have had a certain amount of medical training. And you hear all sorts of things from them.

MRS. LINDE [*begins sewing again; short silence*]. Does Dr. Rank call in every day?

NORA. Every single day. He was Torvald's best friend as a boy, and he's a good friend of *mine*, too. Dr. Rank is almost like one of the family.

MRS. LINDE. But tell me—is he really genuine? What I mean is: doesn't he sometimes rather turn on the charm?

NORA. No, on the contrary. What makes you think that?

MRS. LINDE. When you introduced me yesterday, he claimed he'd often heard my name in this house. But afterwards I noticed your husband hadn't the faintest idea who I was. Then how is it that Dr. Rank should. . . .

NORA. Oh yes, it was quite right what he said, Kristine. You see Torvald is so terribly in love with me that he says he wants me all to himself. When we were first married, it even used to make him sort of jealous if I only as much as mentioned any of my old friends from back home. So of course I stopped doing it. But I often talk to Dr. Rank about such things. He likes hearing about them.

MRS. LINDE. Listen, Nora! In lots of ways you are still a child. Now, I'm a good deal older than you, and a bit more experienced. I'll tell you something: I think you ought to give up all this business with Dr. Rank.

NORA. Give up what business?

MRS. LINDE. The whole thing, I should say. Weren't you saying yesterday something about a rich admirer who was to provide you with money. . . .

NORA. One who's never existed, I regret to say. But what of it?

MRS. LINDE. Has Dr. Rank money?

NORA. Yes, he has.

MRS. LINDE. And no dependents?

NORA. No, nobody. But . . . ?

MRS. LINDE. And he comes to the house every day?

NORA. Yes, I told you.

MRS. LINDE. But how can a man of his position want to pester you like this?

NORA. I simply don't understand.

MRS. LINDE. Don't pretend, Nora. Do you think I don't see now who you borrowed the twelve hundred from?

NORA. Are you out of your mind? Do you really think that? A friend of ours who comes here every day? The whole situation would have been absolutely intolerable.

MRS. LINDE. It *really* isn't him?

NORA. No, I give you my word. It would never have occurred to me for one moment. . . . Anyway, he didn't have the money to lend then. He didn't inherit it till later.

MRS. LINDE. Just as well for you, I'd say, my dear Nora.

NORA. No, it would never have occurred to me to ask Dr. Rank. . . . All the same I'm pretty certain if I were to ask him. . . .

MRS. LINDE. But of course you won't.

NORA. No, of course not. I can't ever imagine it being necessary. But I'm quite certain if ever I were to mention it to Dr. Rank. . . .

MRS. LINDE. Behind your husband's back?

NORA. I have to get myself out of that other business. That's also behind his back. I *must* get myself out of that.

MRS. LINDE. Yes, that's what I said yesterday. But . . .

NORA [*walking up and down*]. A man's better at coping with these things than a woman. . . .

MRS. LINDE. Your own husband, yes.

NORA. Nonsense! [*Stops.*] When you've paid everything you owe, you do get your IOU back again, don't you?

MRS. LINDE. Of course.

NORA. And you can tear it up into a thousand pieces and burn it—the nasty, filthy thing!

MRS. LINDE [*looking fixedly at her, puts down her sewing and slowly rises*]. Nora, you are hiding something from me.

NORA. Is it so obvious?

MRS. LINDE. Something has happened to you since yesterday morning. Nora, what is it?

NORA [*going towards her*]. Kristine! [*Listens.*] Hush! There's Torvald back. Look, you go and sit in there beside the children for the time being. Torvald can't stand the sight of mending lying about. Get Anne Marie to help you.

MRS. LINDE [*gathering a lot of the things together*]. All right, but I'm not leaving until we have thrashed this thing out.

[*She goes into the room, left; at the same time* HELMER *comes in from the hall.*]

NORA [*goes to meet him*]. I've been longing for you to be back, Torvald, dear.

HELMER. Was that the dressmaker. . . ?

NORA. No, it was Kristine; she's helping me with my costume. I think it's going to look very nice. . .

HELMER. Wasn't that a good idea of mine, now?

NORA. Wonderful! But wasn't it also nice of me to let you have your way?

HELMER [*taking her under the chin*]. Nice of you—because you let your husband have his way? All right, you little rogue, I know you didn't mean it that way. But I don't want to disturb you. You'll be wanting to try the costume on, I suppose.

NORA. And I dare say you've got work to do?

HELMER. Yes. [*Shows her a bundle of papers.*] Look at this. I've been down at the Bank. . . .

[*He turns to go into his study.*]

NORA. Torvald!

HELMER [*stopping*]. Yes.

NORA. If a little squirrel were to ask ever so nicely . . . ?

HELMER. Well?

NORA. Would you do something for it?

HELMER. Naturally I would first have to know what it is.

NORA. Please, if only you would let it have its way, and do what it wants, it'd scamper about and do all sorts of marvellous tricks.

HELMER. What is it?

NORA. And the pretty little sky-lark would sing all day long. . . .

HELMER. Huh! It does that anyway.

NORA. I'd pretend I was an elfin child and dance a moonlight dance for you, Torvald.

HELMER. Nora—I hope it's not that business you started on this morning?

NORA [*coming closer*]. Yes, it is, Torvald. I implore you!

HELMER. You have the nerve to bring that up again?

NORA. Yes, yes, you *must* listen to me. You must let Krogstad keep his job at the Bank.

HELMER. My dear Nora, I'm giving his job to Mrs. Linde.

NORA. Yes, it's awfully sweet of you. But couldn't you get rid of somebody else in the office instead of Krogstad?

HELMER. This really is the most incredible obstinacy! Just because you go and make some thoughtless promise to put in a good word for him, you expect me . . .

NORA. It's not that, Torvald. It's for your own sake. That man writes in all the nastiest papers, you told me that yourself. He can do you no end of harm. He terrifies me to death. . . .

HELMER. Aha, now I see. It's your memories of what happened before that are frightening you.

NORA. What do you mean?

HELMER. It's your father you are thinking of.

NORA. Yes . . . yes, that's right. You remember all the nasty insinuations those wicked people put in the papers about Daddy? I honestly think they would have had him dismissed if the Ministry hadn't sent you down to investigate, and you hadn't been so kind and helpful.

HELMER. My dear little Nora, there is a considerable difference between your father and me. Your father's professional conduct was not entirely above suspicion. Mine is. And I hope it's going to stay that way as long as I hold this position.

NORA. But nobody knows what some of these evil people are capable of. Things could be so nice and pleasant for us here, in the peace and quiet of our home—you and me and the children, Torvald! That's why I implore you. . . .

HELMER. The more you plead for him, the more impossible you make it for me to keep him on. It's already known down at the Bank that I am going to give Krogstad his notice. If it ever got around that the new manager had been talked over by his wife. . . .

NORA. What of it?

HELMER. Oh, nothing! As long as the little woman gets her own stubborn way. . . ! Do you want me to make myself a laughing stock in the office? . . . Give people the idea that I am susceptible to any kind of outside pressure? You can imagine how soon I'd feel the consequences of that! Anyway, there's one other consideration that makes it impossible to have Krogstad in the Bank as long as I am manager.

NORA. What's that?

HELMER. At a pinch I might have overlooked his past lapses. . . .

NORA. Of course you could, Torvald!

HELMER. And I'm told he's not bad at his job, either. But we knew each other rather well when we were younger. It was one of those rather rash friendships that prove embarrassing in later life. There's no reason why you shouldn't know we were once on terms of some familiarity. And he, in his tactless way, makes no attempt to hide the fact, particularly when other people are present. On the contrary, he thinks he has every right to treat me as an equal, with his 'Torvald this' and 'Torvald that' every time he opens his mouth. I find it extremely irritating, I can tell you. He would make my position at the Bank absolutely intolerable.

NORA. Torvald, surely you aren't serious?

HELMER. Oh? Why not?

NORA. Well, it's all so petty.

HELMER. What's that you say? Petty? Do you think I'm petty?

NORA. No, not at all, Torvald dear! And that's why . . .

HELMER. Doesn't make any difference! . . . You call my motives petty; so I must be petty too. Petty! Indeed! Well, we'll put a stop to that, once and for all. [*He opens the hall door and calls.*] Helene!

NORA. What are you going to do?

HELMER [*searching among his papers*]. Settle things. [THE MAID *comes in.*] See this letter? I want you to take it down at once. Get hold of a messenger and get him to deliver it. Quickly. The address is on the outside. There's the money.

MAID. Very good, sir.

[*She goes with the letter.*]

HELMER [*putting his papers together*]. There now, my stubborn little miss.

NORA [*breathless*]. Torvald . . . what was that letter?

HELMER. Krogstad's notice.

NORA. Get it back, Torvald! There's still time! Oh, Torvald, get it back! Please for my sake, for your sake, for the sake of the children! Listen, Torvald, please! You don't realize what it can do to us.

HELMER. Too late.

NORA. Yes, too late.

HELMER. My dear Nora, I forgive you this anxiety of yours, although it is actually a bit of an insult. Oh, but it is, I tell you! It's hardly flattering to suppose that anything this miserable pen-pusher wrote could frighten *me*! But I forgive you all the same, because it is rather a sweet way of showing how much you love me. [*He takes her in his arms.*] This is how things must be, my own darling Nora. When it comes to the point, I've enough strength and enough courage, believe me, for whatever happens. You'll find I'm man enough to take everything on myself.

NORA [*terrified*]. What do you mean?

HELMER. Everything, I said. . . .

NORA [*in command of herself*]. That is something you shall never, never do.

HELMER. All right, then we'll share it, Nora—as man and wife. That's what we'll do. [*Caressing her.*] Does that make you happy now? There, there, don't look at me with those eyes, like a little frightened dove. The whole thing is sheer imagination.—Why don't you run through the tarantella and try out the tambourine? I'll go into my study and shut both the doors, then I won't hear anything. You can make all the noise you want. [*Turns in the doorway.*] And when Rank comes, tell him where he can find me.

[*He nods to her, goes with his papers into his room, and shuts the door behind him.*]

NORA [*wild-eyed with terror, stands as though transfixed*]. He's quite capable of doing it! He would do it! No matter what, he'd do it.— No, never in this world! Anything but that! Help? Some way out. . . ? [*The door-bell rings in the hall.*] Dr. Rank. . . ! Anything but that, *anything*! [*She brushes her hands over her face, pulls herself together and opens the door into the hall. DR. RANK is standing outside hanging up his fur coat. During what follows it begins to grow dark.*] Hello, Dr. Rank. I recognized your ring. Do you mind not going in to Torvald just yet, I think he's busy.

RANK. And you?

[*DR. RANK comes into the room and she closes the door behind him.*]

NORA. Oh, you know very well I've always got time for you.

RANK. Thank you. A privilege I shall take advantage of as long as I am able.

NORA. What do you mean—as long as you are able?

RANK. Does that frighten you?

NORA. Well, it's just that it sounds so strange. Is anything likely to happen?

RANK. Only what I have long expected. But I didn't think it would come quite so soon.

NORA [*catching at his arm*]. What have you found out? Dr. Rank, you must tell me!

RANK. I'm slowly sinking. There's nothing to be done about it.

NORA [*with a sigh of relief*]. Oh, it's *you* you're . . . ?

RANK. Who else? No point in deceiving onself. I am the most wretched of all my patients, Mrs. Helmer. These last few days I've made a careful analysis of my internal economy. Bankrupt! Within a month I shall probably be lying rotting up there in the churchyard.

NORA. Come now, what a ghastly thing to say!

RANK. The whole damned thing is ghastly. But the worst thing is all the ghastliness that has to be gone through first. I only have one more test to make; and when that's done I'll know pretty well when the final disintegration will start. There's something I want to ask you. Helmer is a sensitive soul; he loathes anything that's ugly. I don't want him visiting me. . . .

NORA. But Dr. Rank. . . .

RANK. On no account must he. I won't have it. I'll lock the door on him.—As soon as I'm absolutely certain of the worst, I'll send you my visiting card with a black cross on it. You'll know then the final horrible disintegration has begun.

NORA. Really, you are being quite absurd today. And here was I hoping you would be in a thoroughly good mood.

RANK. With death staring me in the face? Why should I suffer for another man's sins? What justice is there in that? Somewhere, somehow, every single family must be suffering some such cruel retribution. . . .

NORA [*stopping up her ears*]. Rubbish! Do cheer up!

RANK. Yes, really the whole thing's nothing but a huge joke. My poor innocent spine must do penance for my father's gay subaltern life.

NORA [*by the table, left*]. Wasn't he rather partial to asparagus and *pâté de foie gras*?

RANK. Yes, he was. And truffles.

NORA. Truffles, yes. And oysters, too, I believe?

RANK. Yes, oysters, oysters, of course.

NORA. And all the port and champagne that goes with them. It does seem a pity all these delicious things should attack the spine.

RANK. Especially when they attack a poor spine that never had any fun out of them.

NORA. Yes, that is an awful pity.

RANK [*looks at her sharply*]. Hm. . . .

NORA [*after a pause*]. Why did you smile?

RANK. No, it was you who laughed.

NORA. No, it was you who smiled, Dr. Rank!

RANK [*getting up*]. You are a bigger rascal than I thought you were.

NORA. I feel full of mischief today.

RANK. So it seems.

NORA [*putting her hands on his shoulders*]. Dear, dear Dr. Rank, you mustn't go and die on Torvald and me.

RANK. You wouldn't miss me for long. When you are gone, you are soon forgotten.

NORA [*looking at him anxiously*]. Do you think so?

RANK. People make new contacts, then . . .

NORA. Who make new contacts?

RANK. Both you and Helmer will, when I'm gone. You yourself are already well on the way, it seems to me. What was this Mrs. Linde doing here last night?

NORA. Surely you aren't jealous of poor Kristine?

RANK. Yes, I am. She'll be my successor in this house. When I'm done for, I can see this woman. . . .

NORA. Hush! Don't talk so loud, she's in there.

RANK. Today as well? There you are, you see!

NORA. Just to do some sewing on my dress. Good Lord, how absurd you are! [*She sits down on the sofa.*] Now Dr. Rank, cheer up. You'll see tomorrow how nicely I can dance. And you can pretend I'm doing it just for you—and for Torvald as well, of course. [*She takes various things out of the box.*] Come here, Dr. Rank. I want to show you something.

RANK [*sits*]. What is it?

NORA. Look!

RANK. Silk stockings.

NORA. Flesh-coloured! Aren't they lovely! Of course, it's dark here now, but tomorrow. . . . No, no, no, you can only look at the feet. Oh well, you might as well see a bit higher up, too.

RANK. Hm. . . .

NORA. Why are you looking so critical? Don't you think they'll fit?

RANK. I couldn't possibly offer any informed opinion about that.

NORA [*looks at him for a moment*]. Shame on you. [*Hits him lightly across the ear with the stockings.*] Take that! [*Folds them up again.*]

RANK. And what other delights am I to be allowed to see?

NORA. Not another thing. You are too naughty. [*She hums a little and searches among her things.*]

RANK [*after a short pause*]. Sitting here so intimately like this with you, I can't imagine . . . I simply cannot conceive what would have become of me if I had never come to this house.

NORA [*smiles*]. Yes, I rather think you do enjoy coming here.

RANK [*in a low voice, looking fixedly ahead*]. And the thought of having to leave it all . . .

NORA. Nonsense. You aren't leaving.

RANK [*in the same tone*]. . . . without being able to leave behind even the slightest token of gratitude, hardly a fleeting regret even . . . nothing but an empty place to be filled by the first person that comes along.

NORA. Supposing I were to ask you to . . . ? No . . .

RANK. What?

NORA. . . . to show me the extent of your friendship . . .

RANK. Yes?

NORA. I mean . . . to do me a tremendous favour. . . .

RANK. Would you really, for once, give me that pleasure?

NORA. You have no idea what it is.

RANK. All right, tell me.

NORA. No, really I can't, Dr. Rank. It's altogether too much to ask . . . because I need your advice and help as well. . . .

RANK. The more the better. I cannot imagine what you have in mind. But tell me anyway. You do trust me, don't you?

NORA. Yes, I trust you more than anybody I know. You are my best and my most faithful friend. I know that. So I will tell you. Well then, Dr. Rank, there is something you must help me to prevent. You know how deeply, how passionately Torvald is in love with me. He would never hesitate for a moment to sacrifice his life for my sake.

RANK [*bending towards her*]. Nora . . . do you think he's the only one who . . . ?

NORA [*stiffening slightly*]. Who . . . ?

RANK. Who wouldn't gladly give his life for your sake.

NORA [*sadly*]. Oh!

RANK. I swore to myself you would know before I went. I'll never have a better opportunity. Well, Nora! Now you know. And now you know too that you can confide in me as in nobody else.

NORA [*rises and speaks evenly and calmly*]. Let me past.

RANK [*makes way for her, but remains seated*]. Nora. . . .

NORA [*in the hall doorway*]. Helene, bring the lamp in, please. [*Walks over to the stove.*] Oh, my dear Dr. Rank, that really was rather horrid of you.

RANK [*getting up*]. That I have loved you every bit as much as anybody? Is *that* horrid?

NORA. No, but that you had to go and tell me. When it was all so unnecessary. . . .

RANK. What do you mean? Did you know. . . ?

[THE MAID *comes in with the lamp, puts it on the table, and goes out again.*]

RANK. Nora . . . Mrs. Helmer . . . I'm asking you if you knew?

NORA. How can I tell whether I did or didn't. I simply can't tell you. . . . Oh, how could you be so clumsy, Dr. Rank! When everything was so nice.

RANK. Anyway, you know now that I'm at your service, body and soul. So you can speak out.

NORA [*looking at him*]. After this?

RANK. I beg you to tell me what it is.

NORA. I can tell you nothing now.

RANK. You must. You can't torment me like this. Give me a chance— I'll do anything that's humanly possible.

NORA. You can do nothing for me now. Actually, I don't really need any help. It's all just my imagination, really it is. Of course! [*She sits down in the rocking-chair, looks at him and smiles.*] I must say, you are a nice one, Dr. Rank! Don't you feel ashamed of yourself, now the lamp's been brought in?

RANK. No, not exactly. But perhaps I ought to go—for good?

NORA. No, you mustn't do that. You must keep coming just as you've always done. You know very well Torvald would miss you terribly.

RANK. And *you*?

NORA. I always think it's tremendous fun having you.

RANK. That's exactly what gave me wrong ideas. I just can't puzzle you out. I often used to feel you'd just as soon be with me as with Helmer.

NORA. Well, you see, there are those people you love and those people you'd almost rather *be* with.

RANK. Yes, there's something in that.

NORA. When I was a girl at home, I loved Daddy best, of course. But I also thought it great fun if I could slip into the maids' room. For one thing they never preached at me. And they always talked about such exciting things.

RANK. Aha! So it's their role I've taken over!

NORA [*jumps up and crosses to him*]. Oh, my dear, kind Dr. Rank, I didn't mean that at all. But you can see how it's a bit with Torvald as it was with Daddy. . . .

[THE MAID *comes in from the hall.*]

MAID. Please, ma'am. . . !

[*She whispers and hands her a card.*]

NORA [*glances at the card*]. Ah!

[*She puts it in her pocket.*]

RANK. Anything wrong?

NORA. No, no, not at all. It's just . . . it's my new costume. . . .

RANK. How is that? There's your costume in there.

NORA. That one, yes. But this is another one. I've ordered it. Torvald mustn't hear about it. . . .

RANK. Ah, so that's the big secret, is it!

NORA. Yes, that's right. Just go in and see him, will you? He's in the study. Keep him occupied for the time being. . . .

RANK. Don't worry. He shan't escape me.

[*He goes into Helmer's study.*]

NORA [*to the maid*]. Is he waiting in the kitchen?

MAID. Yes, he came up the back stairs. . . .

NORA. But didn't you tell him somebody was here?

MAID. Yes, but it was no good.

NORA. Won't he go?

MAID. No, he won't till he's seen you.

NORA. Let him in, then. But quietly. Helene, you mustn't tell anybody about this. It's a surprise for my husband.

MAID. I understand, ma'am. . . .

[*She goes out.*]

NORA. Here it comes! What I've been dreading! No, no, it can't happen, it *can't* happen.

[*She walks over and bolts Helmer's door. The maid opens the hall door for* KROGSTAD *and shuts it again behind him. He is wearing a fur coat, over-shoes, and a fur cap.*]

NORA [*goes towards him*]. Keep your voice down, my husband is at home.

KROGSTAD. What if he is?

NORA. What do you want with me?

KROGSTAD. To find out something.

NORA. Hurry, then. What is it?

KROGSTAD. You know I've been given notice.

NORA. I couldn't prevent it, Mr. Krogstad, I did my utmost for you, but it was no use.

KROGSTAD. Has your husband so little affection for you? He knows what I can do to you, yet he dares. . . .

NORA. You don't imagine he knows about it!

KROGSTAD. No, I didn't imagine he did. It didn't seem a bit like my good friend Torvald Helmer to show that much courage. . . .

NORA. Mr. Krogstad, I must ask you to show some respect for my husband.

KROGSTAD. Oh, sure! All due respect! But since you are so anxious to keep this business quiet, Mrs. Helmer, I take it you now have a rather clearer idea of just what it is you've done, than you had yesterday.

NORA. Clearer than *you* could ever have given me.

KROGSTAD. Yes, being as I am such a rotten lawyer. . . .

NORA. What do you want with me?

KROGSTAD. I just wanted to see how things stood, Mrs. Helmer. I've been thinking about you all day. Even a mere money-lender, a hack journalist, a—well, even somebody like me has a bit of what you might call feeling.

NORA. Show it then. Think of my little children.

KROGSTAD. Did you or your husband think of mine? But what does it matter now? There was just one thing I wanted to say: you needn't take this business too seriously. I shan't start any proceedings, for the present.

NORA. Ah, I knew you wouldn't.

KROGSTAD. The whole thing can be arranged quite amicably. Nobody need know. Just the three of us.

NORA. My husband must never know.

KROGSTAD. How can you prevent it? Can you pay off the balance?

NORA. No, not immediately.

KROGSTAD. Perhaps you've some way of getting hold of the money in the next few days.

NORA. None I want to make use of.

KROGSTAD. Well, it wouldn't have been very much help to you if you had. Even if you stood there with the cash in your hand and to spare, you still wouldn't get your IOU back from me now.

NORA. What are you going to do with it?

KROGSTAD. Just keep it—have it in my possession. Nobody who isn't implicated need know about it. So if you are thinking of trying any desperate remedies . . .

NORA. Which I am. . . .

KROGSTAD. . . . if you happen to be thinking of running away . . .

NORA. Which I am!

KROGSTAD. . . . or anything worse . . .

NORA. How did you know?

KROGSTAD. . . . forget it!

NORA. How did you know I was thinking of *that*?

KROGSTAD. Most of us think of *that*, to begin with. I did, too; but I didn't have the courage. . . .

NORA [*tonelessly*]. I haven't either.

KROGSTAD [*relieved*]. So you haven't the courage either, eh?

NORA. No, I haven't! I haven't!

KROGSTAD. It would also be very stupid. There'd only be the first domestic storm to get over. . . . I've got a letter to your husband in my pocket here. . . .

NORA. And it's all in there?

KROGSTAD. In as tactful a way as possible.

NORA [*quickly*]. He must never read that letter. Tear it up. I'll find the money somehow.

KROGSTAD. Excuse me, Mrs. Helmer, but I've just told you. . . .

NORA. I'm not talking about the money I owe you. I want to know how much you are demanding from my husband, and I'll get the money.

KROGSTAD. I want no money from your husband.

NORA. What do you want?

KROGSTAD. I'll tell you. I want to get on my feet again, Mrs. Helmer; I want to get to the top. And your husband is going to help me. For the last eighteen months I've gone straight; all that time it's been hard going; I was content to work my way up, step by step. Now I'm being kicked out, and I won't stand for being taken back again as an act of charity. I'm going to get to the top, I tell you. I'm going back into that Bank—with a better job. Your husband is going to create a new vacancy, just for me. . . .

NORA. He'll never do that!

KROGSTAD. He will do it. I know him. He'll do it without so much as a whimper. And once I'm in there with him, you'll see what's what. In less than a year I'll be his right-hand man. It'll be Nils Krogstad, not Torvald Helmer, who'll be running that Bank.

NORA. You'll never live to see that day!

KROGSTAD. You mean you . . . ?

NORA. Now I have the courage.

KROGSTAD. You can't frighten me! A precious pampered little thing like you. . . .

NORA. I'll show you! I'll show you!

KROGSTAD. Under the ice, maybe? Down in the cold, black water? Then being washed up in the spring, bloated, hairless, unrecognizable. . . .

NORA. You can't frighten me.

KROGSTAD. You can't frighten me, either. People don't do that sort of thing, Mrs. Helmer. There wouldn't be any point to it, anyway, I'd still have him right in my pocket.

NORA. Afterwards? When I'm no longer . . .

KROGSTAD. Aren't you forgetting that your reputation would then be entirely in my hands? [NORA *stands looking at him, speechless.*] Well, I've warned you. Don't do anything silly. When Helmer gets my letter, I expect to hear from him. And don't forget: it's him who is forcing me off the straight and narrow again, your own husband! That's something I'll never forgive him for. Goodbye, Mrs. Helmer.

[*He goes out through the hall.* NORA *crosses to the door, opens it slightly, and listens.*]

NORA. He's going. He hasn't left the letter. No, no, that would be impossible! [*Opens the door further and further.*] What's he doing? He's stopped outside. He's not going down the stairs. Has he changed his mind? Is he . . . ? [*A letter falls into the letter-box. Then* KROGSTAD'S *footsteps are heard receding as he walks downstairs.* NORA *gives a stifled cry, runs across the room to the sofa table; pause.*] In the letter-box! [*She creeps stealthily across to the hall door.*] There it is! Torvald, Torvald! It's hopeless now!

MRS. LINDE [*comes into the room, left, carrying the costume*]. There, I think that's everything. Shall we try it on?

NORA [*in a low, hoarse voice*]. Kristine, come here.

MRS. LINDE [*throws the dress down on the sofa*]. What's wrong with you? You look upset.

NORA. Come here. Do you see that letter? *There*, look! Through the glass in the letter-box.

MRS. LINDE. Yes, yes, I can see it.

NORA. It's a letter from Krogstad.

MRS. LINDE. Nora! It was Krogstad who lent you the money!

NORA. Yes. And now Torvald will get to know everything.

MRS. LINDE. Believe me, Nora, it's best for you both.

NORA. But there's more to it than that. I forged a signature. . . .

MRS. LINDE. Heavens above!

NORA. Listen, I want to tell you something, Kristine, so you can be my witness.

MRS. LINDE. What do you mean 'witness'? What do you want me to . . . ?

NORA. If I should go mad . . . which might easily happen . . .

MRS. LINDE. Nora!

NORA. Or if anything happened to me . . . which meant I couldn't be here. . . .

MRS. LINDE. Nora, Nora! Are you out of your mind?

NORA. And if somebody else wanted to take it all upon himself, the whole blame, you understand. . . .

MRS. LINDE. Yes, yes. But what makes you think . . . ?

NORA. Then you must testify that it isn't true, Kristine. I'm not out of my mind; I'm quite sane now. And I tell you this: nobody else knew anything, I alone was responsible for the whole thing. Remember that!

MRS. LINDE. I will. But I don't understand a word of it.

NORA. Why should you? You see something miraculous is going to happen.

MRS. LINDE. Something miraculous?

NORA. Yes, a miracle. But something so terrible as well, Kristine— oh, it must *never* happen, not for anything.

MRS. LINDE. I'm going straight over to talk to Krogstad.

NORA. Don't go. He'll only do you harm.

MRS. LINDE. There was a time when he would have done anything for me.

NORA. Him!

MRS. LINDE. Where does he live?

NORA. How do I know. . . ? Wait a minute. [*She feels in her pocket.*] Here's his card. But the letter, the letter. . . !

HELMER [*from his study, knocking on the door*]. Nora!

NORA [*cries out in terror*]. What's that? What do you want?

HELMER. Don't be frightened. We're not coming in. You've locked the door. Are you trying on?

NORA. Yes, yes, I'm trying on. It looks so nice on me, Torvald.

MRS. LINDE [*who has read the card*]. He lives just round the corner.

NORA. It's no use. It's hopeless. The letter is there in the box.

MRS. LINDE. Your husband keeps the key?

NORA. Always.

MRS. LINDE. Krogstad must ask for his letter back unread, he must find some sort of excuse. . . .

NORA. But this is just the time that Torvald generally . . .

MRS. LINDE. Put him off! Go in and keep him busy. I'll be back as soon as I can.

[*She goes out hastily by the hall door.* NORA *walks over to Helmer's door, opens it and peeps in.*]

NORA. Torvald!

HELMER [*in the study*]. Well, can a man get into his own living-room again now? Come along, Rank, now we'll see . . . [*In the doorway.*] But what's this?

NORA. What, Torvald dear?

HELMER. Rank led me to expect some kind of marvellous transformation.

RANK [*in the doorway*]. That's what I thought too, but I must have been mistaken.

NORA. I'm not showing myself off to anybody before tomorrow.

HELMER. Nora dear, you look tired. You haven't been practising too hard?

NORA. No, I haven't practised at all yet.

HELMER. You'll have to, though.

NORA. Yes, I certainly must, Torvald. But I just can't get anywhere without your help: I've completely forgotten it.

HELMER. We'll soon polish it up.

NORA. Yes, do help me, Torvald. Promise? I'm so nervous. All those people. . . . You must devote yourself exclusively to me this evening. Pens away! Forget all about the office! Promise me, Torvald dear!

HELMER. I promise. This evening I am wholly and entirely at your service . . . helpless little thing that you are. Oh, but while I remember, I'll just look first . . .

[*He goes towards the hall door.*]

NORA. What do you want out there?

HELMER. Just want to see if there are any letters.

NORA. No, don't, Torvald!

HELMER. Why not?

NORA. Torvald, *please*! There aren't any.

HELMER. Just let me see.

[*He starts to go.* NORA, *at the piano, plays the opening bars of the tarantella.*]

HELMER [*at the door, stops*]. Aha!

NORA. I shan't be able to dance tomorrow if I don't rehearse it with you.

HELMER [*walks to her*]. Are you really so nervous, Nora dear?

NORA. Terribly nervous. Let me run through it now. There's still time before supper. Come and sit here and play for me, Torvald dear. Tell me what to do, keep me right—as you always do.

HELMER. Certainly, with pleasure, if that's what you want.

[*He sits at the piano.* NORA *snatches the tambourine out of the box, and also a long gaily-coloured shawl which she drapes round herself, then with a bound she leaps forward.*]

NORA [*shouts*]. Now play for me! Now I'll dance!

[HELMER *plays and* NORA *dances;* DR. RANK *stands at the piano behind Helmer and looks on.*]

HELMER [*playing*]. Not so fast! Not so fast!

NORA. I can't help it.

HELMER. Not so wild, Nora!

NORA. This is how it has to be.

HELMER [*stops*]. No, no, that won't do at all.

NORA [*laughs and swings the tambourine*]. Didn't I tell you?

RANK. Let me play for her.

HELMER [*gets up*]. Yes, do. Then I'll be better able to tell her what to do.

[RANK *sits down at the piano and plays.* NORA *dances more and more wildly.* HELMER *stands by the stove giving her repeated directions as she dances; she does not seem to hear them. Her hair comes undone and falls about her shoulders; she pays no attention and goes on dancing.* MRS. LINDE *enters.*]

MRS. LINDE [*standing as though spellbound in the doorway*]. Ah. . . !

NORA [*dancing*]. See what fun we are having, Kristine.

HELMER. But my dear darling Nora, you are dancing as though your life depended on it.

NORA. It does.

HELMER. Stop, Rank! This is sheer madness. Stop, I say.

[RANK *stops playing and* NORA *comes to a sudden halt.*]

HELMER [*crosses to her*]. I would never have believed it. You have forgotten everything I ever taught you.

NORA [*throwing away the tambourine*]. There you are, you see.

HELMER. Well, some more instruction is certainly needed there.

NORA. Yes, you see how necessary it is. You must go on coaching me right up to the last minute. Promise me, Torvald?

HELMER. You can rely on me.

NORA. You mustn't think about anything else but me until after tomorrow . . . mustn't open any letters . . . mustn't touch the letter-box.

HELMER. Ah, you are still frightened of what that man might . . .

NORA. Yes, yes, I am.

HELMER. I can see from your face there's already a letter there from him.

NORA. I don't know. I think so. But you mustn't read anything like that now. We don't want anything horrid coming between us until all this is over.

RANK [*softly to* HELMER]. I shouldn't cross her.

G

HELMER [*puts his arm round her*]. The child must have her way. But tomorrow night, when your dance is done. . . .

NORA. Then you are free.

MAID [*in the doorway, right*]. Dinner is served, madam.

NORA. We'll have champagne, Helene.

MAID. Very good, madam.

[*She goes.*]

HELMER. Aha! It's to be quite a banquet, eh?

NORA. With champagne flowing until dawn. [*Shouts.*] And some maca-roons, Helene . . . lots of them, for once in a while.

HELMER [*seizing her hands*]. Now, now, not so wild and excitable! Let me see you being my own little singing bird again.

NORA. Oh yes, I will. And if you'll just go in . . . you, too, Dr. Rank. Kristine, you must help me to do my hair.

RANK [*softly, as they leave*]. There isn't anything . . . anything as it were, impending, is there?

HELMER. No, not at all, my dear fellow. It's nothing but these childish fears I was telling you about.

[*They go out to the right.*]

NORA. Well?

MRS. LINDE. He's left town.

NORA. I saw it in your face.

MRS. LINDE. He's coming back tomorrow evening. I left a note for him.

NORA. You shouldn't have done that. You must let things take their course. Because really it's a case for rejoicing, waiting like this for the miracle.

MRS. LINDE. What is it you are waiting for?

NORA. Oh, you wouldn't understand. Go and join the other two. I'll be there in a minute.

[MRS. LINDE *goes into the dining-room.* NORA *stands for a moment as though to collect herself, then looks at her watch.*]

NORA. Five. Seven hours to midnight. Then twenty-four hours till the next midnight. Then the tarantella will be over. Twenty-four and seven? Thirty-one hours to live.

HELMER [*in the doorway, right*]. What's happened to our little sky-lark?

NORA [*running towards him with open arms*]. Here she is!

ACT THREE

The same room. The round table has been moved to the centre of the room, and the chairs placed round it. A lamp is burning on the table. The door to the hall stands open. Dance music can be heard coming from the floor above. MRS. LINDE *is sitting by the table, idly turning over the pages of a book; she tries to read, but does not seem able to concentrate. Once or twice she listens, tensely, for a sound at the front door.*

MRS. LINDE [*looking at her watch*]. Still not here. There isn't much time left. I only hope he hasn't . . . [*She listens again.*] Ah, there he is. [*She goes out into the hall, and cautiously opens the front door. Soft footsteps can be heard on the stairs. She whispers.*] Come in. There's nobody here.

KROGSTAD [*in the doorway*]. I found a note from you at home. What does it all mean?

MRS. LINDE. I *had* to talk to you.

KROGSTAD. Oh? And did it have to be here, in this house?

MRS. LINDE. It wasn't possible over at my place, it hasn't a separate entrance. Come in. We are quite alone. The maid's asleep and the Helmers are at a party upstairs.

KROGSTAD [*comes into the room*]. Well, well! So the Helmers are out dancing tonight! Really?

MRS. LINDE. Yes, why not?

KROGSTAD. Why not indeed!

MRS. LINDE. Well then, Nils. Let's talk.

KROGSTAD. Have we two anything more to talk about?

MRS. LINDE. We have a great deal to talk about.

KROGSTAD. I shouldn't have thought so.

MRS. LINDE. That's because you never really understood me.

KROGSTAD. What else was there to understand, apart from the old, old story? A heartless woman throws a man over the moment something more profitable offers itself.

MRS. LINDE. Do you really think I'm so heartless? Do you think I found it easy to break it off.

KROGSTAD. Didn't you?

MRS. LINDE. You didn't really believe that?

KROGSTAD. If that wasn't the case, why did you write to me as you did?

MRS. LINDE. There was nothing else I could do. If I had to make the break, I felt in duty bound to destroy any feeling that you had for me.

KROGSTAD [*clenching his hands*]. So that's how it was. And all that . . . was for money!

MRS. LINDE. You mustn't forget I had a helpless mother and two young brothers. We couldn't wait for you, Nils. At that time you hadn't much immediate prospect of anything.

KROGSTAD. That may be. But you had no right to throw me over for somebody else.

MRS. LINDE. Well, I don't know. Many's the time I've asked myself whether I was justified.

KROGSTAD [*more quietly*]. When I lost you, it was just as if the ground had slipped away from under my feet. Look at me now: a broken man clinging to the wreck of his life.

MRS. LINDE. Help might be near.

KROGSTAD. It was near. Then you came along and got in the way.

MRS. LINDE. Quite without knowing, Nils. I only heard today it's you I'm supposed to be replacing at the Bank.

KROGSTAD. If you say so, I believe you. But now you do know, aren't you going to withdraw?

MRS. LINDE. No, that wouldn't benefit you in the slightest.

KROGSTAD. Benefit, benefit. . . . ! I would do it just the same.

MRS. LINDE. I have learned to go carefully. Life and hard, bitter necessity have taught me that.

KROGSTAD. And life has taught me not to believe in pretty speeches.

MRS. LINDE. Then life has taught you a very sensible thing. But deeds are something you surely must believe in?

KROGSTAD. How do you mean?

MRS. LINDE. You said you were like a broken man clinging to the wreck of his life.

KROGSTAD. And I said it with good reason.

MRS. LINDE. And I am like a broken woman clinging to the wreck of her life. Nobody to care about, and nobody to care for.

KROGSTAD. It was your own choice.

MRS. LINDE. At the time there was no other choice.

KROGSTAD. Well, what of it?

MRS. LINDE. Nils, what about us two castaways joining forces.

KROGSTAD. What's that you say?

MRS. LINDE. Two of us on *one* wreck surely stand a better chance than each on his own.

KROGSTAD. Kristine!

MRS. LINDE. Why do you suppose I came to town?

KROGSTAD. You mean, you thought of me?

MRS. LINDE. Without work I couldn't live. All my life I have worked, for as long as I can remember; that has always been my one great joy. But now I'm completely alone in the world, and feeling horribly empty and forlorn. There's no pleasure in working only for yourself. Nils, give me somebody and something to work for.

KROGSTAD. I don't believe all this. It's only a woman's hysteria, wanting to be all magnanimous and self-sacrificing.

MRS. LINDE. Have you ever known me hysterical before?

KROGSTAD. Would you really do this? Tell me—do you know all about my past?

MRS. LINDE. Yes.

KROGSTAD. And you know what people think about me?

MRS. LINDE. Just now you hinted you thought you might have been a different person with me.

KROGSTAD. I'm convinced I would.

MRS. LINDE. Couldn't it still happen?

KROGSTAD. Kristine! You know what you are saying, don't you? Yes, you do. I can see you do. Have you really the courage. . . ?

MRS. LINDE. I need someone to mother, and your children need a mother. We two need each other. Nils, I have faith in what, deep down, you are. With you I can face anything.

KROGSTAD [*seizing her hands*]. Thank you, thank you, Kristine. And I'll soon have everybody looking up to me, or I'll know the reason why. Ah, but I was forgetting. . . .

MRS. LINDE. Hush! The tarantella! You must go!

KROGSTAD. Why? What is it?

MRS. LINDE. You hear that dance upstairs? When it's finished they'll be coming.

KROGSTAD. Yes, I'll go. It's too late to do anything. Of course, you know nothing about what steps I've taken against the Helmers.

MRS. LINDE. Yes, Nils, I do know.

KROGSTAD. Yet you still want to go on. . . .

MRS. LINDE. I know how far a man like you can be driven by despair.

KROGSTAD. Oh, if only I could undo what I've done!

MRS. LINDE. You still can. Your letter is still there in the box.

KROGSTAD. Are you sure?

MRS. LINDE. Quite sure. But . . .

KROGSTAD [*regards her searchingly*]. Is that how things are? You want to save your friend at any price? Tell me straight. Is that it?

MRS. LINDE. When you've sold yourself *once* for other people's sake, you don't do it again.

KROGSTAD. I shall demand my letter back.

MRS. LINDE. No, no.

KROGSTAD. Of course I will, I'll wait here till Helmer comes. I'll tell him he has to give me my letter back . . . that it's only about my notice . . . that he mustn't read it. . . .

MRS. LINDE. No, Nils, don't ask for it back.

KROGSTAD. But wasn't that the very reason you got me here?

MRS. LINDE. Yes, that was my first terrified reaction. But that was yesterday, and it's quite incredible the things I've witnessed in this house in the last twenty-four hours. Helmer must know everything. This unhappy secret must come out. Those two must have the whole thing out between them. All this secrecy and deception, it just can't go on.

KROGSTAD. Well, if you want to risk it. . . . But one thing I can do, and I'll do it at once. . . .

MRS. LINDE [*listening*]. Hurry! Go, go! The dance has stopped. We aren't safe a moment longer.

KROGSTAD. I'll wait for you downstairs.

MRS. LINDE. Yes, do. You must see me home.

KROGSTAD. I've never been so incredibly happy before.

[*He goes out by the front door. The door out into the hall remains standing open.*]

MRS. LINDE [*tidies the room a little and gets her hat and coat ready*]. How things change! How things change! Somebody to work for . . . to live for. A home to bring happiness into. Just let me get down to it. . . . I wish they'd come. . . . [*Listens.*] Ah, there they are. . . . Get my things.

[*She takes her coat and hat. The voices of* HELMER *and* NORA *are heard outside. A key is turned and* HELMER *pushes* NORA *almost forcibly into the hall. She is dressed in the Italian costume, with a big black shawl over it. He is in evening dress, and over it a black cloak, open.*]

NORA [*still in the doorway, reluctantly*]. No, no, not in here! I want to go back up again. I don't want to leave so early.

HELMER. But my dearest Nora . . .

NORA. Oh, please, Torvald, I beg you. . . . *Please*, just for another hour.

HELMER. Not another minute, Nora my sweet. You remember what we agreed. There now, come along in. You'll catch cold standing there.

[*He leads her, in spite of her resistance, gently but firmly into the room.*]

MRS. LINDE. Good evening.

NORA. Kristine!

HELMER. Why, Mrs. Linde. You here so late?

MRS. LINDE. Yes. You must forgive me but I did so want to see Nora all dressed up.

NORA. Have you been sitting here waiting for me?

MRS. LINDE. Yes, I'm afraid I wasn't in time to catch you before you went upstairs. And I felt I couldn't leave again without seeing you.

HELMER [*removing* NORA's *shawl*]. Well take a good look at her. I think I can say she's worth looking at. Isn't she lovely, Mrs. Linde?

MRS. LINDE. Yes, I must say. . . .

HELMER. Isn't she quite extraordinarily lovely? That's what everybody at the party thought, too. But she's dreadfully stubborn . . . the sweet little thing! And what shall we do about that? Would you believe it, I nearly had to use force to get her away.

NORA. Oh Torvald, you'll be sorry you didn't let me stay, even for half an hour.

HELMER. You hear that, Mrs. Linde? She dances her tarantella, there's wild applause—which was well deserved, although the performance was perhaps rather realistic . . . I mean, rather more so than was strictly necessary from the artistic point of view. But anyway! The main thing is she was a success, a tremendous success. Was I supposed to let her stay after that? Spoil the effect? No thank you! I took my lovely little Capri girl—my capricious little Capri girl, I might say—by the arm, whisked her once round the room, a curtsey all round, and then—as they say in novels—the beautiful vision vanished. An exit should always be effective, Mrs. Linde. But I just can't get Nora to see that. Phew! It's warm in here. [*He throws his cloak over a chair and opens the door to his study.*] What? It's dark. Oh yes, of course. Excuse me. . . .

[*He goes in and lights a few candles.*]

NORA [*quickly, in a breathless whisper*]. Well?

MRS. LINDE [*softly*]. I've spoken to him.

NORA. And . . . ?

MRS. LINDE. Nora . . . you must tell your husband everything.

NORA [*tonelessly*]. I knew it.

MRS. LINDE. You've got nothing to fear from Krogstad. But you must speak.

NORA. I won't.

MRS. LINDE. Then the letter will.

NORA. Thank you, Kristine. Now I know what's to be done. Hush . . . !

HELMER [*comes in again*]. Well, Mrs. Linde, have you finished admiring her?

MRS. LINDE. Yes. And now I must say good night.

HELMER. Oh, already? Is this yours, this knitting?

MRS. LINDE [*takes it*]. Yes, thank you. I nearly forgot it.

HELMER. So you knit, eh?

MRS. LINDE. Yes.

HELMER. You should embroider instead, you know.

MRS. LINDE. Oh? Why?

HELMER. So much prettier. Watch! You hold the embroidery like this in the left hand, and then you take the needle in the right hand, like this, and you describe a long, graceful curve. Isn't that right?

MRS. LINDE. Yes, I suppose so. . . .

HELMER. Whereas knitting on the other hand just can't help being ugly. Look! Arms pressed into the sides, the knitting needles going up and down—there's something Chinese about it. . . . Ah, that was marvellous champagne they served tonight.

MRS. LINDE. Well, good night, Nora! And stop being so stubborn.

HELMER. Well said, Mrs. Linde!

MRS. LINDE. Good night, Mr. Helmer.

HELMER [*accompanying her to the door*]. Good night, good night! You'll get home all right, I hope? I'd be only too pleased to . . . But you haven't far to walk. Good night, good night! [*She goes; he shuts the door behind her and comes in again.*] There we are, got rid of her at last. She's a frightful bore, that woman.

NORA. Aren't you very tired, Torvald?

HELMER. Not in the least.

NORA. Not sleepy?

HELMER. Not at all. On the contrary, I feel extremely lively. What about you? Yes, you look quite tired and sleepy.

NORA. Yes, I'm very tired. I just want to fall straight off to sleep.

HELMER. There you are, you see! Wasn't I right in thinking we shouldn't stay any longer.

NORA. Oh, everything you do is right.

HELMER [*kissing her forehead*]. There's my little sky-lark talking common sense. Did you notice how gay Rank was this evening?

NORA. Oh, was he? I didn't get a chance to talk to him.

HELMER. I hardly did either. But it's a long time since I saw him in such a good mood. [*Looks at* NORA *for a moment or two, then comes nearer her.*] Ah, it's wonderful to be back in our own home again, and quite alone with you. How irresistibly lovely you are, Nora!

NORA. Don't look at me like that, Torvald!

HELMER. Can't I look at my most treasured possession? At all this loveliness that's mine and mine alone, completely and utterly mine.

NORA [*walks round to the other side of the table*]. You mustn't talk to me like that tonight.

HELMER [*following her*]. You still have the tarantella in your blood, I see. And that makes you even more desirable. Listen! The guests are beginning to leave now. [*Softly.*] Nora . . . soon the whole house will be silent.

NORA. I should hope so.

HELMER. Of course you do, don't you, Nora my darling? You know, whenever I'm out at a party with you . . . do you know why I never talk to you very much, why I always stand away from you and only steal a quick glance at you now and then . . . do you know why I do that? It's because I'm pretending we are secretly in love, secretly engaged and nobody suspects there is anything between us.

NORA. Yes, yes. I know your thoughts are always with me, of course.

HELMER. And when it's time to go, and I lay your shawl round those shapely, young shoulders, round the exquisite curve of your neck . . . I pretend that you are my young bride, that we are just leaving our wedding, that I am taking you to our new home for the first time . . . to be alone with you for the first time . . . quite alone with your young and trembling loveliness! All evening I've been longing for you, and nothing else. And as I watched you darting and swaying in the tarantella, my blood was on fire . . . I couldn't bear it any longer . . . and that's why I brought you down here with me so early. . . .

NORA. Go away, Torvald! Please leave me alone. I won't have it.

HELMER. What's this? It's just your little game isn't it, my little Nora. Won't! Won't! Am I not your husband. . . ?

[*There is a knock on the front door.*]

NORA [*startled*]. Listen . . . ! ·

HELMER [*going towards the hall*]. Who's there?

RANK [*outside*]. It's me. Can I come in for a minute?

HELMER [*in a low voice, annoyed*]. Oh, what does he want now? [*Aloud.*] Wait a moment. [*He walks across and opens the door.*] How nice of you to look in on your way out.

RANK. I fancied I heard your voice and I thought I would just look in.

[*He takes a quick glance round.*] Ah yes, this dear, familiar old place! How cosy and comfortable you've got things here, you two.

HELMER. You seemed to be having a pretty good time upstairs yourself.

RANK. Capital! Why shouldn't I? Why not make the most of things in this world? At least as much as one can, and for as long as one can. The wine was excellent. . . .

HELMER. Especially the champagne.

RANK. You noticed that too, did you? It's incredible the amount I was able to put away.

NORA. Torvald also drank a lot of champagne this evening.

RANK. Oh?

NORA. Yes, and that always makes him quite merry.

RANK. Well, why shouldn't a man allow himself a jolly evening after a day well spent?

HELMER. Well spent? I'm afraid I can't exactly claim that.

RANK [*clapping him on the shoulder*]. But I can, you see!

NORA. Dr. Rank, am I right in thinking you carried out a certain laboratory test today?

RANK. Exactly.

HELMER. Look at our little Nora talking about laboratory tests!

NORA. And may I congratulate you on the result?

RANK. You may indeed.

NORA. So it was good?

RANK. The best possible, for both doctor and patient—certainty!

NORA [*quickly and searchingly*]. Certainty?

RANK. Absolute certainty. So why shouldn't I allow myself a jolly evening after that?

NORA. Quite right, Dr. Rank.

HELMER. I quite agree. As long as you don't suffer for it in the morning.

RANK. Well, you never get anything for nothing in this life.

NORA. Dr. Rank . . . you are very fond of masquerades, aren't you?

RANK. Yes, when there are plenty of amusing disguises. . . .

NORA. Tell me, what shall we two go as next time?

HELMER. There's frivolity for you . . . thinking about the next time already!

RANK. We two? I'll tell you. You must go as Lady Luck. . . .

HELMER. Yes, but how do you find a costume to suggest *that*?

RANK. Your wife could simply go in her everyday clothes. . . .

HELMER. That was nicely said. But don't you know what you would be?

RANK. Yes, my dear friend, I know exactly what I shall be.

HELMER. Well?

RANK. At the next masquerade, I shall be invisible.

HELMER. That's a funny idea!

RANK. There's a big black cloak . . . haven't you heard of the cloak of invisibility? That comes right down over you, and then nobody can see you.

HELMER [*suppressing a smile*]. Of course, that's right.

RANK. But I'm clean forgetting what I came for. Helmer, give me a cigar, one of the dark Havanas.

HELMER. With the greatest of pleasure.

[*He offers his case.*]

RANK [*takes one and cuts the end off*]. Thanks.

NORA [*strikes a match*]. Let me give you a light.

RANK. Thank you. [*She holds out the match and he lights his cigar.*] And now, goodbye!

HELMER. Goodbye, goodbye, my dear fellow!

NORA. Sleep well, Dr. Rank.

RANK. Thank you for that wish.

NORA. Wish me the same.

RANK. You? All right, if you want me to. . . . Sleep well. And thanks for the light.

[*He nods to them both, and goes.*]

HELMER [*subdued*]. He's had a lot to drink.

NORA [*absently*]. Very likely.

[HELMER *takes a bunch of keys out of his pocket and goes out into the hall.*]

NORA. Torvald . . . what do you want there?

HELMER. I must empty the letter-box, it's quite full. There'll be no room for the papers in the morning. . . .

NORA. Are you going to work tonight?

HELMER. You know very well I'm not. Hello, what's this? Somebody's been at the lock.

NORA. At the lock?

HELMER. Yes, I'm sure of it. Why should that be? I'd hardly have thought the maids . . . ? Here's a broken hair-pin. Nora, it's one of yours. . . .

NORA [*quickly*]. It must have been the children. . . .

HELMER. Then you'd better tell them not to. Ah . . . there . . . I've managed to get it open. [*He takes the things out and shouts into the kitchen.*] Helene! . . . Helene, put the light out in the hall. [*He comes into the room again with the letters in his hand and shuts the hall door.*] Look how it all mounts up. [*Runs through them.*] What's this?

NORA. The letter! Oh no, Torvald, no!

HELMER. Two visiting cards . . . from Dr. Rank.

NORA. From Dr. Rank?

HELMER [*looking at them*]. Dr. Rank, Medical Practitioner. They were on top. He must have put them in as he left.

NORA. Is there anything on them?

HELMER. There's a black cross above his name. Look. What an uncanny idea. It's just as if he were announcing his own death.

NORA. He is.

HELMER. What? What do you know about it? Has he said anything to you?

NORA. Yes. He said when these cards came, he would have taken his last leave of us. He was going to shut himself up and die.

HELMER. Poor fellow! Of course I knew we couldn't keep him with us very long. But so soon. . . . And hiding himself away like a wounded animal.

NORA. When it has to happen, it's best that it should happen without words. Don't you think so, Torvald?

HELMER [*walking up and down*]. He had grown so close to us. I don't think I can imagine him gone. His suffering and his loneliness seemed almost to provide a background of dark cloud to the sunshine of our lives. Well, perhaps it's all for the best. For him at any rate. [*Pauses.*] And maybe for us as well, Nora. Now there's just the two of us. [*Puts his arms round her.*] Oh, my darling wife, I can't hold you close enough. You know, Nora . . . many's the time I wish you were threatened by some terrible danger so I could risk everything, body and soul, for your sake.

NORA [*tears herself free and says firmly and decisively*]. Now you must read your letters, Torvald.

HELMER. No, no, not tonight. I want to be with you, my darling wife.

NORA. Knowing all the time your friend is dying. . . ?

HELMER. You are right. It's been a shock to both of us. This ugly thing has come between us . . . thoughts of death and decay. We must try to free ourselves from it. Until then . . . we shall go our separate ways.

NORA [*her arms round his neck*]. Torvald . . . good night! Good night!

HELMER [*kisses her forehead*]. Goodnight, my little singing bird. Sleep well, Nora, I'll just read through my letters.

[*He takes the letters into his room and shuts the door behind him.*]

NORA [*gropes around her, wild-eyed, seizes Helmer's cloak, wraps it round herself, and whispers quickly, hoarsely, spasmodically*]. Never see him again. Never, never, never. [*Throws her shawl over her head.*] And never see the children again either. Never, never. Oh, that black icy water. Oh, that bottomless . . . ! If only it were all over! He's got it now. Now he's reading it. Oh no, no! Not yet! Torvald, goodbye . . . and my children. . . .

[*She rushes out in the direction of the hall; at the same moment* HELMER *flings open his door and stands there with an open letter in his hand.*]

HELMER. Nora!

NORA [*shrieks*]. Ah!

HELMER. What is this? Do you know what is in this letter?

NORA. Yes, I know. Let me go! Let me out!

HELMER [*holds her back*]. Where are you going?

NORA [*trying to tear herself free*]. You mustn't try to save me, Torvald!

HELMER [*reels back*]. True! Is it true what he writes? How dreadful! No, no, it can't possibly be true.

NORA. It *is* true. I loved you more than anything else in the world.

HELMER. Don't come to me with a lot of paltry excuses!

NORA [*taking a step towards him*]. Torvald. . . !

HELMER. Miserable woman . . . what is this you have done?

NORA. Let me go. I won't have you taking the blame for me. You mustn't take it on yourself.

HELMER. Stop play-acting! [*Locks the front door.*] You are staying here to give an account of yourself. Do you understand what you have done? Answer me! Do you understand?

NORA [*looking fixedly at him, her face hardening*]. Yes, now I'm really beginning to understand.

HELMER [*walking up and down*]. Oh, what a terrible awakening this is. All these eight years . . . this woman who was my pride and joy . . . a hypocrite, a liar, worse than that, a criminal! Oh, how utterly squalid it all is! Ugh! Ugh! [NORA *remains silent and looks fixedly at him.*] I should have realized something like this would happen. I should have seen it coming. All your father's irresponsible ways. . . . Quiet! All your father's irresponsible ways are coming out in you. No religion, no morals, no sense of duty. . . . Oh, this is my punishment for turning a blind eye to him. It was for your sake I did it, and this is what I get for it.

NORA. Yes, this.

HELMER. Now you have ruined my entire happiness, jeopardized my whole future. It's terrible to think of. Here I am, at the mercy of a thoroughly unscrupulous person; he can do whatever he likes with me, demand anything he wants, order me about just as he chooses . . . and I daren't even whimper. I'm done for, a miserable failure, and it's all the fault of a feather-brained woman!

NORA. When I've left this world behind, you will be free.

HELMER. Oh, stop pretending! Your father was just the same, always ready with fine phrases. What good would it do me if you left this world behind, as you put it? Not the slightest bit of good. He can still let it all come out, if he likes; and if he does, people might even suspect me of being an accomplice in these criminal acts of yours. They might even think I was the one behind it all, that it was I who pushed you into it! And it's you I have to thank for this . . . and when I've taken such good care of you, all our married life. Now do you understand what you have done to me?

NORA [*coldly and calmly*]. Yes.

HELMER. I just can't understand it, it's so incredible. But we must see about putting things right. Take that shawl off. Take it off, I tell you! I must see if I can't find some way or other of appeasing him. The thing must be hushed up at all costs. And as far as you and I are concerned, things must appear to go on exactly as before. But only in the eyes of the world, of course. In other words you'll go on living here; that's understood. But you will not be allowed to bring up the children, I can't trust you with them. . . . Oh, that I should have to say this to the woman I loved so dearly, the woman I still. . . . Well, that must be all over and done with. From now on, there can be no question of happiness. All we can do is save the bits and pieces from the wreck, preserve appearances. . . . [*The front door-bell rings.* HELMER *gives a start.*] What's that? So late? How terrible, supposing. . . . If he should . . . ? Hide, Nora! Say you are not well.

[NORA *stands motionless.* HELMER *walks across and opens the door into the hall.*]

MAID [*half dressed, in the hall*]. It's a note for Mrs. Helmer.

HELMER. Give it to me. [*He snatches the note and shuts the door.*] Yes, it's from him. You can't have it. I want to read it myself.

NORA. You read it then.

HELMER [*by the lamp*]. I hardly dare. Perhaps this is the end, for both of us. Well, I *must* know. [*He opens the note hurriedly, reads a few lines, looks at another enclosed sheet, and gives a cry of joy.*] Nora! [NORA *looks at him inquiringly.*] Nora! I must read it again. Yes, yes, it's true! I am saved! Nora, I am saved!

NORA. And me?

HELMER. You too, of course, we are both saved, you as well as me. Look, he's sent your IOU back. He sends his regrets and apologies for what he has done. . . . His luck has changed. . . . Oh, what does it matter what he says. We are saved, Nora! Nobody can do anything to you now. Oh, Nora, Nora . . . but let's get rid of this disgusting thing first. Let me see. . . . [*He glances at the IOU.*] No, I don't want to see it. I don't want it to be anything but a dream. [*He tears up the IOU and both letters, throws all the pieces into the stove and watches them burn.*] Well, that's the end of that. He said in his note you'd known since Christmas Eve. . . . You must have had three terrible days of it, Nora.

NORA. These three days haven't been easy.

HELMER. The agonies you must have gone through! When the only way out seemed to be. . . . No, let's forget the whole ghastly thing. We can rejoice and say: It's all over! It's all over! Listen to me, Nora! You don't seem to understand: it's all over! Why this grim look on your face? Oh, poor little Nora, of course I understand. You can't bring yourself to believe I've forgiven you. But I have, Nora, I swear it. I forgive you everything. I know you did what you did because you loved me.

NORA. That's true.

HELMER. You loved me as a wife should love her husband. It was simply that you didn't have the experience to judge what was the best way of going about things. But do you think I love you any the less for that; just because you don't know how to act on your own responsibility? No, no, you just lean on me, I shall give you all the advice and guidance you need. I wouldn't be a proper man if I didn't find a woman doubly attractive for being so obviously helpless. You mustn't dwell on the harsh things I said in that first moment of horror, when I thought everything was going to come crashing down about my ears. I have forgiven you, Nora, I swear it! I have forgiven you!

NORA. Thank you for your forgiveness.

[*She goes out through the door, right.*]

HELMER. No, don't go! [*He looks through the doorway.*] What are you doing in the spare room?

NORA. Taking off this fancy dress.

HELMER [*standing at the open door*], Yes, do. You try and get some rest, and set your mind at peace again, my frightened little song-bird. Have a good long sleep; you know you are safe and sound under my wing. [*Walks up and down near the door.*] What a nice, cosy little home we have here, Nora! Here you can find refuge. Here I shall hold you like a hunted dove I have rescued unscathed from the cruel talons of the hawk, and calm your poor beating heart. And that will come, gradually, Nora, believe me. Tomorrow you'll see everything quite differently. Soon everything will be just as it was before. You won't need me to keep on telling you I've forgiven you; you'll feel convinced of it in your own heart. You don't really imagine me ever thinking of turning you out, or even of reproaching you? Oh, a real man isn't made that way, you know, Nora. For a man, there's something indescribably moving and very satisfying in knowing that he has forgiven his wife—forgiven her, completely and genuinely, from the depths of his heart. It's as though it made her his property in a double sense: he has, as it were, given her a new life, and she becomes in a way both his wife and at the same time his child. That is how you will seem to me after today, helpless, perplexed little thing that you are. Don't you worry your pretty little head about anything, Nora. Just you be frank with me,

and I'll take all the decisions for you. .... What's this? Not in bed?
You've changed your things?

NORA [*in her everyday dress*]. Yes, Torvald, I've changed.

HELMER. What for? It's late.

NORA. I shan't sleep tonight.

HELMER. But my dear Nora. . . .

NORA [*looks at her watch*]. It's not so terribly late. Sit down, Torvald.
We two have a lot to talk about.

[*She sits down at one side of the table.*]

HELMER. Nora, what is all this? Why so grim?

NORA. Sit down. It'll take some time. I have a lot to say to you.

HELMER [*sits down at the table opposite her*]. You frighten me, Nora.
I don't understand you.

NORA. Exactly. You don't understand me. And I have never understood you, either—until tonight. No, don't interrupt. I just want
you to listen to what I have to say. We are going to have things
out, Torvald.

HELMER. What do you mean?

NORA. Isn't there anything that strikes you about the way we two are
sitting here?

HELMER. What's that?

NORA. We have now been married eight years. Hasn't it struck you
this is the first time you and I, man and wife, have had a serious
talk together?

HELMER. Depends what you mean by 'serious'.

NORA. Eight whole years—no, more, ever since we first knew each
other—and never have we exchanged one serious word about
serious things.

HELMER. What did you want me to do? Get you involved in worries
that you couldn't possibly help me to bear?

NORA. I'm not talking about worries. I say we've never once sat down together and seriously tried to get to the bottom of anything.

HELMER. But, my dear Nora, would that have been a thing for you?

NORA. That's just it. You have never understood me . . . I've been greatly wronged, Torvald. First by my father, and then by you.

HELMER. What! Us two! The two people who loved you more than anybody?

NORA [shakes her head]. You two never loved me. You only thought now nice it was to be in love with me.

HELMER. But, Nora, what's this you are saying?

NORA. It's right, you know, Torvald. At home, Daddy used to tell me what he thought, then I thought the same. And if I thought differently, I kept quiet about it, because he wouldn't have liked it. He used to call me his baby doll, and he played with me as I used to play with my dolls. Then I came to live in your house. . . .

HELMER. What way is that to talk about our marriage?

NORA [imperturbably]. What I mean is: I passed out of Daddy's hands into yours. You arranged everything to your tastes, and I acquired the same tastes. Or I pretended to . . . I don't really know . . . I think it was a bit of both, sometimes one thing and sometimes the other. When I look back, it seems to me I have been living here like a beggar, from hand to mouth. I lived by doing tricks for you, Torvald. But that's the way you wanted it. You and Daddy did me a great wrong. It's your fault that I've never made anything of my life.

HELMER. Nora, how unreasonable . . . how ungrateful you are! Haven't you been happy here?

NORA. No, never. I thought I was, but I wasn't really.

HELMER. Not . . . not happy!

NORA. No, just gay. And you've always been so kind to me. But our house has never been anything but a play-room. I have been your doll wife, just as at home I was Daddy's doll child. And the children in turn have been my dolls. I thought it was fun when you came and played with me, just as they thought it was fun when I went and played with them. That's been our marriage, Torvald.

HELMER. There is some truth in what you say, exaggerated and hysterical though it is. But from now on it will be different. Play-time is over; now comes the time for lessons.

NORA. Whose lessons? Mine or the children's?

HELMER. Both yours and the children's, my dear Nora.

NORA. Ah, Torvald, you are not the man to teach me to be a good wife for you.

HELMER. How can you say that?

NORA. And what sort of qualifications have I to teach the children?

HELMER. Nora!

NORA. Didn't you say yourself, a minute or two ago, that you couldn't trust me with that job.

HELMER. In the heat of the moment! You shouldn't pay any attention to that.

NORA. On the contrary, you were quite right. I'm not up to it. There's another problem needs solving first. I must take steps to educate myself. You are not the man to help me there. That's something I must do on my own. That's why I'm leaving you.

HELMER [*jumps up*]. What did you say?

NORA. If I'm ever to reach any understanding of myself and the things around me, I must learn to stand alone. That's why I can't stay here with you any longer.

HELMER. Nora! Nora!

NORA. I'm leaving here at once. I dare say Kristine will put me up for tonight. . . .

HELMER. You are out of your mind! I won't let you! I forbid you!

NORA. It's no use forbidding me anything now. I'm taking with me my own personal belongings. I don't want anything of yours, either now or later.

HELMER. This is madness!

NORA. Tomorrow I'm going home—to what used to be my home, I mean. It will be easier for me to find something to do there.

HELMER. Oh, you blind, inexperienced . . .

NORA. I must set about *getting* experience, Torvald.

HELMER. And leave your home, your husband and your children? Don't you care what people will say?

NORA. That's no concern of mine. All I know is that this is necessary for *me*.

HELMER. This is outrageous! You are betraying your most sacred duty.

NORA. And what do you consider to be my most sacred duty?

HELMER. Does it take me to tell you that? Isn't it your duty to your husband and your children?

NORA. I have another duty equally sacred.

HELMER. You have not. What duty might *that* be?

NORA. My duty to myself.

HELMER. First and foremost, you are a wife and mother.

NORA. That I don't believe any more. I believe that first and foremost I am an individual, just as much as you are—or at least I'm going to try to be. I know most people agree with you, Torvald, and that's also what it says in books. But I'm not content any more with what most people say, or with what it says in books. I have to think things out for myself, and get things clear.

HELMER. Surely you are clear about your position in your own home? Haven't you an infallible guide in questions like these? Haven't you your religion?

NORA. Oh, Torvald, I don't really know what religion is.

HELMER. What do you say!

NORA. All I know is what Pastor Hansen said when I was confirmed. He said religion was this, that and the other. When I'm away from all this and on my own, I'll go into that, too. I want to find out whether what Pastor Hansen told me was right—or at least whether it's right for *me*.

HELMER. This is incredible talk from a young woman! But if religion cannot keep you on the right path, let me at least stir your conscience. I suppose you do have some moral sense? Or tell me—perhaps you don't?

NORA. Well, Torvald, that's not easy to say. I simply don't know. I'm really very confused about such things. All I know is my ideas about such things are very different from yours. I've also learnt that the law is different from what I thought; but I simply can't get it into my head that that particular law is right. Apparently a woman has no right to spare her old father on his death-bed, or to save her husband's life, even. I just don't believe it.

HELMER. You are talking like a child. You understand nothing about the society you live in.

NORA. No, I don't. But I shall go into that too. I must try to discover who is right, society or me.

HELMER. You are ill, Nora. You are delirious. I'm half inclined to think you are out of your mind.

NORA. Never have I felt so calm and collected as I do tonight.

HELMER. Calm and collected enough to leave your husband and children?

NORA. Yes.

HELMER. Then only one explanation is possible.

NORA. And that is?

HELMER. You don't love me any more.

NORA. Exactly.

HELMER. Nora! Can you say that!

NORA. I'm desperately sorry, Torvald. Because you have always been so kind to me. But I can't help it. I don't love you any more.

HELMER [*struggling to keep his composure*]. Is that also a 'calm and collected' decision you've made?

NORA. Yes, absolutely calm and collected. That's why I don't want to stay here.

HELMER. And can you also account for how I forfeited your love?

NORA. Yes, very easily. It was tonight, when the miracle didn't happen. It was then I realized you weren't the man I thought you were.

HELMER. Explain yourself more clearly. I don't understand.

NORA. For eight years I have been patiently waiting. Because, heavens, I knew miracles didn't happen every day. Then this devastating business started, and I became absolutely convinced the miracle *would* happen. All the time Krogstad's letter lay there, it never so much as crossed my mind that you would ever submit to that man's conditions. I was absolutely convinced you would say to him: Tell the whole wide world if you like. And when that was done . . .

HELMER. Yes, then what? After I had exposed my own wife to dis-honour and shame . . . !

NORA. When that was done, I was absolutely convinced you would come forward and take everything on yourself, and say: I am the guilty one.

HELMER. Nora!

NORA. You mean I'd never let you make such a sacrifice for my sake? Of course not. But what would my story have counted for against yours?—That was the miracle I went in hope and dread of. It was to prevent it that I was ready to end my life.

HELMER. I would gladly toil day and night for you, Nora, enduring all manner of sorrow and distress. But nobody sacrifices his *honour* for the one he loves.

NORA. Hundreds and thousands of women have.

HELMER. Oh, you think and talk like a stupid child.

NORA. All right. But you neither think nor talk like the man I would want to share my life with. When you had got over your fright— and you weren't concerned about me but only about what might happen to you—and when all danger was past, you acted as though nothing had happened. I was your little sky-lark again, your little doll, exactly as before; except you would have to protect it twice as carefully as before, now that it had shown itself to be so weak and fragile. [*Rises.*] Torvald, that was the moment I realised that for eight years I'd been living with a stranger, and had borne him three children. . . . Oh, I can't bear to think about it! I could tear myself to shreds.

HELMER [*sadly*]. I see. I see. There is a tremendous gulf dividing us. But, Nora, is there no way we might bridge it?

NORA. As I am now, I am no wife for you.

HELMER. I still have it in me to change.

NORA. Perhaps . . . if you have your doll taken away.

HELMER. And be separated from you! No, no, Nora, the very thought of it is inconceivable.

NORA [*goes into the room, right*]. All the more reason why it must be done.

[*She comes back with her outdoor things and a small travelling bag which she puts on the chair beside the table.*]

HELMER. Nora, Nora, not now! Wait till the morning.

NORA [*putting on her coat*]. I can't spend the night in a strange man's room.

HELMER. Couldn't we go on living here like brother and sister. . . . ?

NORA [*tying on her hat*]. You know very well that wouldn't last. [*She draws the shawl round her.*] Goodbye, Torvald. I don't want to see the children. I know they are in better hands than mine. As I am now, I can never be anything to them.

HELMER. But some day, Nora, some day. . . ?

NORA. How should I know? I've no idea what I might turn out to be.

HELMER. But you are my wife, whatever you are.

NORA. Listen, Torvald, from what I've heard, when a wife leaves her husband's house as I am doing now, he is absolved by law of all responsibility for her. I can at any rate free you from all responsibility. You must not feel in any way bound, any more than I shall. There must be full freedom on both sides. Look, here's your ring back. Give me mine.

HELMER. That too?

NORA. That too.

HELMER. There it is.

NORA. Well, that's the end of that. I'll put the keys down here. The maids know where everything is in the house—better than I do, in fact. Kristine will come in the morning after I've left to pack up the few things I brought with me from home. I want them sent on.

HELMER. The end! Nora, will you never think of me?

NORA. I dare say I'll often think about you and the children and this house.

HELMER. May I write to you, Nora?

NORA. No, never. I won't let you.

HELMER. But surely I can send you . . .

NORA. Nothing, nothing.

HELMER. Can't I help you if ever you need it?

NORA. I said 'no'. I don't accept things from strangers.

HELMER. Nora, can I never be anything more to you than a stranger?

NORA [*takes her bag*]. Ah, Torvald, only by a miracle of miracles. . . .

HELMER. Name it, this miracle of miracles!

NORA. Both you and I would have to change to the point where . . . Oh, Torvald, I don't believe in miracles any more.

HELMER. But I *will* believe. Name it! Change to the point where. . . ?

NORA. Where we could make a real marriage of our lives together. Goodbye!
     [*She goes out through the hall door.*]

HELMER [*sinks down on a chair near the door, and covers his face with his hands*]. Nora! Nora! [*He rises and looks round.*] Empty! She's gone! [*With sudden hope.*] The miracle of miracles. . . ?

     [*The heavy sound of a door being slammed is heard from below.*]

GHOSTS

[Gengangere]

A DOMESTIC DRAMA IN THREE ACTS
(1881)

CHARACTERS

MRS. HELENE ALVING, widow of Captain (and Chamberlain) Alving

OSWALD ALVING, her son, an artist

PASTOR MANDERS

JACOB ENGSTRAND, a carpenter

REGINE ENGSTRAND, in service with Mrs. Alving

The action takes place on Mrs. Alving's country estate by one of the large fjords of Western Norway

ACT ONE

A spacious garden room, with one door on the left wall, and two on the right. In the centre of the room stands a round table, with chairs round it; books, periodicals, and newspapers are lying on the table. Downstage, left, is a window, and near it a small sofa with a work-table in front of it. The room is continued at the back of the stage into an open and rather narrower conservatory, the walls of which are extensively glazed. In the right wall of the conservatory is a door that leads out into the garden. Through the glass wall may be glimpsed a gloomy fjord landscape, shrouded in steady rain.

JACOB ENGSTRAND is standing beside the door into the garden. His left leg is somewhat deformed, and he wears a boot with a built-up wooden sole. REGINE, with an empty garden syringe in her hand, is trying to prevent him coming any further.

REGINE [*keeping her voice low*]. What do you want? Stay where you are. You are dripping wet.

ENGSTRAND. It's God's own rain, my child.

REGINE. More like the devil's, you mean.

ENGSTRAND. Lord, the things you say, Regine. [*Takes a few limping steps into the room.*] But what I wanted to tell you was . . .

REGINE. Stop clumping about with that foot, man! The young master's upstairs asleep.

ENGSTRAND. Asleep? At this time of day?

REGINE. That's got nothing to do with you.

ENGSTRAND. I was out having a few drinks last night. . . .

REGINE. That I can well believe.

ENGSTRAND. Well, we are frail creatures, all of us, my child . . .

REGINE. We are that.

ENGSTRAND. . . . and many are the temptations of this world, you know . . . but still, there was I up and at work at half-past five this morning.

REGINE. Yes, yes, but off you go now. I'm not standing for having *rendez-vous's* here with you.

ENGSTRAND. Having what, did you say?

REGINE. I'm not going to have anybody finding you here. So, away you go.

ENGSTRAND [*comes a few steps closer*]. I'm damned if I'm going before I've had a word with you. I'll have that work down at the school-house finished by this afternoon, and I'm taking the night boat home, back to town.

REGINE [*mutters*]. Pleasant journey!

ENGSTRAND. Thank you, my child. You see tomorrow, the Orphanage is being opened, and I expect there'll be a lot of drinking and such like going on. And nobody's going to say about Jacob Engstrand that he can't resist temptation when it comes along.

REGINE. Huh!

ENGSTRAND. There'll be a lot of posh people here tomorrow. And they're expecting Pastor Manders from town as well.

REGINE. He'll be here today.

ENGSTRAND. There you are, you see. Got to be damned careful I don't put my foot in it with him, you know.

REGINE. Aha! So *that's* it!

ENGSTRAND. So what's it?

REGINE [*looks hard at him*]. What are you going to try and talk him into this time?

ENGSTRAND. Sh! Are you crazy? *Me* talk Pastor Manders into anything? Oh no, Pastor Manders has been far too good to me for *that*. But look, what I really wanted to talk to you about was me going back home again tonight.

REGINE. The sooner the better, as far as I'm concerned.

ENGSTRAND. Yes, but I want you to come with me, Regine.

REGINE [*open-mouthed*]. You want me to. . . . What did you say?

ENGSTRAND. I said I want you to come home with me.

REGINE [*scornfully*]. Not likely! You'll never get me coming home with you.

ENGSTRAND. Oh? We'll see about that.

REGINE. Yes, I'll say we will. *Me*? Who's been brought up here by a lady like Mrs. Alving . . . ? Who's been treated like one of the family, almost. . . ? Expect me to go home with you? To a place like that? Puh!

ENGSTRAND. What the devil. . . ? Setting yourself up against your own father, you little bitch?

REGINE [*mutters, without looking at him*]. Often enough you've said I wasn't any concern of yours.

ENGSTRAND. Huh! You are not going to bother your head about that. . . ?

REGINE. And what about all the times you've sworn at me and called me a . . . ? *Fi donc!*

ENGSTRAND. I'll be damned if I ever used such filthy language.

REGINE. Oh, I know well enough what language you used.

ENGSTRAND. Well, but only when I'd had a few . . . h'm. Many are the temptations of this world, Regine.

REGINE. Ugh!

ENGSTRAND. Or else when your mother started her nagging. I had to have something to get my own back on her, my girl. Always so stuck-up, she was. [*Mimics.*] 'Let me go, Engstrand. Let me be. I was three years in service at Rosenvold, with Chamberlain Alving, I was.' [*Laughs.*] My God! She couldn't ever forget that the captain was made a chamberlain while she was in service there.

REGINE. Poor mother! You drove her to her death the way you tormented her.

ENGSTRAND [*shrugs*]. Oh, that's right! Blame me for everything.

REGINE [*turns away, under her breath*]. Ugh! And then that leg!

ENGSTRAND. What's that you say, my girl?

REGINE. *Pied de mouton.*

ENGSTRAND. Is that English?

REGINE. Yes.

ENGSTRAND. Ah, you've learned quite a lot out here, and that might come in very handy now, Regine.

REGINE [*after a short silence*]. And what did you want with me in town?

ENGSTRAND. How can you ask what a father wants with his only child? I'm a lonely, deserted widower, aren't I?

REGINE. Oh, don't come that fiddle-faddle with me. What do you want me there for?

ENGSTRAND. Well, the thing is I've been thinking of going in for something new.

REGINE [*sneers*]. How many times haven't I heard *that* one before! But you always made a mess of it.

ENGSTRAND. Yes, but just you watch me this time, Regine! Damn me if . . .

REGINE [*stamps her foot*]. Stop that swearing!

ENGSTRAND. Sh! sh! You are right enough there, my girl! I just wanted to say this: I've saved quite a bit of money out of this Orph'anage job.

REGINE. Have you? How nice for you.

ENGSTRAND. Because what can you spend your money on, stuck out here in the country?

REGINE. What about it?

ENGSTRAND. Well, you see, I'd thought of putting the money into something worthwhile. A sort of hotel for seamen. . . .

REGINE. Ugh!

ENGSTRAND. A real classy hotel, I mean . . . not one of them cheap dumps for deckhands. By God, no! It'd be for captains and mates and . . . and real classy people, you know.

REGINE. And I'd have to . . . ?

ENGSTRAND. To lend a hand, that's right. Just help to look after the place, if you know what I mean. You wouldn't have such a hell of a lot to do, my girl. You could do pretty well what you liked.

REGINE. Oh, really!

ENGSTRAND. There has to be some women about the place, that's clear. Because we'd want a bit of fun in the evenings, singing and dancing and that sort of thing. These are seafaring men, you've got to remember, roaming the high seas. [*Comes closer.*] Now don't be such a fool as to stand in your own way, Regine. What can you do with yourself out here? Is it going to be any use to you, all this education the lady's lavished on you? You'll be looking after the children in the new Orphanage, they tell me. What sort of thing is that for a girl like you, eh? Are you all that keen on working your-self to death for the sake of a lot of dirty little brats?

REGINE. No, if things worked out as *I* wanted them to. . . . Well, it could happen. It could happen!

ENGSTRAND. What could happen?

REGINE. Never you mind. . . . Have you managed to put a lot of money by?

ENGSTRAND. What with one thing and another, it might be about seven or eight hundred crowns.

REGINE. Not bad.

ENGSTRAND. Enough to make a start with, my girl.

REGINE. You didn't think of giving me any of it?

ENGSTRAND. No, I'm damned if I did.

REGINE. Don't even think of sending me a bit of stuff for a dress?

ENGSTRAND. Come back to town with me, and you can have plenty of dresses.

REGINE. Puh, I can manage that on my own if I want.

ENGSTRAND. Ah, but it's better with a father's hand to guide you, Regine. I can get a nice little house that's going in Little Harbour Road. They're not asking a big deposit; and it could be a kind of Sailors' Home, see?

REGINE. But I don't *want* to come with *you*! I don't want anything to do with you. Now get away!

ENGSTRAND. I bet you damn well wouldn't stay very long with me, my girl. Not much chance of that. Not if you played your cards properly. Pretty little piece you've turned into, this last year or two. . . .

REGINE. Well. . . ?

ENGSTRAND. It wouldn't be long before some ship's officer would turn up . . . maybe even a captain. . . .

REGINE. I wouldn't marry anybody like that. Sailors have no *savoir vivre*.

ENGSTRAND. What's that they haven't got?

REGINE. I know what sailors are, let me tell you. No use marrying *them*.

ENGSTRAND. You don't have to marry them. It can still be worth your while. [*More confidentially.*] That Englishman, now . . . the one with the yacht . . . he paid three hundred dollars . . . and she wasn't any prettier than you.

REGINE [*going towards him*]. Get out!

ENGSTRAND [*retreating*]. Now, now, you wouldn't hit me, would you!

REGINE. Wouldn't I! You say one word about Mother, and I'll let you have it. Get out, I say! [*Drives him towards the door into the garden.*] And don't go slamming any doors. Young Mr. Alving. . .

ENGSTRAND. He's asleep, I know. You seem very concerned about this young Mr. Alving. [*Softly.*] Aha! It wouldn't be *him* . . . eh?

REGINE. Out, and quick about it! You're barmy, man! No, not that way. There's Pastor Manders coming. Down the back stairs.

ENGSTRAND [*towards the right*]. All right, I'm going. But you just have a talk with *him*, coming in there. *He's* the man to tell you what a child owes its father. Because after all I am your father, you know. I can prove it from the Parish Register.

[*He goes out through the other door which* REGINE *opens for him, and closes again after him.* REGINE *hastily looks at herself in the mirror, dabs herself with her handkerchief and straightens her collar; then she busies herself with the flowers.* PASTOR MANDERS, *in topcoat, carrying an umbrella and with a small satchel slung over his shoulder, enters the conservatory from the garden.*]

MANDERS. Good morning, Miss Engstrand.

REGINE [*turning round in glad surprise*]. Why it's Pastor Manders! Good morning, Pastor. Is the steamer in already?

MANDERS. Just arrived. [*He comes into the room.*] Miserable rainy weather we've been having lately.

REGINE [*following him*]. A blessing for the farmers, though, Pastor.

MANDERS. Ah, you are quite right. We townsfolk so rarely think of that. [*He begins to take off his topcoat.*]

REGINE. Oh, please let me help you. There! Goodness, how wet it is. I'll just hang it up in the hall. And your umbrella . . . I'll leave it up somewhere, so it can be drying.

[*She takes the things out through the second door, right.* PASTOR MANDERS *takes his satchel and lays it along with his hat on a chair. Meanwhile* REGINE *returns.*]

MANDERS. Ah, it's good to get indoors. And how are things out here? All right, I hope.

REGINE. Yes, thank you.

MANDERS. But pretty busy, I imagine, getting ready for tomorrow?

REGINE. Oh yes, there's plenty to do.

MANDERS. And Mrs. Alving is at home, I trust?

REGINE. Yes, of course. She's just upstairs seeing to some cocoa for Mr. Oswald.

MANDERS. Ah yes . . . I heard down at the quay that Oswald is supposed to have arrived.

REGINE. Yes, he came the day before yesterday. We hadn't been expecting him till today.

MANDERS. Fit and well, I hope?

REGINE. Yes, thank you, quite well. But horribly tired after his journey. He did the whole trip from Paris in one. . . . I mean he travelled all the way without a break. I think he's having a little sleep now, so perhaps we'd better talk just a little bit quieter.

MANDERS. Sh! We'll be very quiet.

REGINE [*moving an armchair into place beside the table*]. Do sit down, Pastor Manders, and make yourself comfortable. [*He sits down; she places a footstool under his feet.*] There now! Nice and comfortable?

MANDERS. Splendid, thank you. [*Looks at her.*] You know, Miss Engstrand, I do believe you've grown since I saw you last.

REGINE. Do you think so, Pastor? Mrs. Alving says I've also filled out.

MANDERS. Filled out? Oh, yes, a little perhaps . . . quite nicely.

[*Short pause.*]

REGINE. Should I go and tell Mrs. Alving?

MANDERS. Thank you, but there's no hurry, my dear. . . . Tell me, Regine, how is your father getting on out here?

REGINE. Fairly well, thank you, Pastor.

MANDERS. He looked in to see me last time he was in town.

REGINE. Did he? He's always glad to have a talk with you, Pastor.

MANDERS. And you run across and see him pretty regularly, I suppose?

REGINE. Me? Oh yes, I do, whenever I have a moment. . . .

MANDERS. Your father is not a particularly strong character, Miss Engstrand. He sorely needs a guiding hand.

REGINE. Oh yes, that's very likely.

MANDERS. He needs somebody near and dear to him to turn to, some-body whose judgement he respects. He admitted that himself quite frankly the last time he came to see me.

REGINE. Yes, he mentioned something of the kind to me too. But I don't know that Mrs. Alving would want to let me go . . . especially now we've got the new Orphanage to run. And then again, I would hate to leave Mrs. Alving, because she's always been so kind to me.

MANDERS. But a daughter's duty, my good girl. . . . Of course we'd have to get the consent of your mistress first.

REGINE. But I'm not sure it's quite the thing for me, at my age, to keep house for a single man.

MANDERS. What! But my dear Miss Engstrand, we happen to be talking about your own father.

REGINE. Yes, that may be, but all the same. . . . Now, if it was in a *good* house with a proper gentleman . . .

MANDERS. But my dear Regine. . . .

REGINE. . . . Somebody I could feel affection and respect for, and be a sort of daughter to . . .

MANDERS. Yes, but my dear, good child . . .

REGINE. Then I should be quite happy to go back to town. It's awfully lonely out here . . . and you know well enough yourself, Pastor, what it's like to be alone in the world. And I think I can honestly say I'm both willing and able. You don't know of any place like that for me, Pastor, do you?

MANDERS. Who, me? No, to be quite honest, I don't.

REGINE. But dear, dear Pastor Manders . . . you will think of me, won't you, if ever . . .

MANDERS [*gets up*]. Yes, that I will, Miss Engstrand.

REGINE. Because if I . . .

MANDERS. Would you be so kind as to fetch Mrs. Alving?

REGINE. I'll see to it at once, Pastor.

[REGINE *goes out, left.* PASTOR MANDERS *walks up and down the room a few times, stands at the back of the room for a moment with his hands clasped behind his back, looking out at the garden. Then he again comes back near the table, picks up a book and looks at the title page; he gives a start and looks at several more.*]

MANDERS. H'm! Indeed!

[MRS. ALVING *enters through the door, left. She is followed by* REGINE *who immediately goes off again, right.*]

MRS. ALVING [*holds out her hand*]. Welcome, Pastor.

MANDERS. Good morning, Mrs. Alving. Here I am, just as I promised.

MRS. ALVING. Punctual, as ever.

MANDERS. But it wasn't easy getting away, believe me. All these blessed committees and things I've been put on. . . .

MRS. ALVING. All the nicer of you to come so promptly. Now we can get our business settled before dinner. But where's your suitcase?

MANDERS [*hurriedly*]. I left my things down at the store. I'll stay there tonight.

MRS. ALVING [*suppressing a smile*]. Can't you be persuaded even yet to stay the night in my house?

MANDERS. No, no, Mrs. Alving, thanks all the same. I'll stay down there again as usual. It's so handy for catching the boat.

MRS. ALVING. Well, have it your own way. All the same, I really do think a couple of old things like us. . . .

MANDERS. Dear me, you will have your little joke, won't you? Well, of course you must be feeling extremely pleased with yourself today. First the celebrations tomorrow, and then having Oswald at home.

MRS. ALVING. Yes, just fancy! Isn't it marvellous! It's more than two years since he was last home. Now he's promised to stay with me the whole winter.

MANDERS. Has he now? There's a nice dutiful son for you. Because I imagine the attractions of living in Rome or Paris are altogether different.

MRS. ALVING. Yes, but you see here at home he has his mother. Ah, my dear, darling boy . . . he still has a soft spot for his mother!

MANDERS. I must say it would be a sad thing if leaving home and taking up Art and all that interfered with his natural feelings.

MRS. ALVING. Ah, it's right what you say. But there isn't any danger of that with him, no really there isn't. It will be fun to see if you recognize him again. He'll be coming down later. He's just upstairs having a little rest on the sofa. But do sit down, my dear Pastor.

MANDERS. Thank you. You are sure it's quite convenient. . . ?

MRS. ALVING. Yes, of course it is.

[*She sits down at the table.*]

MANDERS. Good. Let's see then. . . . [*He goes over to the chair on which his satchel is lying, takes a sheaf of papers out of it, sits down at the opposite side of the table and looks for a clear space to put his papers down.*] First of all we have . . . [*Breaking off.*] Tell me, Mrs. Alving, how did *these* books get *here*?

MRS. ALVING. These books? They are books *I* am reading.

MANDERS. You read that sort of thing?

MRS. ALVING. Of course I do.

MANDERS. Do you think reading that sort of thing makes you feel any better, or any happier?

MRS. ALVING. I feel, as it were, more confident.

MANDERS. Strange. How?

MRS. ALVING. Well, I find it seems to explain and confirm a lot of the things I had been thinking myself. That's the strange thing, Pastor Manders . . . there's really nothing new in these books; there's nothing there but what most people think and believe already. It's just that most people either haven't really considered these things, or won't admit them.

MANDERS. Good God! Do you seriously believe that most people . . . ?

MRS. ALVING. Yes, I do.

MANDERS. Yes, but surely not in this country? Not here?

MRS. ALVING. Oh yes, here too.

MANDERS. Well, I must say. . . !

MRS. ALVING. Anyway, what is it in fact you've got against these books?

MANDERS. Got against them? You don't think I waste my time examining publications of that kind, surely?

MRS. ALVING. Which means you know absolutely nothing about what you are condemning?

MANDERS. I have read sufficient about these publications to disapprove of them.

MRS. ALVING. Yes, but your own personal opinion. . . .

MANDERS. My dear lady, there are many occasions in life when one must rely on others. That's the way of the world, and things are best that way. How else would society manage?

MRS. ALVING. Well, you may be right.

MANDERS. Not that I want to deny, of course, that these books can have a considerable fascination. Nor can I blame you for wanting to get to know something about the new trends of thought which, so they tell me, are current in the great world outside—that world in which you have allowed your son so much rein for so long. But . . .

MRS. ALVING. But . . . ?

MANDERS [*lowering his voice*]. But one doesn't talk about it, Mrs. Alving. One doesn't have to account to all and sundry for what one reads and thinks in the privacy of one's own room.

MRS. ALVING. No, of course not. I quite agree.

MANDERS. Think for a moment of the responsibilities you have towards this Orphanage. You decided to found it at a time when your opinions and beliefs were very different from what they are now—as far as *I* can judge, anyway.

MRS. ALVING. Yes, yes, I quite admit that. But about the Orphanage. . . .

MANDERS. That's right, we were going to discuss the Orphanage. Still . . . caution, dear lady! Now let's get down to business. [*Opens an envelope and takes some papers out.*] You see these?

MRS. ALVING. The deeds?

MANDERS. Complete, and in order. It wasn't easy getting them ready in time, believe me. I had to bring a certain amount of pressure to bear. The authorities are painfully conscientious when it comes to drawing up agreements. But anyway, here they are. [*He turns over the papers.*] Here is the deed of conveyance for the site known as Solvik, being part of the Rosenvold estate, together with the buildings newly erected thereon, the school, the school house and the chapel. And here is the authorization for the bequest and for the regulations of the institution. Would you like to see.... [*Reads.*] Regulations for the Captain Alving Memorial Home.

MRS. ALVING [*looks long at the paper*]. So there it is.

MANDERS. I chose 'Captain' rather than 'Chamberlain' for the name. 'Captain' looks less ostentatious.

MRS. ALVING. Yes, just as you think best.

MANDERS. And in this Bank Book you have details of the capital sum, the interest on which is to cover the running expenses of the Orphanage.

MRS. ALVING. Thank you. But it would be a great convenience if you would please hold on to them.

MANDERS. With pleasure. I think we'll leave the money in the bank for the time being. The interest isn't very attractive, it's true—four per cent. at six months' notice. If in time we could find some good mortgage investment . . . a first mortgage it would have to be, of course, and absolutely sound . . . then we could discuss the thing again in more detail.

MRS. ALVING. Yes, yes, dear Pastor Manders, you know best about these things.

MANDERS. Anyway, I'll keep my eyes open. . . . But there's just one other thing I've been meaning to ask you several times.

MRS. ALVING. And what is that?

MANDERS. Are the Orphanage buildings to be insured or not?

MRS. ALVING. Yes, of course they must be insured.

MANDERS. Ah, but wait a moment Mrs. Alving. Let's examine this matter more closely.

MRS. ALVING. I keep everything insured—the buildings, the contents, the crops and the stock.

MANDERS. Naturally. On your own property. I do the same . . . of course. But this is quite a different thing, you see. The Orphanage is, as it were, to be dedicated to a higher purpose.

MRS. ALVING. Yes, but . . .

MANDERS. As for me personally, I don't honestly see anything objectionable in covering ourselves against all possible contingencies...

MRS. ALVING. Nor do I.

MANDERS. ... but what about the people round here, how would they react? That's something you know better than I.

MRS. ALVING. H'm, people's reactions. ...

MANDERS. Would there be any considerable body of responsible opinion—really responsible opinion—that might take exception to it?

MRS. ALVING. Well, what actually is it you mean by responsible opinion?

MANDERS. I'm thinking principally of men in independent and influential positions of the kind that makes it difficult not to attach a certain importance to their opinions.

MRS. ALVING. Oh, there are plenty here of the kind that might very easily take exception if ...

MANDERS. Well, there you are! In town we have plenty of that kind. You've only got to think of all those who support my colleague! It would be so terribly easy to interpret things as meaning that neither you nor I had a proper faith in Divine Providence.

MRS. ALVING. But as far as you are concerned, my dear Pastor, you know perfectly well yourself. ...

MANDERS. Yes, I know, I know ... my conscience is clear, that's true enough. But all the same, we might not be able to stop people from seriously misrepresenting us. And that in turn might well have an inhibiting effect on the activities of the Orphanage.

MRS. ALVING. Well, if *that* were to be the case ...

MANDERS. Nor can I altogether disregard the difficult ... I might well call it painful position, I might conceivably find myself in. All the influential people in town have been talking about this Orphanage. It's partly intended to benefit the town, of course, and people are hoping it will help considerably towards reducing the burden on the rates. But since I have acted as your adviser and looked after the business side of things, I rather fear the more zealous ones would turn on *me* in the first place. . . .

MRS. ALVING. Yes, that risk you mustn't run.

MANDERS. To say nothing of the attacks that would undoubtedly be made on me in certain papers and periodicals. . . .

MRS. ALVING. You've said enough, my dear Pastor Manders. That settles it.

MANDERS. So you don't want any insurance?

MRS. ALVING. No, we'll let it go.

MANDERS [*leaning back in his chair*]. But if there did happen to be an accident? You never know . . . would you be able to make good the damage?

MRS. ALVING. No, I can tell you straight, I wouldn't.

MANDERS. Well, you know, Mrs. Alving . . . this is really a grave responsibility we are taking upon ourselves.

MRS. ALVING. But *can* we do anything else, do you think?

MANDERS. No, that's just it. In fact, we *can't*. We mustn't run the risk of giving people the wrong impression; and mustn't at any cost give offence to the general public.

MRS. ALVING. You mustn't anyway, a clergyman.

MANDERS. And really I think we may assume that an institution of this kind will have luck on its side . . . indeed that it will enjoy a very special measure of protection.

MRS. ALVING. Let us hope so, Pastor Manders.

MANDERS. So we leave things as they are?

MRS. ALVING. Yes, certainly.

MANDERS. Good. Just as you wish. [*Notes down.*] Well, then—no insurance.

MRS. ALVING. Incidentally, it's odd you should happen to mention this today . . .

MANDERS. I had often thought of asking you about it. . . .

MRS. ALVING. . . . because yesterday we nearly had a fire down there.

MANDERS. What!

MRS. ALVING. Well, it wasn't anything very much. Some shavings caught fire in the carpenter's shop.

MANDERS. Where Engstrand works?

MRS. ALVING. Yes. They say he's sometimes rather careless with matches.

MANDERS. He has a lot on his mind, that man . . . all sorts of worries. From what I hear, he's trying very hard to turn over a new leaf, thank God.

MRS. ALVING. Oh? Who told you that?

MANDERS. He told me so himself. He's a good workman, too.

MRS. ALVING. Oh yes, when he's sober.

MANDERS. Ah, it's sad, that failing of his! He says he's very often driven to it because of his bad leg. The last time he was in town, I really felt very touched. He came and thanked me so sincerely for getting him this work here, so he could be beside Regine.

MRS. ALVING. He doesn't see much of her.

MANDERS. Oh yes. He has a word with her every day, he told me so himself.

MRS. ALVING. Oh well, it could be.

MANDERS. He feels he needs somebody to stand by him when temptation comes along. *That's* what is so likeable about Jacob Engstrand— the fact that he comes along so helplessly, so full of self-reproach, to confess his failings. The last time he looked in to see me. . . . Look, Mrs. Alving, suppose he desperately needed Regine back home with him again . . .

MRS. ALVING [*rises quickly*]. Regine!

MANDERS. . . . *You* mustn't try to prevent it.

MRS. ALVING. I will. I most certainly will try to prevent it. Anyway
. . . Regine is going to work in the Orphanage.

MANDERS. But remember, he *is* her father. . . .

MRS. ALVING. Oh, I know best what sort of a father he's been to her.
No, she's not going back to him if I can help it.

MANDERS [*rises*]. But dear Mrs. Alving, you mustn't get so worked-
up about it. It's sad the way you misjudge poor Engstrand. It's almost
as though you were terrified. . . .

MRS. ALVING [*calmer*]. That's as may be. I have taken Regine into my
house and in my house she shall remain. [*Listens.*] Sh! my dear Pastor
Manders, I don't want to hear any more about it. [*Her face lights up
with joy.*] Listen! There's Oswald coming downstairs. Let's think
about *him* now.

[OSWALD ALVING *enters by the door, left; he has on a light overcoat,
carries his hat in his hand, and is smoking a large Meerschaum pipe.*]

OSWALD [*remains standing in the doorway*]. Oh, I beg your pardon . . .
I thought you were in the study. [*Comes forward.*] Good morning,
Pastor.

MANDERS [*staring*]. Ah . . . ! Astounding . . . !

MRS. ALVING. Well, what have you got to say about him *now*, Pastor
Manders.

MANDERS. I say . . . I say . . . But is it really . . . ?

OSWALD. Yes, it really is the Prodigal Son, Pastor.

MANDERS. But my dear young friend. . . .

OSWALD. Well, the exile returned, then.

MRS. ALVING. Oswald is thinking of the time when you were so very
much against the idea of his becoming an artist.

MANDERS. Some decisions often seem to mortal view unwise at the
time, but later. . . . [*Shakes his hand.*] Welcome, welcome! Really,
my dear Oswald . . . I can call you Oswald, can't I?

OSWALD. What else would you call me?

MANDERS. Good. What I wanted to say, my dear Oswald, was *this*— you mustn't think I want to condemn out of hand all artists and their ways. I assume there are many who can still preserve some integrity of soul even in their circumstances.

OSWALD. We must hope so.

MRS. ALVING [*beaming with pleasure*]. I know one who has preserved his integrity, both of soul and of body. Just look at him, Pastor Manders.

OSWALD [*pacing up and down*]. Mother dear, please. . . !

MANDERS. Oh, indubitably . . . nobody will deny that. And already you've begun to make a name for yourself. There have often been things in the paper about you, and extremely favourable too. Well that is . . . I believe things seem to have fallen off a bit of late.

OSWALD [*near the conservatory*]. I haven't been doing much painting lately.

MRS. ALVING. Even an artist must rest now and again.

MANDERS. I can well imagine that. Then he gathers strength in preparation for something big.

OSWALD. Yes. . . . Mother, how soon will dinner be ready?

MRS. ALVING. In just half an hour. He's got a good appetite, thank God.

MANDERS. And a taste for tobacco, too.

OSWALD. I found Father's pipe in the little room upstairs, and . . .

MANDERS. Aha! So that was it!

MRS. ALVING. What?

MANDERS. When Oswald was standing there in the door, with that pipe in his mouth, he looked the very spit and image of his father.

OSWALD. Really?

MRS. ALVING. How can you say that! Oswald takes after me.

MANDERS. Yes, but there's something about the corners of the mouth, something about the lips, that reminds one exactly of Alving . . . at least when he is smoking.

MRS. ALVING. Not at all. Oswald is much more like a clergyman about the mouth, I would say.

MANDERS. Yes, yes, quite a lot of my colleagues have a similar expression.

MRS. ALVING. But put that pipe away now, my dear boy. I don't want smoke in here.

OSWALD [*does so*]. Certainly. I just wanted to try it. Because I smoked it once before, as a child.

MRS. ALVING. You?

OSWALD. Yes. I was quite small at the time. And I remember I went up to Father's room one evening when he was feeling rather pleased with himself.

MRS. ALVING. You can't remember anything of those years.

OSWALD. I can. I distinctly remember he sat me on his knee and gave me the pipe to smoke. 'Smoke, lad,' he said, 'go on, lad, smoke!' And I smoked as hard as I could, till I felt I was going quite pale and great beads of sweat stood out on my forehead. Then he roared with laughter. . . .

MANDERS. Most extraordinary!

MRS. ALVING. My dear Pastor, it's only something Oswald has dreamt.

OSWALD. No, Mother, I certainly didn't dream it. Because—don't you remember—you came in and carried me off to the nursery. Then I was sick, and I saw you were crying. . . . Did Father often play tricks like that?

MANDERS. When he was young, he was always full of the joys of living. . . .

OSWALD. And still managed to accomplish such a lot in life. So much that was good and useful, though he wasn't very old when he died.

MANDERS. Yes, you certainly bear the name of a fine, enterprising man, my dear Oswald Alving. I trust it will be an incentive to you. . . .

OSWALD. Yes, it ought to be.

MANDERS. It was nice of you to come home for these celebrations in his honour.

OSWALD. That's the least I could do for Father.

MRS. ALVING. The really nice thing is that he is letting me keep him here a while.

MANDERS. You are going to be at home over the winter, I hear.

OSWALD. I'm going to be at home indefinitely, Pastor. . . . Ah, it *is* nice to be home again.

MRS. ALVING [*beaming*]. Yes, isn't it, Oswald?

MANDERS [*looking sympathetically at him*]. You left home at a very early age, my dear Oswald.

OSWALD. I did. Sometimes I wonder whether it wasn't *too* early.

MRS. ALVING. Not at all. It's a good thing for a bright lad. Especially when he's an only child. You don't want him staying at home with his mother and father getting spoilt.

MANDERS. That's a very moot point, Mrs. Alving. A child's proper place is and must be the home.

OSWALD. I rather think I agree with the pastor there.

MANDERS. Look at your own son. There's no reason why we shouldn't talk about it in front of him. What has been the result in his case? There he is—twenty-six, twenty-seven years old, and never had an opportunity of knowing what a proper home is like.

OSWALD. I beg your pardon, Pastor . . . you are quite wrong there.

MANDERS. Oh? I thought you had been moving more or less exclusively in artistic circles.

OSWALD. I have.

MANDERS. And mostly among the younger artists.

OSWALD. Yes.

MANDERS. But I thought most of those people couldn't afford to set up a home and start a family.

OSWALD. Plenty of them can't afford to get married, Pastor Manders.

MANDERS. Yes. That's what I am saying.

OSWALD. Yet they can still have a home. And some of them *do*. And very proper and very comfortable homes they are.

[MRS. ALVING *follows with close attention, and nods but says nothing.*]

MANDERS. But I'm not talking about bachelor establishments. By 'home' I mean a place for a family, where a man lives with his wife and children.

OSWALD. Yes, or with his children and his children's mother.

MANDERS [*startled, clasps his hands*]. Good heavens!

OSWALD. Well?

MANDERS. Live with his children's mother!

OSWALD. Well, would you rather he abandoned his children's mother?

MANDERS. So it's illicit relationships you are talking about. These so-called sham marriages!

OSWALD. I have never noticed anything particularly sham about these people's lives together.

MANDERS. But how is it possible for any young man or woman with . . . with the slightest sense of decency to consent to live in that fashion . . . openly, for all the world to see!

OSWALD. But what are they to do? A poor young artist . . . a poor girl. . . . It costs money to get married. What are they to do?

MANDERS. What are they to do? Yes, Mr. Alving, I'll tell you what they are to do. They should have kept away from each other from the very start—that's what they should have done!

OSWALD. That kind of talk won't get you very far with eager young people in love.

MRS. ALVING. No, that won't get you very far!

MANDERS [*continuing*]. To think the authorities tolerate such things! That this sort of thing goes on openly! [*Facing* MRS. ALVING.] Hadn't I good reason to be so deeply concerned about your son? Moving in circles where blatant immorality is rampant, where it's even become the accepted thing. . . .

OSWALD. I'll tell you something, Pastor Manders. I have been a regular Sunday visitor in some of these unconventional homes. . . .

MANDERS. On Sundays, even!

OSWALD. Yes, surely that's when people should enjoy themselves? But never have I heard one word that could give offence, let alone seen anything that could be called immoral. No, do you know where and when I *have* encountered immorality in artistic circles?

MANDERS. No, thank God!

OSWALD. Well then, permit me to tell you. When some of our model husbands and fathers took themselves a trip to Paris to have a look round on the loose . . . and condescended to drop in on the artists in their modest haunts, that's when I've met it. Then we got to know what was what. These gentlemen were able to tell us about places and things we'd never even dreamt of.

MANDERS. What? Are you insinuating that respectable men from this country would . . . ?

OSWALD. Have you never heard these respectable men when they get home again? Never heard them holding forth about the outrageous immorality that's to be found abroad?

MANDERS. Yes, of course. . . .

MRS. ALVING. I have too.

OSWALD. Well, you can believe every word they say. Some of them are experts. [*Clutching his head.*] Oh, when I think of that glorious, free life out there . . . smeared by this filth.

MRS. ALVING. You mustn't excite yourself, Oswald. It's not good for you.

OSWALD. Yes, you are right, Mother. It's bad for my health. It's this confounded tiredness, you know. Well, I'll take a little walk before dinner. Forgive me, Pastor Manders, I know you can't agree with all this. But I just had to say it.

[*He goes out through the second door, right.*]

MRS. ALVING. My poor boy. . . !

MANDERS. Yes, you may well say so. So this is what he's come to. [MRS. ALVING *looks at him in silence.* MANDERS *walks up and down.*] He called himself the Prodigal Son. Alas . . . it's true! [MRS. ALVING *continues to look at him.*] And what do you say to all this?

MRS. ALVING. I say Oswald was right in every single word he said.

MANDERS [*stops short*]. Right! Right! To have standards like that!

MRS. ALVING. Living here alone, I have come round to the same way of thinking myself, Pastor Manders. But I've never had the courage to say so. All right, now my boy shall speak for me.

MANDERS. Then you are greatly to be pitied, Mrs. Alving. But now I have something very serious to say to you. No longer as your business executor and adviser, nor even as you and your husband's life-long friend do I stand before you now. It is as your priest, standing now as he stood once before at that most critical moment of your life.

MRS. ALVING. And what does my priest have to say to me?

MANDERS. Let me first refresh your memory, Mrs. Alving. The time is well chosen. Tomorrow is the tenth anniversary of your husband's death. Tomorrow a memorial is to be unveiled in his honour. Tomorrow I shall address the assembled company. But today I want to speak to you alone.

MRS. ALVING. Very well, Pastor Manders. Go on!

MANDERS. You remember how, after little more than a year of married life, you stood on the very brink of disaster? How you left house and home. . . . How you ran away from your husband. . . . Yes, Mrs. Alving, ran away, and refused to go back to him, no matter how much he begged and pleaded?

MRS. ALVING. Have you forgotten how utterly miserable I felt that first year?

MANDERS. All this demanding to be happy in life, it's all part of this same wanton idea. What right have people to happiness? No, we have our duty to do, Mrs. Alving! And your duty was to stand by the man you had chosen, and to whom you were bound by sacred ties.

MRS. ALVING. You know very well what sort of life my husband was living in those days, the excesses he committed.

MANDERS. I know quite well the rumours that were going about. And I would be the last person to condone his conduct as a young man, assuming these rumours told the truth. But it is not a wife's place to sit in judgement on her husband. Your duty should have been to bear with humility that cross which a higher power had judged proper for you. But instead you have the effrontery to cast away the cross, you abandon the man whose stumbling steps you should have guided, you go and risk your own good name, and . . . very nearly jeopardize other people's reputations into the bargain.

MRS. ALVING. Other people's? *One* other person's, you mean?

MANDERS. It was extremely inconsiderate of you to seek refuge with *me*.

MRS. ALVING. With our priest? With our close friend?

MANDERS. Precisely for that reason. . . . Yes, you should thank God I possessed the necessary strength of mind . . . that I managed to dissuade you from your hysterical intentions, and that it was granted to me to lead you back into the path of duty, and home to your lawful husband.

MRS. ALVING. Yes, Pastor Manders, that certainly was your doing.

MANDERS. I was only the humble instrument of a higher power. And the fact that I made you return to the path of duty and obedience, hasn't that proved a tremendous blessing to you ever since? Didn't things go just as I had prophesied? Didn't Alving turn his back on his profligate ways, as a decent man should? And didn't he, from then on, live a quite irreproachable and affectionate life with you for the rest of his days? Didn't he become a great benefactor to this district? And didn't he help and encourage you, so much that you eventually came to collaborate with him in all his enterprises? And a very efficient helpmate you were, too. . . . Oh, I know that, Mrs. Alving. Credit where credit is due. . . . But then I come to the next big mistake in your life.

MRS. ALVING. What do you mean?

MANDERS. Just as you once denied your duty as a wife, you have since denied it as a mother.

MRS. ALVING. Ah. . . !

MANDERS. All your life, you've always been quite disastrously selfish and stubborn. In everything you have done, you have tended to be headstrong and undisciplined. Never would you tolerate any kind of restraint. Anything that became an encumbrance to you in your life, you had no scruples or hesitations about throwing it off, as though it were a burden you could dispose of as and when you pleased. It didn't suit you any longer to be a wife, so you left your husband. You found it irksome being a mother, so you put your child out with strangers.

MRS. ALVING. Yes, that's true. I did do that.

MANDERS. With the result that you are now a stranger to him.

MRS. ALVING. No, no, I'm not!

MANDERS. You are! You must be! And what is he like, now you've got him back? Stop and think, Mrs. Alving. You did your husband great wrong—the fact that you are raising this memorial to him shows you recognize that. You should also recognize the wrong you have done your son. There may still be time to lead him back from the paths of iniquity. Turn back yourself, and save what can perhaps still be saved in him. Because, Mrs. Alving [*with raised forefinger*], you are in truth a very guilty mother. . . . I see it as my duty to tell you this.

[*Silence.*]

MRS. ALVING [*slowly, and with control*]. You have had your say, Pastor Manders. And tomorrow you will make a speech in my husband's memory. I shall not speak tomorrow. But now I'm going to talk to you just as you have talked to me.

MANDERS. Of course, you want to make excuses for what you did. . . .

MRS. ALVING. No. I just want to tell you something.

MANDERS. Well?

MRS. ALVING. None of these things you have been saying about my husband and me and our life together after you had led me back to the path of duty, as you put it—absolutely none of these things do you know from first-hand. From that moment on, you—our closest friend, who regularly used to call every day—you never once set foot in our house.

MANDERS. You and your husband moved out of town immediately afterwards.

MRS. ALVING. Yes. And never once while my husband was alive did you come and see us. It was business that finally forced you to come and visit me, when you had to see about the Orphanage.

MANDERS [*in a low, uncertain voice*]. Helene, if this is meant as a reproach, I must ask you to bear in mind . . .

MRS. ALVING. . . . the consideration you owed to your position. Oh, yes! Also that I was a runaway wife. One can never be too careful where such reckless women are concerned.

MANDERS. My dear . . . Mrs. Alving, that is a gross exaggeration. . . .

MRS. ALVING. All right, all right. I just wanted to say *this*: that when you pass judgement on my married life, you are simply taking it for granted that popular opinion is right.

MANDERS. Well? What then?

MRS. ALVING. But now, Pastor Manders, now I'm going to tell you the truth. I swore to myself that one day you should know. You and you alone!

MANDERS. And what is the truth, then?

MRS. ALVING. The truth is this: my husband was just as debauched when he died as he had been all his life.

MANDERS [*fumbling for a chair*]. What did you say?

MRS. ALVING. After nineteen years of marriage, just as debauched—in his pleasures, at any rate—as he was before you married us.

MANDERS. Those youthful indiscretions . . . those irregularities . . . excesses, if you like . . . you call that a debauched life!

MRS. ALVING. That was the expression our doctor used.

MANDERS. I don't understand you.

MRS. ALVING. Nor is it necessary.

MANDERS. I feel quite dazed. Am I to believe that your entire married life . . . all those years together with your husband . . . were nothing but a façade.

MRS. ALVING. Precisely that. Now you know.

MANDERS. This is something . . . I find very hard to accept. I just don't understand. It's beyond me. How was it possible. . . ? How could a thing like that be kept hidden?

MRS. ALVING. That was the endless battle I fought, day after day. When we had Oswald, I rather thought Alving improved a little. But it didn't last long. And then I had to battle twice as hard, fight tooth and nail to prevent anybody from knowing what sort of person my child's father was. And you know, of course, how charming Alving could be. Nobody could believe anything but good of him. He was one of those people whose reputation is proof against anything they may do. But then, Pastor Manders . . . something else you must know . . . then came the most hideous thing of all.

MANDERS. More hideous than this?

MRS. ALVING. I put up with things, although I knew very well what was going on in secret outside this house. But when it came to scandal within these very walls. . . .

MANDERS. What's that you say! Here!

MRS. ALVING. Yes, here in our own home. In there [*points to the first door right*] in the dining-room, that's where I first got wind of it. I was doing something in there, and the door was standing ajar. Then I heard our maid come in from the garden with some water for the plants over there.

MANDERS. Well. . . ?

MRS. ALVING. Shortly afterwards I heard my husband come in, too. I heard him say something to her in a low voice. And then I heard. . . . [*With a short laugh.*] Oh, I can still hear it, so devastating and yet at the time so ludicrous . . . I heard my own maid whisper: 'Let me go, Mr. Alving! Leave me alone!'

MANDERS. How unseemly! How indiscreet of him! But I'm sure it was no more than an indiscretion, Mrs. Alving, please believe me.

MRS. ALVING. I soon knew what to believe. My husband had his way
with the girl. . . . And *that* affair had its consequences, Pastor
Manders.

MANDERS [*as though stunned*]. And all that in this very house! In this
house!

MRS. ALVING. I had to put up with a lot in this house. To keep him at
home in the evenings . . . and at nights . . . I had to join him in secret
drinking orgies up in his room. I had to sit there with him, just the
two of us drinking, and listen to his obscene, stupid remarks, and
then struggling with him to get him dragged into his bed. . . .

MANDERS [*shaken*]. How could you bear it?

MRS. ALVING. I had to bear it for the sake of my little boy. But then
came that final humiliation when my own servant girl . . . Then
I swore to myself that this would have to stop! So I took control in
the house . . . complete control . . . over him and everything else.
Because now I had a weapon against him, you see, and he didn't dare
say anything. That was the time Oswald was sent away. He was
getting on for seven, and beginning to notice things and ask questions, as children do. That was something I couldn't bear. I felt the
child would somehow be poisoned simply by breathing the foul air
of this polluted house. That was why I sent him away. And now
you understand why he was never allowed to set foot in this place
as long as his father was alive. Nobody knows what that cost me.

MANDERS. What a terrible ordeal for you.

MRS. ALVING. I'd never have stood it if it hadn't been for my work.
And I think I can say I have worked! The extensions to the estate,
the improvements, all those useful innovations Alving got the credit
for—do you imagine he was capable of anything like that? *Him*,
sprawling there all day long on the sofa reading an old government
gazette! No. And I will tell you this as well: I was the one who
urged him on when he had his occasional more lucid intervals; and
it was I who was left to run everything when he started kicking
over the traces again, or lapsed into moaning and self-pity.

MANDERS. And this is the man you are raising a memorial to.

MRS. ALVING. Such is the power of a bad conscience.

MANDERS. Bad. . . ? What do you mean?

MRS. ALVING. I was obsessed by the thought that inevitably the truth must come out sometime and be believed. So the Orphanage was meant as it were to kill any rumours, and sweep away any misgivings.

MANDERS. I must say you haven't failed in that respect, Mrs. Alving.

MRS. ALVING. There was also one other reason. I didn't want Oswald, my son, to inherit a single thing from his father.

MANDERS. So it's Alving's money that . . . ?

MRS. ALVING. Yes. The money I have donated, year by year, to this Orphanage adds up exactly—and I've calculated it very carefully— exactly to the amount that made Lieutenant Alving such a good match in his day.

MANDERS. I don't understand. . . .

MRS. ALVING. That was my purchase price . . . I don't want any of that money to pass to Oswald. Anything my son gets is to come from me, and that's that.

[OSWALD ALVING *enters through the second door, right; he has taken off his hat and coat outside.*]

MRS. ALVING [*going towards him*]. Back already? My dear, dear boy!

OSWALD. Yes, what can you do outside in this everlasting rain? But I hear dinner's ready. Splendid!

REGINE [*with a parcel, from the dining-room*]. A parcel's come for you, Mrs. Alving.

[*She hands it to her.*]

MRS. ALVING [*with a glance at* PASTOR MANDERS]. The song sheets for tomorrow, presumably.

MANDERS. H'm. . . .

REGINE. And dinner is served.

MRS. ALVING. Good. We'll be there in a moment. I just want to. . .

[*She begins to open the parcel.*]

REGINE [*to* OSWALD]. Would Mr. Alving like white or red wine?

OSWALD. Both, please, Miss Engstrand.

REGINE. *Bien.* . . . Very good, Mr. Alving.

[*She goes into the dining-room.*]

OSWALD. I may as well help to draw the corks. . . .

[*He also goes into the dining-room; the door swings half open after him.*]

MRS. ALVING [*who has opened the parcel*]. Yes, quite right. Here are the song sheets, Pastor Manders.

MANDERS [*with folded hands*]. How I shall ever have the face to give my speech tomorrow . . . !

MRS. ALVING. Oh, you'll manage it somehow.

MANDERS [*in a low voice, so as not to be heard in the dining-room*]. Yes, we mustn't have any scandal, of course.

MRS. ALVING [*quietly but firmly*]. No. But *then* this long, ghastly farce will be over. After tomorrow I shall feel as though that man had never lived in this house. There'll be nobody else here but my son and his mother.

[*From the dining-room comes the sound of a chair being overturned; simultaneously a voice is heard.*]

REGINE'S VOICE [*in a sharp whisper*]. Oswald! Are you mad? Let me go!

MRS. ALVING [*stiffening with horror*]. Ah. . . !

[*She stares wild-eyed towards the half-open door.* OSWALD *can be heard coughing and humming. A bottle is uncorked.*]

MANDERS [*agitated*]. What on earth was that! What's the matter, Mrs. Alving?

MRS. ALVING [*hoarsely*]. Ghosts! Those two in the conservatory . . . come back to haunt us.

MANDERS. What do you say! Regine. . . ? Is *she* . . . ?

MRS. ALVING. Yes. Come. Not a word. . . !

[*She grips* PASTOR MANDERS *by the arm and walks unsteadily towards the dining-room.*]

ACT TWO

The same room. A heavy mist still lies over the landscape. PASTOR
MANDERS *and* MRS. ALVING *come out of the dining-room.*

MRS. ALVING [*still in the doorway*]. Kind of you to say so, Pastor.
[*Calling into the dining-room.*] Aren't you coming, Oswald?

OSWALD [*within*]. No, thank you. I think I'll go out for a bit.

MRS. ALVING. Yes, do. It's a little clearer now. [*She shuts the dining-room door, walks over to the hall door, and calls.*] Regine!

REGINE [*outside*]. Yes, Mrs. Alving?

MRS. ALVING. Go and help with the decorations down in the ironing room.

REGINE. Yes, Mrs. Alving.

[MRS. ALVING *assures herself that* REGINE *is going, then she shuts the door.*]

MANDERS. I suppose he can't hear anything in there?

MRS. ALVING. Not when the door is shut. Anyway, he's going out.

MANDERS. I'm still quite bewildered. How I managed to swallow a single bite of that excellent dinner, I don't know.

MRS. ALVING [*controlling her agitation, walking up and down*]. Nor I. But what's to be done?

MANDERS. Yes, what's to be done? I'm blessed if I know. I'm completely inexperienced in matters of this kind.

MRS. ALVING. I'm convinced nothing disastrous has happened yet.

MANDERS. No, God forbid. But it's a most unfortunate state of affairs, all the same.

MRS. ALVING. The whole thing's only a passing fancy of Oswald's, you can be sure.

MANDERS. Well, as I said, I'm not very well up in these things. But I cannot help feeling. . .

MRS. ALVING. Of course, we must get her out of the house. Immediately. That's quite clear. . . .

MANDERS. Naturally.

MRS. ALVING. But where to? We can't very well. . . .

MANDERS. Where to? Home to her father, of course.

MRS. ALVING. To whom did you say?

MANDERS. To her. . . . Ah, but of course Engstrand isn't. . . . Good heavens, Mrs. Alving, this can't be possible? You must be mistaken, surely?

MRS. ALVING. I'm afraid there's no mistake. Johanna had to confess everything to me, and Alving couldn't deny it. There was nothing else we could do but get the thing hushed up.

MANDERS. I suppose there was nothing else for it.

MRS. ALVING. The girl left at once, and she was given quite a fair amount to keep her mouth shut. The rest she managed for herself when she got to town. She took up with Engstrand again and I dare say dropped a few hints about how much money she had, and told him a tale about some foreigner who was supposed to have put in here that summer with his yacht. So she and Engstrand got married, all in a great hurry. Why, you married them yourself.

MANDERS. But what am I to make of . . . ? I distinctly remember Engstrand coming to arrange about the wedding. He was quite abject, and full of remorse about the foolish thing he and the girl had done.

MRS. ALVING. Of course, he had to take the blame on himself.

MANDERS. But the deceit of the man! And to *me*! I would honestly never have believed it of Jacob Engstrand. Well I shall have something to say to him about that, so he can just look out. . . . The immorality of a match of that sort! And all for money. . . ! How much did the girl have?

MRS. ALVING. Three hundred dollars.

MANDERS. Fancy going and getting married to a fallen woman for three hundred miserable dollars!

MRS. ALVING. What do you say about me, then, going and letting myself be married to a fallen man?

MANDERS. But . . . good heavens! What are you talking about? A fallen man!

MRS. ALVING. Do you imagine when I went to the altar with Alving, he was any purer than Johanna was when Engstrand married her?

MANDERS. But these are two utterly different things. . . .

MRS. ALVING. Not so terribly different, in fact. Admittedly there was a big difference in the price . . . three hundred miserable dollars as against a whole fortune.

MANDERS. But how can you compare things so utterly dissimilar. You had taken counsel with your own heart, and with your family.

MRS. ALVING [*not looking at him*]. I thought you realized where my heart, as you put it, had strayed at that time.

MANDERS [*distantly*]. If I had realized anything of the kind, I would not have been a daily guest in your husband's house.

MRS. ALVING. Well, the fact remains I did not, after all, take counsel with myself.

MANDERS. Well, with your nearest relatives, then, as it was your duty to. With your mother and your two aunts.

MRS. ALVING. Yes, that's true. The three of them reckoned it all up for me. It's incredible how nicely worked out they had it all, showing how it would be sheer madness to turn down an offer like that. If only Mother could look in now and see what had become of all the glory.

MANDERS. Nobody can be held responsible for the way things have turned out. But nevertheless one thing is clear: your marriage was arranged in strict accord with law and order.

MRS. ALVING. Oh, all this law and order! I often think *that's* the cause of all the trouble in the world.

MANDERS. Mrs. Alving, that's a very wrong thing to say.

MRS. ALVING. Well, perhaps it is. But I'm not putting up with it any longer, all these ties and restrictions. I can't stand it! I must work myself free.

MANDERS. What do you mean by that?

MRS. ALVING [*drumming on the window frame*]. I should never have kept it a secret, the kind of life Alving led. But at the time I didn't dare do anything else . . . and it was partly for my own sake. What a coward I was!

MANDERS. Coward?

MRS. ALVING. If people had got to know about it, they'd probably have said 'Poor man, no wonder he lets himself go a bit, with a wife who runs off and leaves him.'

MANDERS. There would have been some justification for saying that.

MRS. ALVING [*looking hard at him*]. If I were the sort of person I should be, I would take Oswald on one side and say: 'Listen, my son, your father was an old reprobate. . . .'

MANDERS. Heavens above!

MRS. ALVING. . . . and then I would tell him everything I've told you . . . the whole lot.

MANDERS. I am really rather shocked at you, Mrs. Alving.

MRS. ALVING. Oh, I know! I know! I find the idea shocking myself. [*Walks away from the window.*] What a coward I am!

MANDERS. Do you call it cowardice, to do what is quite plainly your duty? Have you forgotten that a child is supposed to love and honour its father and mother?

MRS. ALVING. Let's not generalize. The question is: is Oswald supposed to love and honour Captain Alving?

MANDERS. Don't you feel your mother's heart prompting you not to shatter your son's ideals?

MRS. ALVING. But what about the truth?

MANDERS. What about his ideals?

MRS. ALVING. Oh, ideals, ideals! If only I weren't such a coward!

MANDERS. Don't despise ideals, Mrs. Alving . . . that can bring a cruel reckoning. Especially in Oswald's case. Oswald hasn't so very many ideals, unfortunately. But I saw enough to realize that his father represents a kind of ideal to him.

MRS. ALVING. Yes, you are right.

MANDERS. And it was you yourself who gave him these ideas, and your letters encouraged him in them.

MRS. ALVING. Yes, I was doing my duty, observing the proprieties. That's why I lied to my son, year in and year out. Oh, what a coward . . . what a coward I have been!

MANDERS. You have built up a beautiful illusion in your son's mind, Mrs. Alving . . . and really, that's something you shouldn't underestimate.

MRS. ALVING. H'm! Who knows if it is actually such a good thing after all. . . . But I won't stand for any funny business with Regine. He's not going to go and mess up that girl's life.

MANDERS. Good Lord, no! That would be terrible!

MRS. ALVING. If I thought he was serious, and that it would make him happy. . . .

MANDERS. Well? What then?

MRS. ALVING. But it wouldn't. I'm afraid Regine isn't that kind.

MANDERS. What of it? What do you mean?

MRS. ALVING. If only I weren't such a miserable coward, I'd say to him: marry the girl, or come to some arrangement between yourselves. So long as there's nothing underhand.

MANDERS. Merciful heavens! Legal marriage, even! Of all the frightful. . . . Of all the unheard-of . . . !

MRS. ALVING. Unheard-of, you say? Hand on heart, Pastor Manders, do you think there aren't plenty of couples all over the country who are every bit as closely related?

MANDERS. I simply don't understand you.

MRS. ALVING. Oh yes, you do.

I

MANDERS. I suppose you are thinking of the possibility that. . . . Yes, I regret to say family life is in fact not always as pure as it ought to be. But with the sort of thing you are hinting at, nobody can ever really tell . . . not with any certainty, at least. Here, on the other hand. . . ! How you, as a mother, could be willing to allow your . . . !

MRS. ALVING. But I'm *not* willing! I couldn't wish it, not for anything. That's precisely what I'm saying.

MANDERS. No, because you are a coward, as you put it. But supposing you weren't a coward. . . ! God in Heaven, what a shocking union!

MRS. ALVING. Well, for that matter we are all descended from unions of that sort, they say. And who was it arranged things like that here on earth, Pastor Manders?

MANDERS. I do not propose to discuss such questions with you, Mrs. Alving. You are far from having the right attitude of mind. But how you dare call it cowardice. . . !

MRS. ALVING. I'll tell you what I mean. The reason I'm so timid and afraid is that I can never get properly rid of the ghosts that haunt me.

MANDERS. What did you call them?

MRS. ALVING. Ghosts. When I heard Regine and Oswald in there, it was just like seeing ghosts. But then I'm inclined to think that we are all ghosts, Pastor Manders, every one of us. It's not just what we inherit from our mothers and fathers that haunts us. It's all kinds of old defunct theories, all sorts of old defunct beliefs, and things like that. It's not that they actually *live* on in us; they are simply lodged there, and we cannot get rid of them. I've only to pick up a newspaper and I seem to see ghosts gliding between the lines. Over the whole country there must be ghosts, as numerous as the sands of the sea. And here we are, all of us, abysmally afraid of the light.

MANDERS. Aha! So there we see the fruits of your reading. And a nice harvest it is, I must say. Oh, these disgusting, free-thinking pamphlets! Revolting!

MRS. ALVING. You are wrong, my dear Pastor. You were the one who goaded me into doing some thinking. And I shall always be grateful to you for that.

MANDERS. *I* did!

MRS. ALVING. Yes, when you forced me to submit to what you called my duty and my obligations. When you praised as right and proper what my whole mind revolted against, as against some loathsome thing. It was then I began to examine the fabric of your teachings. I began picking at one of the knots, but as soon as I'd got that undone, the whole thing came apart at the seams. It was then I realized it was just tacked together.

MANDERS [*softly, moved*]. And that's all that came of what was the hardest struggle of my life?

MRS. ALVING. Call it rather your most pitiful defeat.

MANDERS. It was my life's greatest victory, Helene; victory over myself.

MRS. ALVING. It was a crime against us both.

MANDERS. Was it a crime to say to you: 'Woman, go back to your lawful husband'? When you came to me, demented, shouting: 'Here I am! Take me!'? Was *that* a crime?

MRS. ALVING. Yes, I think so.

MANDERS. We two don't understand each other.

MRS. ALVING. Not any more, at least.

MANDERS. Never once . . . not in my most secret thoughts . . . have I ever regarded you as anything other than another man's wife.

MRS. ALVING. Really?

MANDERS. Helene. . . .

MRS. ALVING. It's so easy to forget one's own past.

MANDERS. Not me. I'm the same as I always was.

MRS. ALVING [*changing her tone*]. Well, well, well, let's not talk any more about the old days. You are now up to the ears in committee work and other undertakings; and here I go battling on with ghosts, both within and without.

MANDERS. The latter kind I can at least help you to put down. After all the dreadful things I've heard from you today, I cannot in all conscience think of permitting a young defenceless girl to remain in your house.

MRS. ALVING. Don't you think the best thing would be if we could see her settled? Decently married, I mean?

MANDERS. Indubitably. I think in her case it's in every way desirable. Regine is now of an age when. . . . Of course, I'm not an expert in these things, but. . . .

MRS. ALVING. Regine matured very early.

MANDERS. Yes she did, didn't she. I seem to remember she was remarkably well developed physically when I was preparing her for confirmation. But she'd better go home for the present, under her father's care. . . . Ah, but of course Engstrand isn't. . . . To think that he, *he* of all people, could conceal the truth from me like that!

[*There is a knock on the hall door.*]

MRS. ALVING. Who can *that* be? Come in!

ENGSTRAND [*in his Sunday suit, in the doorway*]. Begging your pardon, but . . .

MANDERS. Aha! H'm. . . .

MRS. ALVING. It's you, is it, Engstrand?

ENGSTRAND. . . . there was none of the maids around, so I made so bold as to knock.

MRS. ALVING. Oh, very well, come in. Something you want to see me about?

ENGSTRAND [*comes in*]. No, thanks all the same. It was really the pastor I was wanting a word with.

MANDERS [*walking up and down*]. H'm, indeed. You want to talk to me, do you?

ENGSTRAND. Yes, I'd be awfully glad if . . .

MANDERS [*stops in front of him*]. Well? What is it, may I ask?

ENGSTRAND. Well, it's like this, Pastor. We are being paid off now down there . . . and many thanks to you, ma'am . . . and now everything's finished. And I was thinking it would be a good idea if us that's been working so hard together all this time . . . I was thinking we ought perhaps to finish up this evening with a bit of a service.

MANDERS. A service? Down at the Orphanage?

ENGSTRAND. Yes, but if you don't happen to think it's such a good idea, Pastor. . . .

MANDERS. Oh yes, I do, but . . . H'm. . . .

ENGSTRAND. I often used to say a prayer or two myself down there in the evenings. . . .

MRS. ALVING. Did you?

ENGSTRAND. Yes, now and again. Nothing like a bit of uplift, as you might say. But I'm just a simple, ordinary man with no real gift for it, so help me . . . and then it struck me that since Pastor Manders happened to be here. . . .

MANDERS. Look, Engstrand, first I must ask you something. Are you in the right frame of mind for a meeting of this kind? Do you feel your conscience is clear?

ENGSTRAND. God help us, Pastor, there's not much point in talking about consciences.

MANDERS. Oh yes, there is. That's exactly what we *are* going to talk about. Well? What have you got to say?

ENGSTRAND. Ah . . . it can be pretty bad, conscience can, sometimes.

MANDERS. Well, at least you admit it. But now I want you to tell me straight—what's the real story about Regine?

MRS. ALVING [*quickly*]. Pastor Manders!

MANDERS [*reassuringly*]. Please allow me. . . .

ENGSTRAND. About Regine? Lord, you put the wind up me there! [*Looks at* MRS. ALVING.] There's nothing the matter about Regine, is there?

MANDERS. Let's hope not. What I mean is this: what's the position as far as you and Regine are concerned? You are supposed to be her father, aren't you? Well?

ENGSTRAND [*hesitantly*]. Well . . . h'm . . . you know all about that business about me and poor Johanna.

MANDERS. No more prevarication. Your late wife informed Mrs. Alving of the true state of affairs before she left her service.

ENGSTRAND. Well I'll be. . . ! She did, did she?

MANDERS. So we've found you out, Engstrand.

ENGSTRAND. And she swore by all that was holy . . .

MANDERS. Swore?

ENGSTRAND. Well, took her oath, then. Really solemn.

MANDERS. And all these years you've been hiding the truth from me. From *me*, when I've always gone out of my way to show every confidence in you.

ENGSTRAND. Yes, I'm sorry to say I have that.

MANDERS. Have I deserved this of you, Engstrand? Haven't I always been ready to lend you a helping hand in any way, as far as it lay in my power? Answer me! Haven't I?

ENGSTRAND. Many's the time things would have looked pretty black for me if I hadn't had Pastor Manders.

MANDERS. And this is what I get for it. You get me to make false entries in the church register, and then for years afterwards you withhold the information you owed to me and to truth. Your conduct has been quite indefensible, Engstrand. And that's the end as far as we two are concerned.

ENGSTRAND [*with a sigh*]. Well, that's that, I suppose.

MANDERS. Because I can't see what possible excuse you could have?

ENGSTRAND. You didn't expect her to go round making the scandal worse by talking about it, did you? Now, Pastor, you just imagine yourself now in the same predicament as poor Johanna. . . .

MANDERS. Me?

ENGSTRAND. Good Lord, I don't mean exactly the same. What I mean is, suppose you had something you were ashamed of in the eyes of the world, as they say. We men shouldn't judge a poor woman too harshly, Pastor.

MANDERS. But I'm not. It's you I'm accusing.

ENGSTRAND. Could I ask you one little question, Pastor?

MANDERS. All right.

ENGSTRAND. Isn't it right and proper for a man to try and raise the fallen?

MANDERS. Yes, of course.

ENGSTRAND. And isn't a man bound to keep his promise?

MANDERS. Certainly he is. But. . . .

ENGSTRAND. When Johanna got into trouble on account of that Englishman—or maybe it was an American, or a Russian or whatever they're called—well, she came back to town. Poor thing, she'd already turned me down once or twice before; she only had eyes for the good-looking ones, she had; and of course I had this gammy leg of mine. You'll remember, Pastor, how I once screwed up my courage to go into one of them dance-halls where you get seafaring men carrying on all drunk and disorderly, as the saying goes. And just as I was appealing to them to turn over a new leaf . . .

MRS. ALVING [*over beside the window*]. H'm. . . .

MANDERS. I know, Engstrand. The brutes threw you downstairs. You've told me about that incident before. Your injury does you honour.

ENGSTRAND. I'm not the one to brag about it, Pastor. But what I was going to say was that she came along to me and confessed everything, with weeping and wailing and gnashing of teeth. I must say it fair broke my heart to listen to her.

MANDERS. Did it really, Engstrand. What then?

ENGSTRAND. So then I says to her: this American is off roaming the seven seas. And as for you Johanna, I says, you've committed a sin, you're a fallen woman. But Jacob Engstrand, I says, he's a man that stands firm on his own two feet, he is . . . in a manner of speaking, that is, I meant, Pastor.

MANDERS. I quite understand. Go on.

ENGSTRAND. Well, so then I married her properly and set her on her feet again, so as nobody would get to know about her carrying on with foreigners.

MANDERS. All this is very admirable. What I can't approve of is that you could stoop to accepting money. . . .

ENGSTRAND. Money? Me? Not a cent.

MANDERS [*inquiringly to* MRS. ALVING]. But . . . ?

ENGSTRAND. Oh, yes, wait a minute . . . now I remember. Johanna did have a copper or two. But I wouldn't have anything to do with *that*. Puh, that's Mammon, I says, that's the wages of sin. We'll take that filthy gold—or notes, or whatever it was—and we'll chuck it back at that American, I says. But he was already up and away, over the stormy seas.

MANDERS. Was he now, Engstrand, my good fellow?

ENGSTRAND. Yes. So then Johanna and I agreed that the money was to go towards the child's education. And so it did. And I can account for every cent of it.

MANDERS. But this changes things quite considerably.

ENGSTRAND. That's the way things are, Pastor. And I think I can say I've been a good father to Regine . . . as far as my strength would let me . . . because I'm just a poor sinner, I'm afraid.

MANDERS. Come now, my dear Engstrand. . . .

ENGSTRAND. But I think I can say I was a loving husband to poor Johanna, and I brought up the child and provided a home, as the good book says we should. But it would never have occurred to me to go bragging to Pastor Manders and giving myself a pat on the back just because I'd happened to do a good deed for once in a while. No, when anything like that happens to Jacob Engstrand, he keeps his mouth shut about it. I should say it doesn't happen all that often, I'm afraid. And whenever I go along to see Pastor Manders, I've always plenty to do, talking about my mistakes and short-comings. Because as I said just now, and I say it again: my conscience can be in a pretty bad way, sometimes.

MANDERS. Give me your hand, Jacob Engstrand.

ENGSTRAND. Oh Lord, Pastor. . . .

MANDERS. No beating about the bush! [*Grasps his hand.*] There now!

ENGSTRAND. And please, Pastor, I want to ask you very humbly to forgive me. . . .

MANDERS. You? On the contrary. I'm the one who should be asking you. . . .

ENGSTRAND. Oh, Lord, no!

MANDERS. But yes, I insist. And I do so with all my heart. Please forgive me for misjudging you like that. I only wish there were some way I could show my sincere regret, and my good will. . . .

ENGSTRAND. Would you, Pastor?

MANDERS. With the very greatest of pleasure. . . .

ENGSTRAND. Well, in point of fact there is something. With the bit of money I've put aside out of this job, I was thinking of starting a kind of Seamen's Home down in town.

MRS. ALVING. You *what*?

ENGSTRAND. Yes, the idea is to make it into a kind of home from home, as you might say. Many are the temptations open to a sailor when he sets foot ashore. But in this place of mine, I was thinking he could be sort of under a fatherly eye.

MANDERS. What do you say to that, Mrs. Alving!

ENGSTRAND. Heaven knows I haven't a great deal to make a start with. But if only I could be given a bit of a helping hand. . . .

MANDERS. Yes, yes, we must go into that in more detail. But now, you go on ahead and get things ready, and light the candles and brighten up the place a little. And we'll spend an improving hour together there, my dear Engstrand. Because now I do think you are in the right frame of mind.

ENGSTRAND. Yes, I think I am. Goodbye then, Mrs. Alving, and thank you. And take good care of Regine for me. [*He wipes away a tear.*] Poor Johanna's little girl . . . ah, it's a funny thing . . . but it's just as though she were tied fast to my heartstrings. Yes, it really is.

[*He bows and goes out through the hall.*]

MANDERS. Well, what do you say to our man now, Mrs. Alving? That was a very different explanation we got from him, wasn't it?

MRS. ALVING. Yes, it certainly was.

MANDERS. You see now how extremely careful one has to be when passing judgement on one's fellow men. But then what a real joy it is to discover that one has been mistaken. What do *you* say?

MRS. ALVING. I say you are a great big baby, and always will be.

MANDERS. Me?

MRS. ALVING [*places both hands on his shoulders*]. And I say I could almost feel like hugging you.

MANDERS [*drawing back hastily*]. Bless me, no. . . . What an idea!

MRS. ALVING [*with a smile*]. Oh, you needn't be afraid of me.

MANDERS [*beside the table*]. Sometimes you have such an extravagant way of expressing yourself. I'll just collect up these documents first and put them in my case. [*He does this.*] There now. And now, good-bye for the present. Keep your eyes open when Oswald returns. I'll look in on you again later.

[*He takes his hat and goes out through the hall door.* MRS. ALVING *sighs, looks for a moment out of the window, tidies up the room a little and is about to go into the dining-room but stops with a stifled cry in the doorway.*]

MRS. ALVING. Oswald, are you still in the dining-room!

OSWALD [*in the dining-room*]. I'm just finishing my cigar.

MRS. ALVING. I thought you'd gone for a little walk up the road.

OSWALD. In *this* weather?

[*A glass clinks.* MRS. ALVING *lets the door stand open and sits down with her knitting on the sofa by the window.*]

OSWALD. Wasn't that Pastor Manders who just went out?

MRS. ALVING. Yes, he went down to the Orphanage.

OSWALD. H'm.

[*The glass and the decanter clink again.*]

MRS. ALVING [*with a worried look*]. Oswald dear, you ought to go carefully with that liqueur. It's strong.

OSWALD. It keeps out the damp.

MRS. ALVING. Wouldn't you rather come in here beside me?

OSWALD. I can't smoke in there.

MRS. ALVING. You know it's all right to smoke cigars.

OSWALD. All right, I'll come then. Just another little drop. . . . There now.

[*He comes into the room smoking his cigar and shuts the door behind him. There is a short silence.*]

OSWALD. Where's the pastor gone?

MRS. ALVING. I told you, he's gone down to the Orphanage.

OSWALD. Oh yes, that's right.

MRS. ALVING. You shouldn't sit so long at the table, Oswald.

OSWALD [*holding his cigar behind his back*]. But I find it so pleasant, Mother. [*Pats and caresses her.*] Think what it means to me . . . to be home, to sit at my mother's own table, in my mother's room, and enjoy my mother's delicious cooking.

MRS. ALVING. My dear, dear boy!

OSWALD [*somewhat impatiently walks up and down, smoking*]. What else is there for me to do here? I can't get started on anything.

MRS. ALVING. Oh, can't you?

OSWALD. This dull weather? When there isn't a glimpse of the sun all day? [*Walks across the room.*] Oh, this not being able to work. . . !

MRS. ALVING. Perhaps you should have thought twice about coming home.

OSWALD. Oh no, Mother. I had to.

MRS. ALVING. Because I'd ten times rather sacrifice the joy of having you here than see you. . .

OSWALD [*stops beside the table*]. But tell me, Mother . . . does it really make you so very happy to have me home?

MRS. ALVING. Make me happy!

OSWALD [*crumpling a newspaper*]. I shouldn't have thought it made much difference to you whether I was around or not.

MRS. ALVING. Have you the heart to say that to your mother, Oswald?

OSWALD. Yet you managed to get on quite well without me before.

MRS. ALVING. Yes. I got on without you, that's true.

[*Silence. It begins slowly to grow dusk.* OSWALD *walks up and down the room. He has put the cigar down.*]

OSWALD [*stops beside* MRS. ALVING]. Mother, may I sit beside you on the sofa?

MRS. ALVING [*makes room for him*]. Yes, do, my dear.

OSWALD [*sits down*]. There is something I must tell you, Mother.

MRS. ALVING [*tense*]. Well?

OSWALD [*staring into space*]. Because I can't stand it any longer.

MRS. ALVING. Stand what? What is it?

OSWALD [*as before*]. I couldn't bring myself to write to you about it. And since I got home . . .

MRS. ALVING [*gripping his arm*]. Oswald, what is it?

OSWALD. Yesterday and again today, I tried to shake off these thoughts . . . fight myself free. But it's no use.

MRS. ALVING [*rising*]. You must tell me everything, Oswald!

OSWALD [*drags her down on the sofa again*]. Sit still, and I'll try and tell you . . . I've been complaining of feeling tired after my journey, you know. . . .

MRS. ALVING. Yes? Well?

OSWALD. But that's not what is wrong with me. Not ordinary tiredness. . . .

MRS. ALVING [*tries to jump up*]. You aren't ill, Oswald!

OSWALD [*pulling her down again*]. Sit still, Mother. Take it easy. I'm not really ill, either. Not what people generally call being ill. [*He puts his hands to his head.*] Mother, it's my mind that's given way . . . destroyed . . . I'll never be able to work again!

[*Hiding his face in his hands, he buries his head in her lap, sobbing bitterly.*]

MRS. ALVING [*pale and trembling*]. Oswald! Look at me! No, no, it isn't true!

OSWALD [*looks up with despair in his eyes*]. Never to be able to work again! Never . . . never! Like a living death! Mother, can you imagine anything more horrible?

MRS. ALVING. My poor boy! How did this terrible thing happen to you?

OSWALD [*sitting up again*]. Yes, that's just what I can't for the life of me understand. I've never gone in for reckless living. Not in any sense of the word. You must believe me, Mother. I've never done that.

MRS. ALVING. I'm sure you haven't, Oswald.

OSWALD. And yet a thing like this happens to me! This terrible thing!

MRS. ALVING. Oh, but it will get better, my darling. It's simply over-work, believe me.

OSWALD [*dully*]. That's also what I believed at first. But it isn't.

MRS. ALVING. Tell me everything, from beginning to end.

OSWALD. All right, I will.

MRS. ALVING. When did you first notice anything?

OSWALD. Immediately after the last time I was home, when I got back to Paris. I began to get the most violent pains in the head . . . generally here at the back of the head, it seemed. It was just like having an iron band clamped tight round your neck, and up there.

MRS. ALVING. And then?

OSWALD. At first I didn't think it was anything more than the ordinary headache I'd always suffered from, ever since I was a child.

MRS. ALVING. Yes, yes. . . .

OSWALD. But it wasn't. I soon realized that. I couldn't work any more. I wanted to start on a big new picture. But my skill just seemed to desert me, I felt paralysed, I couldn't concentrate, I felt giddy, everything went round and round. Oh, I was in a terrible state! In the end I sent for the doctor . . . and I learned the truth from him.

MRS. ALVING. What do you mean?

OSWALD. He was one of the leading doctors over there. I had to tell him how I felt. And then he started asking me a whole lot of questions that didn't seem to me to have anything at all to do with it. I couldn't understand what the man was getting at. . . .

MRS. ALVING. Well!

OSWALD. At last he said: there's been something worm-eaten about you since birth. He used that very word: 'vermoulu'.

MRS. ALVING [*tense*]. What did he mean by that?

OSWALD. I couldn't understand it either, and I asked him for a more detailed explanation. And then he said, the old cynic . . . [*Clenches his fist.*] Oh. . . !

MRS. ALVING. What did he say?

OSWALD. He said: the sins of the fathers are visited upon the children.

MRS. ALVING [*rising slowly*]. The sins of the fathers . . . !

OSWALD. I very nearly hit him in the face. . . .

MRS. ALVING [*walks across the floor*]. The sins of the fathers. . . .

OSWALD [*smiling sadly*]. Yes, what do you think? Of course, I assured him that was quite out of the question. But do you think he would give way? No, he wouldn't budge. And it wasn't until I'd produced your letters and translated for him all those bits about Father. . . .

MRS. ALVING. What then. . . ?

OSWALD. Well, then he naturally had to admit that he'd been on the wrong track. Then I learnt the truth. The incredible truth! This blissfully happy life I'd been living with my friends, I should never have indulged in it. It had been too much for my strength. So it was my own fault, you see!

MRS. ALVING. Oswald! Oh no, you mustn't think that!

OSWALD. There was no other possible explanation, he said. *That's* the really terrible thing. A hopeless wreck for the rest of my life . . . and all the result of my own thoughtlessness. All the things I wanted to do in life . . . I daren't even think about them again . . . can't think about them. Oh, if only I could live my life over again . . . undo everything I've done!

[*He throws himself face-down on the sofa.* MRS. ALVING *wrings her hands and walks up and down in silent inner conflict.*]

OSWALD [*after a moment, looks up and remains lying propped on his elbow*]. If only it had been something inherited . . . something one couldn't have helped. But this! The shame of it, throwing everything away like that, wantonly, thoughtlessly . . . happiness, health, everything . . . one's future . . . one's whole life . . . !

MRS. ALVING. No, no, my dear, darling boy! This is impossible. [*Bends over him.*] Things are not as desperate as you think.

OSWALD. Oh, you don't know. . . . [*Jumps up.*] And then there's all the worry I'm causing you, Mother. Many's the time I've half hoped you didn't really care very much about me.

MRS. ALVING. Oh, Oswald, my own boy! The one thing I have in all the world. The one thing I care anything at all about.

OSWALD [*seizes both her hands and kisses them*]. Yes, yes, I can see that. When I'm at home, I can see it all right. And that's almost the hardest thing about it for me.—Still, now you know. And let's not talk about it any more today. I can't bear thinking about it for long. [*Walks across the room.*] Get me something to drink, Mother!

MRS. ALVING. Drink? What do you want to drink now?

OSWALD. Oh, anything. You must have some of that cold punch in the house, haven't you?

MRS. ALVING. Yes, but my dear Oswald. . . !

OSWALD. Don't begrudge me that, Mother. Please! I *must* have something to swill all these nagging thoughts down with. [*He goes into the conservatory.*] How . . . how dark it is here! [MRS. ALVING *pulls the bell-rope, right.*] And this incessant rain! Week after week it can go on, for months on end. Never a glimpse of the sun. All the times I've been home, I can't ever remember having once seen the sun.

MRS. ALVING. Oswald . . . you are thinking of leaving me!

OSWALD. H'm. . . . [*Sighs deeply.*] I'm not thinking of anything. I *can't* think of anything! [*In a low voice.*] I've given up thinking.

REGINE [*from the dining-room*]. You rang, ma'am?

MRS. ALVING. Yes, can we have the lamp in, please?

REGINE. At once, ma'am. It's already lit.

[*She goes out.*]

MRS. ALVING [*walks over to* OSWALD]. Oswald, don't keep anything back from me.

OSWALD. I'm not, Mother. [*He walks over to the table.*] I think I've told you plenty.

[REGINE *brings in the lamp and puts it on the table.*]

MRS. ALVING. And, Regine, you might bring us a half-bottle of champagne.

REGINE. Very good, ma'am.

[*She goes out again.*]

OSWALD [*puts his arm round* MRS. ALVING's *neck.*] That's the style. I knew my mother wouldn't let her son go thirsty.

MRS. ALVING. My poor darling Oswald. How could I possibly refuse you anything now?

OSWALD [*eagerly*]. Is that true, Mother. Do you mean it?

MRS. ALVING. What?

OSWALD. That you couldn't refuse me anything?

MRS. ALVING. But Oswald dear. . .

OSWALD. Hush!

[REGINE *brings in a tray with a half-bottle of champagne and two glasses, which she places on the table.*]

REGINE. Shall I open . . . ?

OSWALD. No, thank you, I'll do it myself.

[REGINE *goes out again.*]

MRS. ALVING [*sits down at the table*]. What was it you thought . . . I couldn't refuse you?

OSWALD [*busy opening the bottle*]. First we'll have a glass . . . or two.

[*The cork pops, he fills one glass and is about to fill the other.*]

MRS. ALVING [*putting her hand over it*]. No, thanks . . . not for me.

OSWALD. All right, for me, then!

[*He empties his glass, re-fills it and empties it again; then he sits down at the table.*]

MRS. ALVING [*expectantly*]. Well?

OSWALD [*without looking at her*]. Tell me . . . I thought you and Pastor Manders were looking strangely . . . h'm . . . subdued, at dinner.

MRS. ALVING. You noticed?

OSWALD. Yes. H'm. . . . [*After a silence.*] Tell me . . . what do you think of Regine?

MRS. ALVING. What do I think of her?

OSWALD. Yes, isn't she marvellous?

MRS. ALVING. Oswald dear, you don't know her as well as I do. . . .

OSWALD. Well?

MRS. ALVING. Unfortunately Regine stayed too long at home. I should have had her here earlier.

OSWALD. Yes, but isn't she marvellous looking, Mother?

[*He fills his glass.*]

MRS. ALVING. Regine has many serious shortcomings. . . .

OSWALD. Well, what's that matter?

[*He drinks again.*]

MRS. ALVING. All the same, I'm fond of her; and I'm responsible for her. I wouldn't for the world want anything to happen to her.

K

OSWALD [*jumps up*]. Mother, Regine is my only hope!

MRS. ALVING [*rising*]. What do you mean by that?

OSWALD. I can't go on bearing all this agony of mind alone.

MRS. ALVING. Haven't you got your mother to bear it with you?

OSWALD. Yes, that's what I thought. That's why I came home to you. But that way's no use. I can see it's no use. I can't stand living here.

MRS. ALVING. Oswald!

OSWALD. I must live a different life, Mother. That's why I must leave you. I don't want you to have to watch it.

MRS. ALVING. My poor boy! But, Oswald, while you are as ill as this. . . .

OSWALD. If it were only the illness, I'd have been quite ready to stay with you, Mother. Because you are the best friend I have in the world.

MRS. ALVING. Yes, Oswald, I am, aren't I?

OSWALD [*wandering restlessly up and down*]. But it's all the torment, the anguish, the remorse . . . and this great mortal dread. Oh . . . this terrible feeling of dread!

MRS. ALVING [*following him*]. Dread? What feeling of dread? What do you mean?

OSWALD. Oh, you mustn't ask me any more. I don't know. I can't describe it to you. [MRS. ALVING *walks over and pulls the bell-rope, right.*] What do you want?

MRS. ALVING. I want my boy to be happy, that's what I want. He mustn't go on brooding like this. [*To* REGINE *who appears in the doorway.*] More champagne. A whole bottle.

[REGINE *goes.*]

OSWALD. Mother!

MRS. ALVING. Perhaps you think we don't know how to live out here in the country?

OSWALD. Isn't she marvellous looking? What a figure! And as sound as a bell!

MRS. ALVING [*sits down at the table*]. Sit down, Oswald, and let's talk things over quietly.

OSWALD [*sits down*]. You probably don't know, Mother, but I have to make it up to Regine for something I've done to her.

MRS. ALVING. *You've* done?

OSWALD. A bit of thoughtlessness . . . or whatever you like to call it. All very innocent, incidentally. When I was last home . . .

MRS. ALVING. Yes?

OSWALD. . . . she was always asking me about Paris, and I used to tell her something of what went on over there. Then one day I remember I happened to say: 'Wouldn't you like to come over yourself?'

MRS. ALVING. Well?

OSWALD. I saw her blush, and then she said: 'Yes, I wouldn't mind at all.' 'All right,' I said, 'we'll see if it can't be managed' . . . or something like that.

MRS. ALVING. Yes?

OSWALD. Of course I'd forgotten the whole thing. But when I happened to ask her a couple of days ago if she was glad I was going to be at home for so long. . .

MRS. ALVING. Yes?

OSWALD. . . . she gave me a funny look and said: 'But what about my trip to Paris?'

MRS. ALVING. Her trip!

OSWALD. And then she came out with it: she'd taken it all seriously, she'd been thinking about me the whole time, she'd even started learning French. . . .

MRS. ALVING. So that's why. . . .

OSWALD. Mother . . . this girl looked so marvellous standing there, so good-looking and vital . . . I'd never really noticed her very much before. . . . Then when she stood there, ready it seemed to take me in her arms . . .

MRS. ALVING. Oswald!

OSWALD. . . . it was then I realized that she was my salvation. Because she was filled with the joy of life.

MRS. ALVING [*starts*]. Joy of life. . . ? Can there be salvation in *that*?

REGINE [*from the dining-room with a bottle of champagne*]. I'm sorry I took so long, but I had to go down to the cellar. . . .

[*She puts the bottle on the table.*]

OSWALD. And fetch another glass.

REGINE [*looks at him in surprise*]. Mrs. Alving's glass is there, Mr. Alving.

OSWALD. Yes, but fetch one for yourself, Regine. [REGINE *starts, and casts a swift timid glance at* MRS. ALVING.] Well?

REGINE [*softly and hesitantly*]. If Mrs. Alving doesn't object. . . .

MRS. ALVING. Fetch the glass, Regine.

[REGINE *goes out to the dining-room.*]

OSWALD [*watching her*]. Have you noticed the way she walks? So firm, so unafraid.

MRS. ALVING. This is impossible, Oswald!

OSWALD. It's all decided. You must see that. It's useless to say anything. [REGINE *enters with an empty glass, which she keeps in her hand.*] Sit down, Regine.

[REGINE *looks inquiringly at* MRS. ALVING.]

MRS. ALVING. Sit down. [REGINE *sits down on a chair beside the dining-room door, still holding the empty glass in her hand.*] Oswald . . . what was that you were saying about the joy of life?

OSWALD. Yes, Mother, the joy of life. . . . You don't see much of that around this place. I never feel it here.

MRS. ALVING. Not even when you are with me?

OSWALD. Never when I'm at home. But you don't understand.

MRS. ALVING. Yes, I do . . . I'm beginning to understand . . . now.

OSWALD. That . . . and the joy of work, too. Well, they are the same thing, in fact. But people here don't know anything about that either.

MRS. ALVING. Perhaps you are right. Oswald, tell me more about this.

OSWALD. Well, all I mean is that people here are brought up to believe that work is a curse, and a sort of punishment for their sins; and that life is some kind of miserable affair, which the sooner we are done with the better for everybody.

MRS. ALVING. A vale of tears, I know. And we do our damnedest to make it that.

OSWALD. But people elsewhere simply won't have that. Nobody really believes in ideas of that sort any more. In other countries they think it's tremendous fun just to be alive at all. Mother, have you noticed how everything I've ever painted has turned on this joy of life? Always and without exception, this joy of life. Light and sunshine and a holiday spirit . . . and radiantly happy faces. That's why I'm frightened to stay at home with you.

MRS. ALVING. Frightened? What have you got to be frightened about, here with me?

OSWALD. I'm frightened that everything I care about would degenerate here into something ugly.

MRS. ALVING [*looks hard at him*]. You think *that* would happen?

OSWALD. I'm convinced it would. Live the same life here as abroad, yet it still wouldn't be the same life.

MRS. ALVING [*who has been listening intently, rises and says with big pensive eyes*]. Now I see the whole thing.

OSWALD. What do you see?

MRS. ALVING. Now I see for the first time. And now I can speak.

OSWALD [*rising*]. I don't understand you, Mother.

REGINE [*who has also risen*]. Perhaps I'd better go?

MRS. ALVING. No, stay here. Now I can speak. Now my boy must know everything. And then you can choose. Oswald! Regine!

OSWALD. Hush! The pastor. . . .

MANDERS [*enters by the hall door*]. There we are! We've had a most heart-warming time down there.

OSWALD. So have we.

MANDERS. Engstrand must be given help with his Seamen's Home. Regine must move in with him and lend a hand. . . .

REGINE. No, thank you, Pastor.

MANDERS [*only notices her now*]. What. . . ? Here, and with a glass in your hand!

REGINE [*quickly puts the glass down*]. Pardon!

OSWALD. Regine is leaving with me, Pastor.

MANDERS. Leaving with you!

OSWALD. Yes, as my wife . . . if she wants it that way.

MANDERS. But good heavens. . . !

REGINE. Don't blame me, Pastor.

OSWALD. Or else she stays here, if I stay.

REGINE [*involuntarily*]. Here!

MANDERS. I'm appalled at you, Mrs. Alving.

MRS. ALVING. Neither of these things will happen. Because now I can speak plainly.

MANDERS. But you mustn't. No, no, no!

MRS. ALVING. Oh yes I can, and I will. And nobody's ideals are going to suffer by it.

OSWALD. Mother, something's being kept from me! What is it?

REGINE [*listening*]. Mrs. Alving! Listen! They are shouting something out there.

[*She goes into the conservatory and looks out.*]

OSWALD [*over to the window, left*]. What's going on? Where's that glare coming from?

REGINE. The Orphanage is on fire!

MRS. ALVING [*towards the window*]. On fire!

MANDERS. On fire? Impossible. I've just been down there.

OSWALD. Where's my hat? Oh, never mind that . . . Father's Orphanage . . . !

[*He runs into the garden.*]

MRS. ALVING. My shawl, Regine! It's all in flames.

MANDERS. Dreadful! Mrs. Alving, *this* is a flaming judgement on this house of iniquity.

MRS. ALVING. Yes, of course. Come on, Regine.

[*She and* REGINE *hurry out through the hall.*]

MANDERS [*clasping his hands*]. And not insured!

[*He goes out the same way.*]

ACT THREE

The room as before. All the doors are standing open. The lamp is still burning on the table. It is dark outside, apart from a faint glow in the background, left.

MRS. ALVING, a large shawl over her head, is standing in the conservatory looking out. REGINE, also with a shawl round her, is standing a little behind her.

MRS. ALVING. Everything burnt. Burnt to the ground.

REGINE. The basement is still burning.

MRS. ALVING. Why doesn't Oswald come. There's nothing to save.

REGINE. Perhaps I should take him his hat down?

MRS. ALVING. Didn't he even have his hat?

REGINE [*pointing into the hall*]. No, it's hanging there.

MRS. ALVING. Leave it. He must be coming by now. I'll go and look myself.

[*She goes into the garden.*]

MANDERS [*enters from the hall*]. Isn't Mrs. Alving here?

REGINE. She's just gone into the garden.

MANDERS. This is the most terrible night I have ever known.

REGINE. Yes, it's a dreadful thing to happen, isn't it, Pastor?

MANDERS. Oh, don't talk about it! I hardly dare think about it even.

REGINE. But how can it have happened. . . ?

MANDERS. Don't ask me, Miss Engstrand! How should I know? You are not also wanting to. . . ? Isn't it enough that your father. . . ?

REGINE. What about him?

MANDERS. Oh, he's driving me to distraction.

ENGSTRAND [*enters from the hall*]. Pastor Manders. . . !

MANDERS [*turns round, startled*]. Are you after me in here, even?

ENGSTRAND. Yes, by God, I must. . . ! Oh, Lord! This is a terrible business, Pastor!

MANDERS [*walking up and down*]. I'm afraid it is!

REGINE. What is?

ENGSTRAND. Well, you see, it was that there service that did it. [*Aside.*] Now we've got him nicely, my girl. [*Aloud.*] And to think that I'm to blame for Pastor Manders being to blame for a thing like this!

MANDERS. But I assure you, Engstrand . . .

ENGSTRAND. But nobody else down there touched the candles apart from you, Pastor.

MANDERS [*halts*]. Yes, so you say. But I honestly can't remember ever having a candle in my hand.

ENGSTRAND. But I quite distinctly *saw* you take the candle and snuff it with your fingers and chuck the end away straight into some shavings.

MANDERS. You saw that?

ENGSTRAND. As plain as anything, I saw it.

MANDERS. I find that utterly incomprehensible. Besides, that is not a thing I'm in the habit of doing—snuffing candles out with my fingers.

ENGSTRAND. Yes, and horrible careless it looked too, I can tell you. But is it really all that serious, Pastor?

MANDERS [*walking restlessly up and down*]. Oh, don't ask me!

ENGSTRAND [*following him about*]. And you hadn't insured it either, eh, Pastor?

MANDERS [*still walking*]. No, no, no. I've told you.

ENGSTRAND. Not insured. And then to go straight away and set the whole place on fire! Lord, what rotten luck!

MANDERS [*mopping the sweat from his brow*]. You may very well say so, Engstrand.

ENGSTRAND. Fancy a thing like that happening to a charitable institution, something that was going to be such a boon to the whole district, as you might say. I don't suppose the papers are going to let *you* off very lightly, Pastor.

MANDERS. No, that's just what I'm thinking. That's just about the worst part of the whole affair. All these spiteful accusations and insinuations. . . ! Oh, it's terrible to think about!

MRS. ALVING [*coming from the garden*]. I can't get him to come away from the fire.

MANDERS. Ah, there you are, Mrs. Alving.

MRS. ALVING. Well, Pastor Manders, so you did get out of giving your speech.

MANDERS. Oh, I would have been only too glad. . . .

MRS. ALVING [*subdued*]. It's best things have turned out this way. That Orphanage wouldn't have done anybody any good.

MANDERS. Don't you think so?

MRS. ALVING. Do *you* think it would?

MANDERS. But it was a terrible calamity, all the same.

MRS. ALVING. Let's be businesslike about it, and not beat about the bush. . . . Are you waiting for Pastor Manders, Engstrand?

ENGSTRAND [*by the hall door*]. As a matter of fact I am.

MRS. ALVING. Have a seat, then, for the time being.

ENGSTRAND. Thanks, but I'd just as soon stand.

MRS. ALVING [*to* MANDERS]. You are leaving by the boat, presumably?

MANDERS. Yes. It leaves in an hour's time.

MRS. ALVING. Please take all the documents away with you again. I don't want to hear another word about this business. I've got other things to think about. . . .

MANDERS. Mrs. Alving. . . .

MRS. ALVING. Later on I'll send you authorization to clear things up as you think best.

MANDERS. I shall be only too delighted to see to that. The original terms of the bequest will have to be completely altered now, I'm afraid.

MRS. ALVING. Naturally.

MANDERS. Well, my idea at the moment is to arrange for the Solvik estate to be made over to the parish. The land cannot by any means be described as entirely valueless. It will always come in useful for something or other. And as for the interest on the capital in the bank, perhaps the best use I could put it to would be to support some scheme that might bring benefit to the town.

MRS. ALVING. Do just what you wish. It makes not the slightest difference to me.

ENGSTRAND. Don't forget my Seamen's Home, Pastor!

MANDERS. Ah, to be sure, there's something in what you say. Well, it must be given careful consideration

ENGSTRAND. Oh, to hell with considering. . . . Oh Lord!

MANDERS [*with a sigh*]. And I'm afraid I don't know how much longer I'll have any say in these things. Or whether public opinion might not compel me to resign. It all depends on the result of the official inquiry into the cause of the fire.

MRS. ALVING. What's that you say?

MANDERS. And it's quite impossible to predict what those findings will be.

ENGSTRAND [*comes closer*]. Oh, no, it isn't. Because there's always Jacob Engstrand and me.

MANDERS. Yes, but . . . ?

ENGSTRAND [*in a low voice*]. And Jacob Engstrand isn't the sort to desert a worthy benefactor in his hour of need, as the saying goes.

MANDERS. Yes, but my dear fellow . . . how . . . ?

ENGSTRAND. Jacob Engstrand is a sort of guardian angel, like, as you might say, Pastor.

MANDERS. No, no. I honestly couldn't allow that.

ENGSTRAND. Oh, you just let things take their course. It's not the first time somebody I know has taken the blame for somebody else.

MANDERS. Jacob! [*Shakes him by the hand.*] Characters like you are rare. Well, you'll get support for your Seamen's Home, you can depend on it. [ENGSTRAND *tries to thank him, but cannot for emotion.* MANDERS *slings his satchel over his shoulder.*] Let's be off now. We'll travel together.

ENGSTRAND [*by the dining-room door, in a low voice to* REGINE]. Come on with me, lass! You could live like a queen!

REGINE [*tosses her head*]. *Merci!*

[*She goes out into the hall to fetch the pastor's things.*]

MANDERS. Goodbye, Mrs. Alving. And may I hope that very soon some sense of order and propriety will find its way into this house.

MRS. ALVING. Goodbye, Manders!

[*Seeing* OSWALD *enter from the garden, she goes straight towards the conservatory.*]

ENGSTRAND [*as he and* REGINE *help* MANDERS *on with his coat*]. Goodbye, my girl. And if you are ever in any difficulty, you know where to find Jacob Engstrand. [*In a low voice.*] Little Harbour Street, h'm... ! [*To* MRS. ALVING *and* OSWALD.] And this place for seafaring men, it's going to be called the 'Captain Alving Home'. And if I can run it *my* way, I think I can promise it'll be a place worthy of the Captain's memory.

MANDERS [*in the doorway*]. H'm . . . h'm! Come along, my dear Engstrand. Goodbye, goodbye!

[*He and* ENGSTRAND *go out through the hall.*]

OSWALD [*goes over to the table*]. What place was that he was talking about?

MRS. ALVING. It's a sort of hostel he and Pastor Manders are thinking of starting.

OSWALD. It will burn down, just like all this.

MRS. ALVING. What gives you that idea?

OSWALD. Everything will burn. There'll be nothing left to remind people of Father. And here am I, burning down too.

[REGINE *looks at him, startled.*]

MRS. ALVING. Oswald! You shouldn't have stayed so long out there, my poor boy.

OSWALD [*sits at the table*]. I almost believe you are right.

MRS. ALVING. Let me dry your face, Oswald, you are all wet.

[*She dries his face with her handkerchief.*]

OSWALD [*not caring, looks fixedly ahead*]. Thank you, Mother.

MRS. ALVING. Aren't you tired, Oswald? Wouldn't you like a sleep, perhaps?

OSWALD [*fearfully*]. No, no . . . not sleep! I never sleep, I just pretend to. [*Dully.*] That will come soon enough.

MRS. ALVING [*looks anxiously at him*]. Yes, you really *are* ill, all the same, my darling boy.

REGINE [*tense*]. Mr. Alving ill?

OSWALD [*impatiently*]. And now shut all the doors! This deadly feeling of dread. . . .

MRS. ALVING. Shut them, Regine.

[REGINE *shuts the doors, and remains standing by the hall door.* MRS. ALVING *takes off her shawl, and* REGINE *does the same.* MRS. ALVING *draws a chair up near* OSWALD, *and sits down beside him.*]

MRS. ALVING. There now, I'm coming to sit beside you. . . .

OSWALD. Yes, do. And Regine must stay here too. Regine must always be near me. You'll give me a helping hand, Regine, won't you?

REGINE. I don't understand. . . .

MRS. ALVING. Helping hand?

OSWALD. Yes . . . when it's necessary.

MRS. ALVING. Oswald, haven't you got your mother to give you a helping hand?

OSWALD. You? [*Smiles.*] No, Mother, you'd never give me that sort of helping hand. [*Laughs dully.*] You! Ha! Ha! [*Looks earnestly at her.*] And yet who has a better right than you. [*Bursts out.*] Why can't you relax a bit with me, Regine? Why don't you call me Oswald?

REGINE [*softly*]. I don't think Mrs. Alving would like it.

MRS. ALVING. Very soon you can. Come over here and sit beside us. [REGINE *sits demurely and hesitantly on the other side of the table.*] And now, my darling, I am going to take a great burden off your poor, tormented mind . . .

OSWALD. You, Mother?

MRS. ALVING. . . . all the remorse and the self-reproach, as you called it, all those things that have been worrying you. . . .

OSWALD. You think you can?

MRS. ALVING. I can now, Oswald. Yes. You were talking earlier about the joy of living. And suddenly I seemed to see my whole life . . . everything in a new light.

OSWALD [*shakes his head*]. I don't understand a word of what you are saying.

MRS. ALVING. You should have seen your father when he was a young lieutenant. *He* had plenty of the joy of living, I can tell you!

OSWALD. Yes, I know.

MRS. ALVING. It cheered you up just to look at him. All that boundless energy and vitality he had!

OSWALD. Well. . . ?

MRS. ALVING. Well, there was this lively, happy boy—and at the time he *was* still like a boy—having to eat his heart out here in this little provincial town; pleasures of a kind it had to offer, but no real joy; no chance of any proper vocation, only an official position to fill; no sign of any kind of work he could throw himself into heart and soul—only business. He never had a single real friend capable of appreciating the joy of life and what it meant—nothing but a lot of lazy, drunken, hangers-on. . . .

OSWALD. Mother. . . !

MRS. ALVING. So then the inevitable happened.

OSWALD. What do you mean . . . the inevitable?

MRS. ALVING. You told me yourself this evening what would happen if you stayed at home.

OSWALD. Are you trying to say that Father. . . ?

MRS. ALVING. Your father could never find any outlet for this tremendous exuberance of his. And I didn't exactly bring very much gaiety into his home, either.

OSWALD. Didn't you?

MRS. ALVING. They'd taught me various things about duty and suchlike, and I'd simply gone on believing them. Everything seemed to come down to duty in the end—*my* duty and *his* duty and . . . I'm afraid I must have made the house unbearable for your poor father, Oswald.

OSWALD. Why did you never write to me about this?

MRS. ALVING. Until now I've never regarded it as anything I could bring myself to talk about to you—his son.

OSWALD. How did you regard it then?

MRS. ALVING [*slowly*]. I saw only one thing: that your father was a broken man before you were even born.

OSWALD [*in a smothered voice*]. Ah. . . !

[*He rises and goes across to the window.*]

MRS. ALVING. And day in and day out, one thought filled my mind: that in fact Regine belonged here in this house . . . just as much as my own son.

OSWALD [*turns quickly*]. Regine. . . !

REGINE [*jumps up startled, and says in a choking voice*]. Me. . . !

MRS. ALVING. Yes. Now you both know.

OSWALD. Regine!

REGINE [*to herself*]. So my mother was that sort.

MRS. ALVING. Your mother was in many ways a fine woman, Regine.

REGINE. Yes, but she was that sort, all the same. Well, sometimes I've thought as much, but. . . . Well, Mrs. Alving, please may I leave straight away?

MRS. ALVING. Do you really want to, Regine?

REGINE. Yes, I do that.

MRS. ALVING. You must please yourself, of course, but . . .

OSWALD [*walks over to* REGINE]. Leave now? But you belong here.

REGINE. *Merci*, Mr. Alving . . . well, now I suppose I can say Oswald. I must say *this* wasn't the way I'd imagined it happening.

MRS. ALVING. Regine, I haven't been altogether frank with you. . . .

REGINE. No, more's the pity! If I'd known Oswald had something wrong with him. . . . And anyway, now that there can never be anything serious between us. . . . No, you don't catch me staying out here in the country, working myself to death looking after invalids.

OSWALD. Not even somebody so close to you?

REGINE. Not likely. A poor girl's got to make the most of things while she's young. Or else you find yourself on the shelf before you know where you are. I've *also* got some of this joy of life as well, Mrs. Alving.

MRS. ALVING. Yes, I'm afraid so. But don't just throw yourself away, Regine.

REGINE. Oh, whatever will be, will be. If Oswald takes after his father, I probably take after my mother, I suppose. Mrs. Alving, may I ask if Pastor Manders knows all this about me?

MRS. ALVING. Pastor Manders knows everything.

REGINE [*busy putting on her shawl*]. Well, I'd better see what I can do about catching that boat, and getting away from here as quick as I can. The pastor's such a nice easy man to get on with. And it strikes me I've just as much right to a bit of that money as that rotten old carpenter.

MRS. ALVING. You're welcome to it, Regine.

REGINE [*looking fixedly at her*]. I think you might have brought me up like a gentleman's daughter, Mrs. Alving. It would have suited me a bit better than this. [*Tosses her head.*] Still, what the hell...! What difference does it make! [*With a bitter glance at the unopened bottle.*] I'll be drinking champagne with the best yet, you see if I'm not.

MRS. ALVING. And if ever you need a home, Regine, come to me.

REGINE. No thank you, Mrs. Alving. Pastor Manders will look after me all right. And if the worst comes to the worst, I know a place I can make my home.

MRS. ALVING. Where is that?

REGINE. The Captain Alving Home.

MRS. ALVING. Regine . . . I can see it now . . . you are going to your ruin.

REGINE. Oh, get away! *Adieu!*

[*She nods and goes out through the hall.*]

OSWALD [*stands at the window looking out*]. Has she gone?

MRS. ALVING. Yes.

OSWALD [*mutters to himself*]. I think it's crazy, this.

MRS. ALVING [*goes and stands behind him and puts her hands on his shoulders*]. Oswald, my dear . . . has this been a big shock to you?

OSWALD [*turns his face towards her*]. All this about Father, you mean?

MRS. ALVING. Yes, your poor unhappy father. I'm so afraid it's been too much for you.

OSWALD. Whatever gives you that idea? Of course, it came as a great surprise; but fundamentally it doesn't make very much difference to me.

MRS. ALVING [*draws her hands back*]. Not much difference! That your father was so utterly unhappy!

OSWALD. Of course, I feel sorry for *him* just as I would for anybody else, but . . .

MRS. ALVING. Is that all! Your own father!

OSWALD [*impatiently*]. Oh, father . . . father! I never knew anything about my father. All I remember about him is that he once made me sick.

MRS. ALVING. What a terrible thought! Surely a child ought to love its father in spite of all?

OSWALD. What if a child has nothing to thank its father for? Never knew him? You don't really believe in this old superstition still, do you? And you so enlightened in other ways?

MRS. ALVING. You call that mere superstition. . . !

OSWALD. Yes, surely you realize that, Mother. It's simply one of those ideas that get around and . . .

MRS. ALVING [*shaken*]. Ghosts!

OSWALD [*walks across the room*]. Yes, call them ghosts if you like.

MRS. ALVING [*wildly*]. Oswald . . . then you don't love me either.

OSWALD. Well, at least I do know you. . . .

MRS. ALVING. Yes, you know me. But is that all!

OSWALD. And I also know how fond you are of me. And that's something I must be grateful to you for. And you can also be extremely useful to me, now I'm a sick man.

MRS. ALVING. Yes I can, can't I, Oswald! Oh, I could almost bless this illness that drove you home to me. I can see I haven't made you completely mine yet—I must still win you.

OSWALD [*impatiently*]. Yes, yes, yes, but these are just empty words. You must remember I'm a sick man, Mother. I can't be bothered very much with other people, I've got enough to think of with myself.

MRS. ALVING [*in a low voice*]. I shall be calm and patient.

OSWALD. And *cheerful*, Mother!

MRS. ALVING. Yes, my darling, you are right. [*She walks over to him.*] Now have I taken away all that remorse, those self-reproaches?

OSWALD. Yes, you have. But who now will take away the feeling of dread?

MRS. ALVING. Dread?

OSWALD [*walks across the room*]. Regine would have done it, just for the asking.

MRS. ALVING. I don't understand you. What's all this about dread . . . and about Regine?

OSWALD. Is it very late, Mother?

MRS. ALVING. It's early morning. [*She looks out from the conservatory.*] Dawn is already breaking over the mountains. And it's going to be fine, Oswald! In a little while you'll be able to see the sun.

OSWALD. I'm looking forward to that. Oh, there might be all sorts of things I could still take a delight in, and live for. . . .

MRS. ALVING. I should just think so!

OSWALD. Even if I can't work, I . . .

MRS. ALVING. Oh, but now you'll soon be able to work again, my darling. Now that you are rid of all those nagging and depressing thoughts that were worrying you.

OSWALD. Yes, you've made me stop imagining things now anyway, and that's a good thing. And if only I can get this last thing settled now. . . . [*Sits down on the sofa.*] Mother, we are going to have a talk . . .

MRS. ALVING. Yes, of course.

[*She pushes an armchair over to the sofa and sits close by him.*]

OSWALD. . . . and meanwhile the sun will be rising. And then you'll know. And then I'll no longer have this feeling of dread.

MRS. ALVING. What am I to know, did you say?

OSWALD [*without listening to her*]. Mother, earlier on this evening didn't you say there was nothing in the world you wouldn't do for me, if I asked you.

MRS. ALVING. Yes, that's what I said!

OSWALD. And you mean that, Mother?

MRS. ALVING. You can depend on me, my dear, darling boy. I have nothing to live for but you.

OSWALD. All right, then I'll tell you. . . . Mother, I know you are quite strong-minded. You must sit quite calmly when you hear what it is.

MRS. ALVING. What terrible thing is this. . . ?

OSWALD. You mustn't scream. Do you hear? Promise me? You'll sit and talk about it quite quietly? Promise me, Mother?

MRS. ALVING. Yes, yes, I promise. But tell me!

OSWALD. Well then, I must tell you that all this about being tired . . . about not being able to bear the thought of work . . . all this isn't the real illness. . . .

MRS. ALVING. What is the illness, then?

OSWALD. The disease I have inherited . . . [*He points to his forehead and adds softly.*] . . . has its seat here.

MRS. ALVING [*almost speechless*]. Oswald! No! no!

OSWALD. Don't scream. I couldn't bear it. Yes, Mother, it sits lurking in here. And it can break out any day, any time.

MRS. ALVING. Oh, how horrible. . . !

OSWALD. Keep calm. That's how things are with me. . . .

MRS. ALVING [*jumping up*]. It's not true, Oswald! It's impossible! It can't be!

OSWALD. I've already had one attack over there. It soon passed. But when they told me how I'd been, I suddenly felt so dreadfully, pitifully afraid. So I set off back home to you as quick as I could.

MRS. ALVING. So this is the feeling of dread. . . !

OSWALD. Yes, and it's so utterly revolting, don't you see. If only it had been some ordinary kind of fatal disease. . . . Because I'm not afraid to die, although I would like to live as long as I can.

MRS. ALVING. Of course, Oswald, you must!

OSWALD. But this is so horribly revolting. To be turned into a helpless child again. To have to be fed, to have to be. . . . Oh, it doesn't bear talking about!

MRS. ALVING. My child will have his mother to look after him.

OSWALD [*jumping up*]. No, never. That's exactly what I don't want. I can't bear the thought that I might lie like that for years . . . till I become old and grey. And in the meantime you might die and leave me. [*He sits in* MRS. ALVING'S *chair.*] For the doctor said it wouldn't necessarily prove fatal immediately. He called it a kind of softening of the brain . . . or something like that. [*Smiles sadly.*] I think that expression sounds so nice. It always makes me think of cherry-red velvet curtains . . . something soft and delicate to the touch.

MRS. ALVING [*screams*]. Oswald!

OSWALD [*jumps up again and walks across the room*]. And now you have taken Regine away from me! If only I'd had her. She'd have given me this helping hand all right.

MRS. ALVING [*walks over to him*]. What do you mean by that, my darling. Is there anything in the world I wouldn't do for you?

OSWALD. When I came round again after that attack over there, the doctor said when it happened again—and it will happen again— there'd be no hope.

MRS. ALVING. How could he be so heartless. . . .

OSWALD. I demanded to know. I told him I had certain arrangements to make. . . . [*He smiles craftily.*] And so I had. [*He takes a little box out of his breast pocket.*] Mother, do you see this?

MRS. ALVING. What is it?

OSWALD. Morphine.

MRS. ALVING [*looks at him in terror*]. Oswald . . . my son!

OSWALD. I've got twelve tablets stored up. . . .

MRS. ALVING [*snatching at it*]. Give me that box, Oswald!

OSWALD. Not yet, Mother.

[*He puts the box back in his pocket.*]

MRS. ALVING. I can't bear this!

OSWALD. You must bear it. Now if I'd had Regine here, I'd have told her how things stood . . . and asked her for this last helping hand. She'd have helped me, I'm sure.

MRS. ALVING. Never!

OSWALD. If she saw me struck down by this ghastly thing, lying there helpless, like an imbecile child, beyond all hope of recovery. . . .

MRS. ALVING. Regine would never have done it, never!

OSWALD. Regine would have done it. Regine was so marvellously light-hearted. And she'd soon have got bored with looking after an invalid like me.

MRS. ALVING. Then thank God Regine isn't here!

OSWALD. Well then, now you'll have to give me this helping hand, Mother.

MRS. ALVING [*with a scream*]. Me!

OSWALD. There's nobody with a better right than you.

MRS. ALVING. Me! Your mother!

OSWALD. All the more reason.

MRS. ALVING. Me! Who gave you life!

OSWALD. I never asked you for life. And what sort of a life is this you've given me? I don't want it! Take it back!

MRS. ALVING. Help! Help!

[*She runs into the hall.*]

OSWALD. Don't leave me! Where are you going?

MRS. ALVING [*in the hall*]. To fetch the doctor, Oswald! Let me get out!

OSWALD [*also in the hall*]. You are not getting out. And nobody's getting in.

[*A key is turned.*]

MRS. ALVING [*comes in again*]. Oswald! Oswald! . . . my child!

OSWALD [*following her*]. If you love me, Mother . . . how can you let me suffer all this unspeakable terror!

MRS. ALVING [*after a moment's silence, says firmly*]. Here is my hand on it.

OSWALD. You will. . . ?

MRS. ALVING. If it becomes necessary. But it won't *be* necessary. No, no, it's quite impossible!

OSWALD. Well, let us hope so. And let's live together as long as we can. Thank you, Mother.

[*He sits in the armchair, which* MRS. ALVING *has moved over to the sofa. Day is dawning; the lamp is still burning on the table.*]

MRS. ALVING [*approaching him cautiously*]. Do you feel calmer now?

OSWALD. Yes.

MRS. ALVING [*bent over him*]. What terrible ideas they were to get into your head, Oswald. But all just imagination. All these upsets have been too much for you. But now you'll be able to have a good long rest. At home, with your mother beside you, my darling. Anything you want you shall have, just like when you were a little boy. There now. The attack's over. You see how quickly it went. Oh, I knew it would. . . . See what a lovely day we're going to have, Oswald? Brilliant sunshine. Now you'll be able to see the place properly.

[*She walks over to the table, and puts out the lamp. Sunrise. The glacier and the mountain peaks in the background gleam in the morning light.*]

OSWALD [*sits motionless in the armchair, with his back to the view; suddenly he says*]. Mother, give me the sun.

MRS. ALVING [*by the table, looks at him startled*]. What do you say?

OSWALD [*repeats dully and tonelessly*]. The sun. The sun.

MRS. ALVING [*across to him*]. Oswald, what's the matter with you? [OSWALD *seems to shrink in his chair, all his muscles go flaccid, his face is expressionless, and his eyes stare vacantly.* MRS. ALVING *quivers with terror.*] What is it? [*Screams.*] Oswald! What's the matter with you! [*Throws herself down on her knees beside him and shakes him.*] Oswald! Oswald! Look at me! Don't you know me?

OSWALD [*tonelessly as before*]. The sun. . . . The sun.

MRS. ALVING [*jumps up in anguish, tears at her hair with both hands, and shouts*]. I can't bear it! [*As though petrified, she whispers.*] I can't bear it! Never! [*Suddenly.*] Where's he put them? [*Hastily fumbling at his breast.*] Here! [*She shrinks back a step or two and screams.*] No, no, no! . . . Yes! . . . No, no!

[*She stands a few paces away from him, with her hands clutching her hair, staring at him in speechless horror.*]

OSWALD [*sits motionless as before, and says*]. The sun. . . . The sun.

SELECT BIBLIOGRAPHY

WORKS OF CRITICISM

(i) general studies, in English, arranged chronologically

Edmund Gosse, *Studies in the Literature of Northern Europe* (London, 1879), pp. 35–69.

Georg Brandes, *Eminent authors of the Nineteenth Century*, tr. Rasmus B. Anderson (New York, 1886), pp. 405–60.

Havelock Ellis, *The New Spirit* (London, 1890), pp. 133–73.

George Bernard Shaw, *The Quintessence of Ibsenism* (London, 1891)—second edition 'completed to the death of Ibsen', London, 1913.

Philip H. Wicksteed, *Four lectures on Henrik Ibsen dealing chiefly with his metrical works* (London, 1892).

F. Anstey [i.e. Thomas Anstey Guthrie], *Mr. Punch's Pocket Ibsen*. A collection of some of the master's best-known dramas. Condensed, revised, and slightly rearranged for the benefit of the earnest student (London, 1893).

'Zanoni' [pseud.], *Ibsen and the Drama* (London, [? 1894]).

H. H. Boyesen, *A Commentary on the Works of Henrik Ibsen* (London, 1894).

Edward Russell, *Ibsen*. A lecture delivered at University College, Liverpool, 26 Jan. 1894 (Liverpool, 1894).

George Bernard Shaw, *Our Theatres in the Nineties*. 3 vols. (London, 1932)—being dramatic criticisms contributed week by week to *The Saturday Review* from Jan. 1895 to May 1898.

Henry James, *The Scenic Art*, ed. Allan Wade (London, 1949), pp. 243–60, 286–94—including: 'On the occasion of Hedda Gabler', *New Review*, June 1891; 'The Master Builder', *Pall Mall Gazette*, 17 Feb. 1893; 'Little Eyolf', 'John Gabriel Borkman', *Harper's Weekly*, 23 Jan., 6 Feb., 1897.

Edward Russell and Percy Cross Standing, *Ibsen on his merits* (London, 1897).

Georg Brandes, *Henrik Ibsen, Bjørnstjerne Bjørnson*. Critical studies (London, 1899).

Max Beerbohm. *Around Theatres* (London, 1953)—being dramatic criticisms May 1898—April 1910, including: 'An hypocrisy in play-going' [on *Hedda Gabler* played in Italian, Oct. 1903], pp. 277–81; 'Ibsen' [an obituary, May 1906], pp. 432–6; 'A memorable performance' [on *Rosmersholm*, Feb. 1908], pp. 497–501.

James Joyce, 'Ibsen's new drama', *Fortnightly Review*, 73, 1900, pp. 575–90.

James Huneker, *Iconoclasts: a book of dramatists* (London, 1905), pp. 1–138.

Arthur Symons, *Figures of Several Centuries* (London, 1916), pp. 222–67: 'Henrik Ibsen', written 1906.

Jeanette Lee, *The Ibsen Secret*. A key to the prose dramas of Henrik Ibsen (London, 1907).

Haldane Macfall, *Ibsen: the man, his art and his significance* (London, 1907).

Montrose, J. Moses, *Henrik Ibsen: the man and his plays* (New York, 1908).

James Huneker, *Egoists: a book of supermen* (London, 1909), pp. 317–39.

Edward Dowden, *Essays, modern and Elizabethan* (London, 1910), pp. 26–60.

Archibald Henderson, *Interpreters of life and the modern spirit* (London, 1911), pp. 157–283.

Otto Heller, *Henrik Ibsen: plays and problems* (New York, 1912).

R. Ellis Roberts, *Henrik Ibsen: a critical study* (London, 1912).

Henry Rose, *Henrik Ibsen: poet, mystic and moralist* (London, 1913).

William Archer, 'The true greatness of Ibsen', a lecture delivered at University College, London. *Edda*, xii, 1919, pp. 175–91.

Carl Burchardt, *Norwegian life and literature* (London, 1920).

Storm Jameson, *Modern Drama in Europe* (London, 1920).

Janko Lavrin, *Ibsen and his creation. A psycho-critical study* (London, 1921).

T. M. Campbell, *Hebbel, Ibsen and the analytical exposition* (Heidelberg, 1922).

Basil King, 'Ibsen and Emilie Bardach', *Century Magazine* (New York), 1923: Oct. pp. 803–15, Nov. pp. 83–92.

Benedetto Croce, *European Literature in the Nineteenth Century* (London, 1924), pp. 326–43.

Hermann J. Weigand, *The modern Ibsen: a reconsideration* (New York, 1925).

Paul Henry Grumman, *Henrik Ibsen: an introduction to his life and works* (New York, 1928).

Elizabeth Robins, *Ibsen and the actress* (London, 1928).

Bonamy Dobrée, *The Lamp and the lute* (Oxford, 1929), pp. 1–20.

Harley Granville-Barker. 'The coming of Ibsen', in *The Eighteen Eighties*, Essays by Fellows of the Royal Society of Literature, ed. Walter de la Mare (Cambridge, 1930), pp. 159–96.

J. G. Robertson, *Essays and addresses on literature* (London, 1935), pp. 147–226.

A. Anstensen, *The Proverb in Ibsen* (Columbia U.P. and London, 1935).

E. M. Forster, *Abinger Harvest* (London, 1936), including chapter on 'Ibsen the Romantic'.

Theodore Jorgenson, *Henrik Ibsen: a study in art and personality* (Northfield, Minn., 1945).

Ronald Peacock, *The Poet in the Theatre* (London, 1946), pp. 65–71.

Brian W. Downs, *Ibsen: the intellectual background* (Cambridge, 1946).

M. C. Bradbrook, *Ibsen the Norwegian* (London, 1948).

P. F. D. Tennant, *Ibsen's Dramatic Technique* (Cambridge, 1948).

Alan Reynolds Thompson, *The Dry Mock* (Berkeley, Cal., 1948), pp. 197–244: 'Ibsen'.

Francis Fergusson, *The Idea of a Theater* (Princeton U.P. and London, 1949)—with special reference to *Ghosts*.

Brian W. Downs, *A study of six plays by Ibsen* (Cambridge, 1950), incl. *A Doll's House*.

Janko Lavrin, *Ibsen: an approach* (London, 1950).

Raymond Williams, *Drama from Ibsen to Eliot* (London, 1952).

John Northam, *Ibsen's Dramatic Method: a study of the prose dramas* (London, 1953).

G. K. Chesterton, *A Handful of Authors* (London, 1953), pp. 134–58: 'Henrik Ibsen', articles written in 1906 and 1928.

J. T. Farrell, *Reflections at Fifty, and other essays* (New York, 1954), pp. 66–96: 'Joyce and Ibsen'.

Francis Bull, *Ibsen: the man and the dramatist*. Taylorian Lecture (Oxford, 1954).

Eric Bentley, *In search of theatre* (London, 1954), pp. 365–80.

Eva Le Gallienne, *Hedda Gabler*, A preface . . . with a new translation (London, 1955); and *The Master Builder*, a translation . . . with a prefatory study (London, 1955).

Einar Haugen, 'Ibsen in America', *Edda*, lvi, 1956, pp. 270–88.

Una Ellis-Fermor, 'Ibsen and Shakespeare as dramatic artists', *Edda*, lvi, 1956, pp. 364–79.

T. R. Henn, *The Harvest of Tragedy* (London, 1956), pp. 172–88: 'A Note on Ibsen'.

F. W. Kaufmann, 'Ibsen's Conception of Truth', *Germanic Review*, xxxii (1957), pp. 83–92.

R. M. Adams, 'Henrik Ibsen: The Fifty-first Anniversary', *Hudson Review*, x (1957), pp. 415–23.

J. B. Priestley, *Literature and Western Man* (London, 1960), pp. 284–9.

J. W. McFarlane, *Ibsen and the Temper of Norwegian Literature* (London, 1960).

Una Ellis-Fermor, *Shakespeare the Dramatist* (London, 1961): chapter on 'Ibsen and Shakespeare as dramatic artists'.

J. Setterquist, *Ibsen and the Beginnings of Anglo-Irish Drama* (Harvard U.P., 1961).

Kenneth Muir, *Last Periods of Shakespeare, Racine and Ibsen* (Liverpool U.P., 1962).

F. L. Lucas, *The Drama of Ibsen and Strindberg* (London, 1962).

G. Wilson Knight, *Ibsen* (Edinburgh, 1962).

J. W. McFarlane (ed.), *Discussions of Ibsen* (Boston, Mass., 1962)—essays by various hands.

M. J. Valency, *The Flower and the Castle* (New York, 1964).

R. Brustein, *The Theatre of Revolt* (New York, 1964, and London, 1965), pp. 35–84: 'Henrik Ibsen'.

Rolf Fjelde (ed.), *Twentieth-Century Views on Ibsen* (New York, 1965)—essays by various hands.

Contemporary Approaches to Ibsen, ed. Daniel Haakonsen (Oslo, 1966)—essays by Francis Fergusson, James McFarlane, John Northam *et al.*

B. W. Downs, *Modern Norwegian Literature 1860–1918* (Cambridge U.P., 1966), pp. 43–64 and 116–32.

M. Meyer, *Henrik Ibsen: the Making of a Dramatist 1828–1864* (London, 1967).

J. W. McFarlane (ed.), *Henrik Ibsen* (Penguin Critical Anthologies, London, 1970).

(ii) some other items relating to the plays in this volume

H. L. Mencken, 'History of a Doll's House', *Theatre* (N.Y.), xii (1910), pp. 41–44.

Einar Haugen, 'Ibsen in America: a forgotten performance and an unpublished letter [concerning *A Doll's House*]', *Journal of English and Germanic Philology*, xxxiii (1934), pp. 396–420.

B. M. Kinck, 'Laura Kieler: the model for Ibsen's Nora', *London Mercury*, Nov. 1937, pp. 12–15.

Roger Dataller, *Drama and Life* (London, 1938), pp. 64–72: 'A Doll's House'.

Edmund Wilson, 'Ghosts', *Literary Review*, iv (1924), pp. 501–2.

Joseph Wood Krutch, 'The Tragic Fallacy [on *Ghosts*]', *Atlantic*, 142 (1928), pp. 606–9.

Eleazer Lecky, '*Ghosts* and *Mourning becomes Electra*: two versions of Fate', *Arizona Quarterly*, xiii (1957), pp. 320–38.

Derek Russell Davis, 'A Re-Appraisal of Ibsen's *Ghosts*', *Family Process*, ii, i, March 1963, pp. 81–94.

Walter Stein, 'No Need of this Hypothesis: *Ghosts* and the Death of God', *Critical Quarterly*, ix, 2, 1967, pp. 109–19.

Reprinted offset in Great Britain by
The Camelot Press Ltd., London and Southampton